DICTIONARY OF LANCASHIRE DIALECT, TRADITION AND FOLKLORE

Dictionary

of
Lancashire
Dialect, Tradition and Folklore

Dr Alan G Crosby, MA

Illustrated by Peter Kearney

Smith
Settle

First published in 2000 by

Smith Settle Ltd
Ilkley Road
Otley
West Yorkshire
LS21 3JP

ISBN   Paperback   1 85825 122 2
       Hardback   1 85825 123 0

Set in ITC Stone Informal & Stone Sans

Designed, printed and bound by
SMITH SETTLE
Ilkley Road, Otley, West Yorkshire LS21 3JP

To Stanley Brown of Lytham, a loved and valued friend
(and a great Lancastrian)

Acknowledgements

I should like to give my special thanks to the many people who helped with this book, and to mention particularly Elsie Baines, Stanley Brown, Elsie Crosby, Emmeline Garnett, Margaret Hanrahan (who, among much other invaluable assistance, lent me her transcript of the St Helens Pig story), Gladys Lang, Brenda McGee, Laura Rafferty, Avril Whitham and Diana Winterbotham. Bill Rollinson, who died just before this book went to press, gave much help and encouragement — he is sadly missed. The contribution of my grandparents, Alexander and May Bagshaw, and of my great-grandmother Elizabeth Routledge, has been extremely important, though of course they were blissfully unaware of the way in which I would one day exploit them. The fine drawings which illustrate the book were drawn by Peter Kearney, who converted inadequate originals into excellent pictures. My family have put up with quite a lot during the preparation of this book — including sudden interruptions during mealtimes as I called out dialect words, and odd scraps of paper lying about the house with dimly-remembered phrases scribbled on them. The book is dedicated, with pleasure in his friendship and thanks for all that I have learned from him, to Stanley Brown, but I also dedicate it to my children, Anna and James, whose heritage (along with a half-share of Yorkshire!) this is.

Foreword

by
Chris Dawson
Chairman, Friends of Real Lancashire

Those who love Lancashire will enjoy yet another authoritative book on the county, by an author who recognises that the county extends far beyond the boundaries of the area currently administered by the 'County Council'. All too often since 1974, unenlightened authors of books on Lancashire have considered only this limited area of the county; not so Dr Crosby, who clearly recognises that Lancashire still extends from the river Mersey in the south to the rivers Brathay and Duddon in the north.

In his extensive introduction the author explains how our language evolved, being influenced over the years by the influx of peoples from other countries, and in later years by universal education, literature and the 'Standard English' of the broadcasters. The Lancashire dialect portrays the language of our ancestors, be they Celtic, Saxon or Scandinavian; or in more recent times Irish and Welsh in that south-west corner of the county around Liverpool. Lancashire's major role in the Industrial Revolution, with its hard work and grinding poverty, helped to shape its customs and traditions, and the dialect poetry and ballads of the late nineteenth century. However, we are urged not to be too sentimental about our past, for much of it would be unacceptable today, the bull baiting and cockfighting, the shinparing — where men would kick one another with iron-tipped clogs — or wife selling; but some might welcome the sight of naked men racing across Whitworth Moor once again, as they did in the past. The introduction is a book in itself.

Although the way we speak today has been influenced in more recent times by outside forces, you will find many of the words and expressions used in everyday conversation listed in this dictionary. It is fascinating to learn why, often without thinking, we use expressions handed down to us by our ancestors. How often have we been asked by someone 'What does that mean?' or 'Why are you doing that?' Well, the answer may be here. We sometimes despair at the wicked ways of modern society, but people in the past were no better, and some of the seemingly innocent customs observed today such as eating pancakes on Shrove Tuesday, dancing round the Maypole on summer days or rushbearing in season, have rather sinister origins, all of which are explained for the reader.

Numerous books have been published in the past to cover various aspects of Lancashire's dialect, culture or traditions, but here you will find a much more comprehensive collection.

Introduction

Cars and computers, Italian holidays and the Internet ... we live in a world which is shrinking fast and where a global culture is developing. Chain-stores and banks, with their unvarying corporate architecture, standardised road signs, even all those black and gold bins and lamp posts which (while many times better than their predecessors) are now a stock feature of any town centre — all these mean that, to most people, regional and local variety seems sadly diminished. The loss in local variations, the creeping uniformity and the prevalence of a mid-Atlantic accent and vocabulary are a matter for growing regret. We may be powerless to prevent many of the changes, but we do not have to acquiesce without a protest. It is in this context that local history, and the study of the past, can be especially rewarding. We can focus upon what makes communities, landscapes and cultures different, highlight their special qualities and characteristics, try to explain their origins and development, and seek to emphasise diversity and variety. Dialects, traditions and folklore are a vital component of the regional differences which survive. In this book I look at those subjects in Lancashire, celebrating some of the characteristics which make the county and its people what they are today.

Dialect and Tradition

Loss of variety and the increasing uniformity are not, of course, confined to architecture and road signs. A comparable trend is apparent when we look at dialect, but here the tendency to standardise is much older. Since the mid-eighteenth century, when cheap, mass-produced printed books began to circulate, the role of dialect has been diminishing. Whether in Lancashire, Tyneside, East Anglia or anywhere else, dialect has always been primarily an oral or spoken language, not a written one.

Partly for this reason, it has usually been considered by the educated members of society to be inferior, both culturally and socially. Dialect was not only 'wrong' to those who spoke 'proper' English, but it also marked someone out as rough, inadequately educated, a country bumpkin or a provincial. In the past it was particularly associated with low levels of literacy. If you could read and write, you would almost certainly be using standard English, not dialect, and therefore only the illiterate would speak dialect — or, at least, that was the easy assumption which was made.

So dialect began to retreat in the face of uniformity, something for which the media and the education system have rightly received much of the blame. The ever-wider use of printing produced, almost inevitably, a standardisation of spelling, and by 1800 it was generally presumed that if a word was not spelled as it was in the dictionary, it was definitely incorrect rather than merely different. The education system, especially after 1870 when universal element-ary schooling was made compulsory, taught that there was only one correct way to spell, that there were inflexible rules of grammar, and that 'nice' speech (Queen's English, as it was called then and now) meant a standard accent as well as standardised spelling.

Dialect, frowned upon and socially unacceptable, was now deliberately challenged on the grounds that it was simply wrong, and in a more literate society, where mass communication was beginning to develop, the countless local idiosyncrasies of speech and vocabulary could not compete on equal terms. In this, local dialects shared the experience of smaller languages, such as Welsh and Irish, which in the nineteenth and early twentieth centuries were dwindling fast before the onward march of English.

The change in the written word came first, because until the 1920s this was all that most people encountered. But, during the next seventy years, the arrival in most homes of first the gramophone, then wireless and radio, and eventually the television, produced dramatic changes in how people spoke — or, at least, in how dialect and accents were perceived. The sound of words altered, as individuals subconsciously changed their speech patterns to conform with what they heard on the wireless and were taught at school. Between the

1920s and the early 1960s, the tortured upper-class (or imitated upper-class) voices of radio announcers and interviewers were regarded as being 'correct', and provincial accents of any sort or origin were regarded as completely unacceptable, except as quaint features of radio interviews.

Other aspects of local culture were also fighting a losing battle in the nineteenth century. There had been an immense diversity of festivals and feast days, local pastimes and sports, and oral traditions of fearsome ghosts and terrifying apparitions. Different parts of England had local names for most everyday objects, and dialect terms for countless ordinary things in life. The ties which bound communities together included the way that the people spoke, and the special events which they enjoyed as part of an annual calendar or cycle of celebrations and commemorations — the saint's day feast, the festivities at harvest time, the particular local food eaten at Eastertide.

Some writers in the time of the late nineteenth century 'folk revival', and others even today, have believed rather optimistically that these ancient customs were somehow more innocent than today's entertainments, and have seen them as clean and wholesome. There is a vague image of apple-cheeked maidens, dressed in white and garlanded with flowers, dancing round maypoles, while a happy well-fed peasantry looks on. In reality, sex was an ever-present theme in traditional customs, and ritualised or actual physical violence was also commonplace. Most of the participants would have been grubby, poorly-nourished, smelly and scruffy by today's standards, as well as a great deal more inebriated and prone to thump friends and neighbours. But these events were local and they were distinctive, and people loved them and enjoyed them even though the original purpose or meaning had in most cases long since been forgotten.

In the nineteenth century, though, many began to disappear. Stories and legends lost their impact in a more sophisticated and better-educated age. Tales which were formerly recited to terrorise children, or entertain drinking companions on dark nights, were rewritten in pretty Victorian prose, stripped of the sex and violence, and lost their powerful impact in the process. The extremely lively entertainments of feasts and wakes were regarded with increasing disapproval by the Church and respectable members of society. The aggressive and rowdy pastimes of labourers and colliers were no longer acceptable. Strange and fascinating rituals on, for example, All Soul's Eve, with their obvious overtones of pre-Christian belief, were frowned upon as being inappropriate in a Christian society where decorum and rationality were promoted. So, in most places these survivals were either suppressed or were replaced by more refined versions. Boisterous harvest feasts became the sober (in both senses of the word) harvest festivals, while the improper merrymaking at Shrovetide became the domestic ritual of making pancakes — the pancakes were always there, but it was what you did after eating them that made the day so enjoyable in the past.

Nevertheless, much does survive, having resisted the process of standardisation and defied properness. There are still plenty of dialect words in use, regional accents not only survive but have enjoyed a new popularity, and many old customs, altered in character perhaps, are still observed today. But the threat is there and growing. For most who want to 'get on' in society, dialect and strong accents are still regarded as a disadvantage — though, if the strong accent is a middle-class Thames Valley one, that is quite acceptable, of course. A much more powerful threat comes from the mass media, and the development of those global patterns that we hear so much about and can do so little to challenge. The customs and the traditions, too, are threatened, but in a different way. They run the serious risk of becoming part of the great heritage culture, where the 'Merrie England' view of the past disguises what was often an unpalatable reality.

This book celebrates Lancashire's dialect, tradition and folklore. It is not an academic book, and that is not my aim in writing it (I emphasise again the word 'celebrate'), but rather it is an affectionate tribute to the heritage of Lancashire and its people over the past three centuries. A book which included every dialect word and pronunciation, every local feast, festival and entertainment, every site of tradition and legend, would be thousands of pages in length.

This is therefore not a comprehensive dictionary, and I make no claims in that respect. All those who read it will think of dozens of words, sayings and stories which have been omitted, and many readers will also take issue with some of the meaning and spellings ('well, that's not what it meant when *we* were children'). This is inevitable for, as I discuss in the next section, the exceptional richness of Lancashire's dialect and traditions is partly the result of innumerable even more local variations and versions of words, phrases and ideas. The same term might be used in Accrington and Rochdale, but it could have slightly — or even widely — different meanings in the two towns. The book is, therefore, a personal selection, intended to entertain as well as to inform.

And now, an explanation of the geographical coverage. I am of course acutely aware that **Real Lancashire** includes Furness and Cartmel, north of the Sands, and that its boundaries extend from the Mersey to the Brathay and the Duddon. This book, however, covers only Lancashire south of the Sands, the bulk of the old county but with that important omission. This is because Furness, although part of Lancashire for 900 years, has very strong cultural ties (especially in terms of its dialect) with Cumberland and Westmorland. North of the Sands has therefore been included with those two counties in the companion volume in this series, William Rollinson's admirable *Cumbrian Dictionary of Dialect, Tradition and Folklore.* Bill died in March 2000, and to the last he considered himself a Lancastrian, for he was born in Barrow-in-Furness and lived for much of his life there and in Ulverston. He agreed with me that our inclusion of Furness in his volume did not reflect any endorsement on our part of the post-1974 local government arrangements.

The Lancashire Dialect

For over 250 years there has been interest in the Lancashire dialect. John Collier, the first major dialect writer in the county, was born in 1708, and in 1746 published his lengthy poem *Tummus and Meary*, which was not only an inspiration to his successors (it has been in print ever since), but was also one of the very earliest serious dialect works to be published in any English region.

The great flowering of published dialect poetry and prose came in the 1850s and 1860s, with the work of a remarkable circle of writers headed by Ben Brierley, Edwin Waugh and Sam Laycock. The period of their creativity was brief, but in the later nineteenth century and through the twentieth, many others have sought, with varying degrees of talent and uncertain levels of success, to capture the detail and flavour of a dialect which by 1900 was already fast-receding in the face of spoken and written uniformity. Whereas the dialect was living and breathing in the 1850s, by the 1920s it was in retreat, and much of the poetry and verse written in the twentieth century has been more nostalgic and wistful, less about mundane everyday realities and more about dreams, than that composed by the great men of the mid-Victorian years.

But what exactly was the Lancashire dialect? With minor exceptions, the writers of the nineteenth and earlier twentieth centuries came from a limited area of the county — that bounded by Blackburn, Rochdale, Oldham, Manchester and Bolton — and their heartland was the district around Rochdale, Milnrow, Middleton, Bolton and Bury. They wrote, of course, in the dialects with which they were familiar, and their attempts to reproduce the pronunciations in phonetic form therefore reflect the speech patterns of those parts of the south-east of the county. Closer investigation, however, shows that this is only one among several major dialect groups within the ancient county. Largely because of their dominant place in the study of the subject, the local versions of the south-east have come to be widely regarded as the 'real' Lancashire dialect, and the dialects of other parts of Lancashire — most notably the south-west — have been correspondingly neglected.

Perhaps we also need to establish what makes a dialect. The answer is complex, but two main elements can be distinguished. The first, and most important in terms of linguistics, is the vocabulary. The use of distinctive local or regional words is of course universal — every language has its dialects (American English is very rich in them) and local terminology is found in them all. In the case of Lancashire's dialects, most of the words commonly thought to be 'Lancashire' are in fact more widely used, being shared with other parts of northern England, including Cumbria and (dangerous to say, but true) Yorkshire. If you read Arnold Kellett's *Yorkshire Dictionary*, a companion volume to this book, you will find that numerous Yorkshire words are also found in Lancashire ... or should it be the other way round?

This is because very few words, whether or not dialect, were created out of nothing and are therefore purely local. Most are instead of ancient derivation, and they can be related to the various languages which have at different periods been spoken in northern England, and which have left their legacy in words and place-names. This common linguistic ground, whereby many Lancashire dialect words are not unique to Lancashire, might not meet with favour among Yorkshire or Lancashire nationalists, but it is a powerful unifying factor in the cultural heritage of the North of England (and, indeed, southern Scotland as well).

In the case of the six ancient counties of northern England, three main languages can be identified. The oldest is the Celtic tongue or tongues (in the North-West called Cymric), spoken before the Romans came to Britain in the first century AD. Cymric remained in use as the everyday speech of most of the population during the Roman period (until about AD 400), and it survived as a living language in the area of later Lancashire until the seventh century. Although it has left few words in dialect speech, it has given us many place-names — Lancashire has more Celtic place-names than any other part of England apart from Cornwall and Cumbria.

However, Cymric, which was closely related to Old Welsh, was gradually pushed out, and eventually eliminated altogether, by Anglo-Saxon, introduced in the seventh century by colonisers from Mercia (to the south) and Northumbria (to the east). Pockets of Cymric-speaking inhabitants may have survived in parts of Lancashire until perhaps AD 900, but the language was ultimately doomed.

Anglo-Saxon, in contrast, forms the basis not only of Lancashire dialect but also of modern English, though in both cases heavily influenced by the third element, the various Scandinavian languages which were brought by settlers from Norway and Denmark in the three centuries before the Norman Conquest.

In eastern England, Danish words were more significant, but in the North-West the prevailing Scandinavian influence was Old Norse, which has not only left us thousands of familiar place-names (and many words which are used to describe landscape features or are to do with farming), but also numerous dialect words and pronunciations. Norse was possibly spoken in parts of the Lake District until the thirteenth century, and was certainly widespread in north Lancashire until the Norman Conquest. The cultural legacies of these three waves of settlement — Celtic, Saxon and Norse — have combined to produce a three-language mix across the region, and to create local dialects which are the product of a 'melting pot'.

Many dialect words also represent survivals from what was once the everyday speech throughout England. As language changes, which it always does, words and forms of speech may die out or alter, but the rate at which this happens is very variable. For example, the use of **thee** and **thou**, well-nigh universal in the fifteenth century, was beginning to be superseded in some areas and classes of society in the sixteenth (but remained sufficiently dominant to be the language of the immensely influential King James' Bible at the start of the seventeenth century), and had largely died out except among the peasantry in south-east England by the late eighteenth century. But it remained in everyday use among all levels of society in other parts of England until much later. In Thomas Hardy's late nineteenth century Wessex novels, *thee* and *thou* are still used, since they were part of the normal speech of ordinary people in the agricultural south-west and south of the country, while in the industrialised and urbanised north-west they also remained standard, and are still heard, though ever less often, in our day. Thus, older Lancashire speech often preserves, and may still reflect, even at the beginning of the twenty-first century, patterns and forms of language which were once commonplace across the country as a whole.

The second major element in dialect is the pronunciation of words, and this is integrally associated with another factor, the rhythms of speech and the intonation. Together they produce what is commonly known as the 'accent'.

This is where knowledge and appreciation of local detail plays a vital part in analysis. We all know that we can distinguish between accents, though some people have a 'good ear' and others cannot differentiate between any but the most obvious. To outsiders, regional accents often seem very standardised: thus, there is commonly supposed to be one Lancashire accent, one Geordie accent, one Birmingham accent and so on, whereas to someone attuned to local variations, all sorts of subtle distinctions emerge.

Within Lancashire — and this is a dangerous subject to introduce — there are four or five major groupings of accents and pronunciations. In the south-east there are the 'Manchester' accents (though tell that to people from Rochdale or Bolton and you'd rightly be jumped on), which are what many people think of as 'Lancashire' (*Coronation Street* being instrumental in this, perhaps). Around Burnley, Blackburn and Preston, Rossendale and Chorley, there are mid- and east-Lancashire accents which display some regional similarities among themselves, although with many differences as well. These accents are often sharper than those further south, and certain letters (such as 'r') have very distinctive pronunciations. In parts of south-east Lancashire, 'door' might be pronounced almost as *dah*, whereas in east Lancashire it is often *dawerr*). In north Lancashire, and especially from Lancaster northwards into the Lune Valley, the accents in contrast begin to take on a Cumbrian intonation, which itself has affinities with the sounds and rhythms of the speech of the north-east and of parts of southern Scotland.

And finally, and perhaps most distinctively, there is the group of accents in south-west Lancashire which are usually given one of the following labels: Liverpool, Merseyside or Scouse. These accents (and their associated dialects) are less obviously related to the standard idea of 'Lancashire talk', and hence have acquired a separate identity. Most people would not think of 'Scouse' as being Lancashire at all, though quite obviously it is one of the county's most important dialects. Although historians and linguists argue strongly about the point, there is a widespread belief that the original accents of south-west Lancashire, including those of Liverpool itself, were more closely related to those of the rest of the county. It is fairly certain that in areas as close to Liverpool as Sefton, Huyton and Gateacre, during the nineteenth century when these parts were rural, a 'typical' Lancashire dialect was spoken, but it is equally likely that the city itself had already by 1800 started to develop its very characteristic speech and diverse vocabulary.

The present accent, with its outstandingly fluid use of words and its distinctive intonation (for example, the guttural 'g' spoken halfway down the throat) is usually explained as being the product of Irish immigration on a very large scale from the 1840s onwards. Evidence produced in support is various, but the agility of the vocabulary and the ultra-fast coining of catchphrases (*Mersey Funnel*, *Paddy's Wigwam*) is compared with an allegedly similar pattern in Dublin ('D' Floozie in d' Jacuzzi' for the Liffey statue erected a few years ago in that fair city). These apparent influences may be at least partly true, especially as Liverpool people themselves have often recognised a separate 'Liverpool Irish' speech, but there are also many other possible influences to be taken into account, notably North Walian accents, and perhaps Scottish and Cumbrian as well. Maybe the individual strands can be identified, but their precise significance cannot readily be assessed, largely because it was only comparatively recently that anybody began to analyse the subject. Nobody bothered, a hundred years or more ago, to record on paper the phonetics and complexities of the city's evolving dialect.

Within these enormously generalised groupings, there are of course countless local variations. If we pick up accents and have that 'good ear', we can tell Blackburn from Burnley, Chorley from Preston, Wigan from Bolton, without too much difficulty. Specialists, native speakers and long-time residents can tell in much greater detail. The slow and thoughtful speech of Audenshaw and Ashton-under-Lyne is quite different from the faster and less careful east end of Manchester pronunciation, just down the road, but my mother, as a child in the 1930s, could tell Openshaw from Higher Openshaw (the accents changed at the canal bridge on Ashton Old Road).

Accent (and pronunciation) is a vital element in dialect, and we must be ever grateful to the poets and writers of the nineteenth century, who not only used a distinctive vocabulary, but also sought to reproduce a pronunciation. The spelling of words in their published works is largely dependent upon what they heard — hence the often very considerable difficulty in actually reading the stuff — but we can try to read their poems and essays aloud, and thereby recapture the flavour of the accents 150 years ago. Today, not only can we hear accents all around us, but we can also listen to the archive recordings made by public bodies such as the superb North West Sound Archive at Clitheroe. Many local organisations are also recording oral history, reminiscences and dialect speech as part of their investigations into local history.

Accents, and pronunciation patterns, are not static. Very important in their changing patterns is the fact that people are themselves mobile. Perhaps the most profound change to the traditional distribution of Lancashire dialects has come not from the media or education but from slum clearance policies and the flight to the suburbs, which have taken accents away from their home areas into pastures new. Fifty years ago, Skelmersdale spoke 'Lancashire', Winsford spoke 'Cheshire'. Today they both speak largely Liverpool. In St Helens in the pre-war period the accent was strongly 'Lancashire', as the following true story, told many years ago by an old man to a friend of mine from the town, demonstrates (note that *oo* serves as any pronoun):

The Tale of a Pig

'Yon fella took 'is pig darn t' market a Sat'day on when oo geet theer oo stopped fer a bit wi owld Garge Thomson. On while thi were yackin' t' pig got loose un ran off. Oo felt it goo, on oo sharted "Ay, t' pig's geet loose". On oo arl looked rarnd on theer oo was, off up t' road. On oo sharted "stop en", on oo started runnin' etter him an oo all jarned in, bur'oo dodged 'em in an' art th' sta's. On oo were off o'ort bridge o'ort canal wi oo ar puffin' etter 'im. Oo cort en jus' afore oo reached t' abbatoir on oo brought en back. By gum, it were a good laugh a tell yer.'

This Lancashire accent is still clear among older residents today, but the town and surrounding areas now have a strong and growing Liverpool presence. Among passengers boarding the stopping trains from Wigan to Liverpool, the accent divide seems to be between Bryn and Garswood: Bryn is Wigan and therefore 'Lancashire', Garswood has overtones of Merseyside.

The changing distribution of the Liverpool accents is perhaps easiest to chart, because the accents themselves are very distinctive, but comparable redistribution has taken place everywhere that population movement has been extensive. In its movement from city to suburbs and beyond, any accent will alter, as it is diluted and mixed with other influences, or changed by class — listen to a lady from a better-off part of Southport, and her accent, though probably of recognisably Liverpudlian origin (even if she might not be happy to admit it), will be vastly different from that of a schoolchild in Kirkby or an old man in Toxteth. Thus the complexities and confusions of accent and dialect continue to evolve.

And as to whether all of this is threatened by progress, the answer is equally mixed. The vocabulary certainly is mixed, as mid-Atlantic words and fashionable slang replace the 'vernacular' (though there has always been fashionable slang). The richness of the words themselves is being lost, as standard terms and nationally-known catchphrases dominate. Much Lancashire dialect vocabulary is to do with occupations such as mining, cotton and agriculture, where not only the words, but also the great trades and industries which gave rise to them, have vanished. Banking, supermarkets and computers do not have regional vocabularies — they do not even have national ones.

But the accents are much harder to eradicate, and they will continue for many long years yet. Perhaps the most convincing demonstration of this is the presence, in Oldham, Rochdale, Bolton, Preston and a host of other towns and cities, of many thousands of citizens, of second- and third-generation Asian origin, who speak purest Oldham, broadest Rochdale, deepest Preston. All is not lost!

Traditions and Folklore

Lancashire is a surprisingly conservative county, despite the fact that for over two centuries it has been heavily industrialised and most of its population has lived in towns. Although historians will always argue about this, the county in the sixteenth century was probably relatively self-contained and introverted, and was certainly regarded with suspicion and dislike by those who lived further south. Some things do not change.

Its regard for the traditional and the familiar could not be better illustrated than by the way that, after the Reformation and the Dissolution of the Monasteries, it clung tenaciously to the old Catholic faith. It was, and it remains, the most Catholic county in England, but that is not simply because of Irish immigration in the nineteenth century — it had been so for 300 years before then.

Lancashire had a complex cultural background. It was on the borderlands, between England and Wales, England and Scotland, England and Ireland, and earlier than that between Saxon and Norse kingdoms, between Romans and Celts. This gave it a very rich legacy of traditions and customs. We can see Celtic characteristics — holy wells, wayside crosses, fire festivals — and we can note the 'typical' medieval religious festivals which evolved into **wakes holidays** and ultimately, perhaps, helped to create Blackpool and its ilk. Other traditions, such as those other familiar foods, **black pudding** and **tripe**, which are now thought of as distinctively Lancashire, were once found everywhere, but their popularity and availability has waned in other areas. Lancashire — conservative, quite content with the old ways — has retained its taste for them. Now they are back in fashion in elegant London restaurants, but here they never went out of fashion.

Many of these customs and traditions were, as noted earlier, either remoulded in a more decorous form in the nineteenth century, or were abolished altogether, but others survived and are proudly proclaimed to this day. Other traditions were created from scratch in the nineteenth century, or were the product of a fierce local patriotism, and loyalty to town or village and county.

Here, Lancashire (like Yorkshire and a few other counties, but perhaps unlike Bedfordshire or Surrey) has nurtured a powerful sense of its own very particular identity. That terrible image with which the county has long been blackened, of mills and smoke and dirt and rain, has paradoxically helped to reinforce its deep local pride and — though we all know that it is a false image — has helped to generate much serious literature, light comedy, art and drawing, drama and music.

Lancashire's sense of the traditional has also been fostered by its recent history. The acute poverty and deprivation which many of its population suffered in the past two centuries — the hardship of grinding labour, the near starvation of food shortages and pitiful wages, the endless domestic tragedies of child mortality and industrial disease, the miserable lot of the desperate Irish immigrant — have given rise to much that is now viewed with pride. The paintings of Lowry, the poetry of the Cotton Famine, the anonymous ballads of the handloom weavers, even, perhaps, the songs of Lennon and McCartney, owe much or all to these aspects of Lancashire's past.

Tradition is not all about morris men in colourful costumes, heritage trails, and Rose Queens. It is about real people and their lives, the events which mattered to them, and the celebrations and customs which diversified their existence. In this book are many traditions which, thankfully, have been abolished, as well as many the loss of which we might regret. We can only be glad that **bull-baiting** and **cock-fighting** are no more, we should not hanker after *purring* and *shinparing* (traditional forms of fighting which involve kicking the opponent senseless with metal-tipped clogs), and we now have divorce instead of **wife-selling**. There is such a thing as progress.

So we should not be too sentimental about much that was familiar in the past. If we could go back in time, even only 100 years, we would be appalled by the dirt, the smell, the filth, the disease, the death, the poverty, the women old at forty and the men laid low by lingering illnesses. Thus, not all the traditions and customs which I list are of the type we'd like to see today.

But others certainly are. I have heard it suggested that men should once more be permitted to race naked across the moors of

Whitworth, that **treacle-dipping** should be revived as a spectator sport, and that **rabbit-jumping** could be in the next-but-one Olympics. Lancashire is a great county (the greatest) and its traditions are a powerful force in shaping that essential fact. Let us celebrate the dialect, traditions and folklore of the county, and strive to maintain all that which is good in that rich historical legacy.

Alan Crosby
Preston 2000

Pronunciation

The traditional forms of pronunciation in the county of course varied from place to place, and there is still an extremely wide variety of local accents and speech rhythms. A **Lancashire accent** is really a myth, because the accent of, say, Ashton is totally different from that of Anfield. What is usually meant by the term 'Lancashire accent' is that from the Manchester area. In 1901, F E Taylor summarised the main features of the familiar and traditional south-east Lancashire pronunciation, and the following table is based on his notes:

a   pronounced flat and short , in contrast to the long southern English form

a   sometimes pronounced as 'o' (**hond** instead of hand)

a   sometimes pronounced as 'e' (**kenell** instead of canal)

d   often pronounced as 't' (**awter't** instead of altered)

ea   pronounced as two letters (**ste'yem**, not 'steem', for steam)

en   used as a past-tense ending for verbs (**we getten**)

h   rarely used, except for emphasis, at the start of words

i   sometimes pronounced 'ee' or 'eigh' (**feight**, **neet**)

i   often pronounced as 'oie' (**foier**, for fire)

i   often pronounced 'eye-u' (**ch'eye'uld** for child)

ing pronounced 'ink'

o generally pronounced 'u' (***cum***, for come, in contrast to the southern English 'cam')

ou pronounced 'eaw' ('o' also said in this way — ***Beauwt'n*** for Bolton)

r in the middle of a word, often omitted (***beth*** for birth)

's often omitted — ***keaw-tail*** for cow's tail

s often omitted in plurals — ***fower year sen*** for four years ago

t often pronounced 'th'

y often used instead of 'g' (***yate***) or 'h' (***yed***)

In addition, there were of course innumerable local pronunciations. For example, Richard Ashworth, in a 1916 lecture on the Rossendale dialect, noted that 'ch' and 'gh' were pronounced in the 'Scotch manner'; while in mid-Lancashire, 't' is often pronounced 'k' in the middle of a word: *'Ah said 'e were menkle'*.

Abbreviations & Symbols

abbr	abbreviation
c	circa
cf	compare with
I	Icelandic
D	Danish
N	Norwegian
OE	Old English (the language of the Anglo-Saxons)
ON	Old Norse (the language of the Vikings)
pron	pronounced
qv	which see

A

aam to mock, to repeat a person's words after him

abide suffer, endure, tolerate; a term formerly in common use throughout England, but in this century tending to be confined to dialect *Ah can't abide cabbitch*

aboon above

acker to stammer or stutter

ackersprit potato, turnip, swede or other root vegetable; the literal meaning is 'land sprout', but the word was often applied particularly to a potato with a profusion of roots

Accrington Pals 11th battalion of the East Lancashire Regiment, raised in September 1914 under the initiative of the mayor of Accrington, John Harwood. Accrington was the smallest borough in Britain which recruited its own battalion: two companies were from the town, three platoons from Burnley, three from Chorley and two from Blackburn. The Accrington Pals went to France in March 1916, and went into action on the first day of the Somme, the notorious 1st July 1916, when 234 of its men were killed and 350 wounded. The battalion also fought at Arras in 1917, and in several other major campaigns in northern France during 1918. In total over 750 men from the battalion were killed, most of them from the towns of Accrington, Chorley and Darwen. Their courage and the terrible waste of their young lives had a deep and abiding impact upon Accrington.

Adam Often symbolising extreme antiquity, Adam appears in several

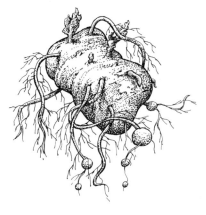

Ackersprit.

1

Lancashire phrases, such as *since Adam were a lad* ('it's been there since …') and *he didn't know me from Adam*.

'addick's water weak or watery liquid, lacking in flavour: a weak cup of tea might be described as *like 'addick's water* (from the pale liquid left after boiling haddock in a lot of water)

addle to earn *addle some brass*

affendole (see *aughendole*)

afterings last of a cow's milk (cf *beestings*)

agate going *the mill's agate, Ah'll get agate*; the word is still in regular use in areas such as Rossendale (from the same Scandinavian root as *gate* (qv), a track or way)

aghendole (see *aughendole*)

agist (pron *a-jyst*, and often abbreviated to *gist* or *gyste*) to let out pasture for grazing cattle; the rights to graze cattle for a consideration upon land

Ainsworth, William Harrison Perhaps the best-known of Lancashire's nineteenth-century authors, Harrison Ainsworth was born in Manchester in 1805 and was educated at Manchester Grammar School. He trained as a solicitor, but his passion for literature and the local history of Lancashire encouraged him to become a novelist. He produced a number of historical romances which were extremely popular in their day, and his best-known work, *The Lancashire witches: a romance of Pendle*, has been continuously in print ever since. It almost single handedly created the present-day 'witch industry' in Pendle, and the novel, with its images of a mysterious, haunted, misty countryside dominated by the brooding presence of the great hill itself, also set the tone for much later writing about Pendle in prose and verse. Ainsworth, one of the bestselling novelists of the nineteenth century, died in 1882.

alder The alder is a common tree in Lancashire, where the extensive wetlands provided an ideal habitat. The dialect form of the name is *oller*, and it has given rise to a number of place-names, such as Allerton in Liverpool and Ollerton near Brinscall, as well as streams called Ellerbeck (as at Lathom and Duxbury). Alder wood was highly valued because, being easily shaped, it was particularly suitable for making clogs.

Common alder.

It was also used as firing for bakers' ovens and kilns.

aliker equivalent to vinegar, but made from soured ale (the 'correct' spelling is *alegar*)

alley narrow space between the looms in a weaving shed, or between *mules* (qv) in a spinning mill; also known as the *wheel gate*. By the 1930s the usual size for this in a spinning mill was approximately forty-two yards (38m) long and six yards (5.5m) wide, and roughly 230 times per hour the mules moved back and forth on their short rails. An *alley* was also, more generally, the back lane or entry between two rows of houses.

alley and jackstones (see *bobber and kibs*)

Alphin and Alderman In ancient local mythology, these were two giants who fell in love with Rimmon, a shepherdess who bathed naked in a moorland stream high in the Pennines above Greenfield. She favoured Alphin, but the jealous Alderman killed his rival by hurling huge rocks at him. In despair Rimmon threw herself to her death from the cliffs on the moor edge. Today, Alphin is the hill (1,544 feet/471m)) on the county boundary between Lancashire and the West Riding south of Greenfield, and Alderman's Hill (1,400 feet/425m) faces it from the Yorkshire side of the valley.

anent (anaunt) against

angry irritated, septic or inflamed (as in a wound or spot)

any road anyway, a direct equivalent of the standard English word, also found in the form *anygate*; has achieved a wider fame since it has become one of the identifiers of 'northern' speech in television programmes since the 1960s

'appy 'arry gloomy and mournful person, a *right misery*

arcades In the late nineteenth century, shopping arcades were particularly fashionable, their wide passageways roofed over with glass and iron, and often entered through an elaborate and architecturally impressive frontage. They provided shelter from the elements, and offered a clean and elegant environment at a time of dirty, wet, sooty streets crowded with horse-drawn traffic. Many Lancashire towns had an arcade: examples include Thwaites Arcade at Blackburn, the Wayfarers Arcade in Southport and the Miller Arcade in Preston. However, many were wantonly destroyed in the 1960s and 1970s, often to be replaced by stark and ugly concrete versions of the same idea, which have worn badly, and lack all the charm of their Victorian and Edwardian predecessors.

ark An *ark* was a chest or coffer, and in the North-West they were a standard item of furniture until the late nineteenth century, being used especially to hold oatmeal. Meal deteriorates very rapidly in contact with air, turning rancid and sour, and it must also be kept absolutely dry. It was therefore rammed down into the *ark*, often

Thwaites Arcade, Blackburn, in 1889.

by being trampled upon, so that as much air as possible was excluded. In 1795 Aikin said that, in the Blackburn area, oats were bought around Michaelmas, fresh from harvest, 'ground to meal, and stored in arks, where they are trodden down hard while new and warm, to serve for the year's bread'.

arr   mark or blemish on the skin

arse-board   tailgate of a cart, also

4

known as the **cart-arse**. This was the sort of term which shocked Victorian sensitivities, and prompted campaigns to stamp out dialect and replace it with with standard English which was considered to be 'nice'.

arval funeral feast, equivalent to a **wake²** (qv), especially in north Lancashire; associated with it were traditions such as the serving of **arval ale** and **arval cakes** or **bread**

'ash Properly, but never in reality, **hash** with a **haitch**, this was the universal Lancashire stew for those who could afford a little more than the barest minimum of food. It is filling and tasty at best, watery and just about warming at worst. There is no recipe and no standard ingredients. Small pieces of any meat, vegetables (especially carrots, onions and potatoes) are cooked gently in water or broth, with or without salt, pepper and herbs, until tender. In my grandmother's house **'ash** was made with small bits of stewing steak, the gravy might include a bit of tinned tomato and — the best bit of all — it was ladled out onto a great slab of bread and HP sauce was dolloped on top. More frugal versions omitted the meat or ended up just as **tater 'ash** which was little more than potato and onion boiled up together with salt and pepper. **Lobscouse** (qv) is the Liverpool equivalent, a near-identical twin.

ashcan 'waterless lavatory' in which ashes from the domestic fire were used to cover the excrement before the cans were (if all went according to plan) tipped by the council scavengers into their nightsoil carts. The contents of the carts were then collected with street sweepings and animal dung, and in the larger towns and cities were sold to farmers as a fertiliser. Thus, much of the human and animal waste of Liverpool ended up on the fields of Burscough and Maghull, brought by canal from the city. Countless fragments of cheap Victorian pottery and glass, the non-biodegradable part of the domestic refuse of a century and more ago, litter the land in these areas to this day.

Ashton, Teddy (see **Clarke, Alan**)

Ashton Memorial James Williamson (1813-1879) was from Keswick but moved to Lancaster in 1827, and there he perfected the mass-production of oilcloth. In the 1850s and 1860s, he built up a huge business manufacturing this cheap, durable and easily-cleaned covering, which helped to transform the domestic circumstances of working-class people. His son, James Williamson II, inherited his father's great fortune, and in 1895 was elevated to the peerage as Lord Ashton. Father and son were the leading local philanthropists, and in 1881 Ashton gave to Lancaster Corporation the tract of open grazing land which became the Williamson Park, and there in 1909 he built the Ashton Memorial as a monument to his late wife. The memorial, one of the county's most

The Ashton Memorial, Lancaster.

dramatic landmarks and an architectural masterpiece, not only commemorated the loss of Lady Ashton, but also — dominating the town and surrounding area — symbolised the all-powerful role which her husband exercised in Lancaster, where he was the largest employer and most influential patron of civic life.

Ashton-under-Lyne Church An ancient legend told how, when the Church of St Michael was being built, a mysterious woman appeared in front of the workmen, who were playing cards, and said that if they turned up an ace she would pay for several yards of the steeple. They duly did so (an ace of spades) and she complied. Harland notes that the trefoil shape of the carved tracery probably 'gave origin to the fable'.

askins, axins banns of marriage (the 'askings') *This month I put up the axins*

asshole, esshole 'ash-hole', that is the hearth or range (to be precise, the space beneath into which the ash dropped). When my aunt was a child in the 1930s, my great-grandfather said to her *'th' art nobbut n'essle-tenter'*, because she was idle and not getting on with her tasks.

attercop (attercrop, attercob) spider (cf *copster*)

aughendole (affendole, aghendole, halfendole, haughendole) half share, or half dole; in the past, a term used in land transactions or when profits or assets were shared, but also in a more colloquial sense to imply something which was half complete; in everyday use, an *aughendole* was a measure of meal (cf *neckleton*)

Aughton Pudding Feast At Aughton in the Lune Valley, a giant pudding was cooked every twenty-one years, allegedly from the early nineteenth century (possibly 1803) until 1886. (The dates don't actually fit, since there was one in 1845.) The 1886 pudding weighed eleven hundredweight (560kg), and took five days and nights to cook. Ingredients included 100 lb (45kg) of flour, 300 lb (135kg) of dried fruit, 150 lb (68kg) of sugar and 900 eggs. The festival was attended by over 8,000 people, and much fun (and pudding) was had by all. The feast then lapsed,

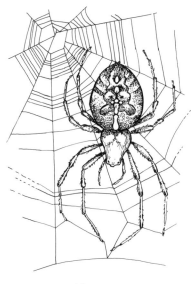

Attercop.

but it was revived in 1971. Its origins are uncertain — one source says that the boiler used was that in which the local basket-makers 'cooked' willows prior to stripping the bark.

axins (see *askins*)

Axon, William Edward Armytage William Axon (1846-1913) lived all his life in Manchester, becoming first the city's deputy chief librarian, and then in 1874 joining the *Manchester Guardian* as a literary reporter. He became a leading figure in Lancashire dialect circles because of his special interest in the surviving Lancashire dialect and in traditional verses and ballads, publishing several volumes on these subjects in the 1870s and 1880s.

awce to begin, to prepare (and, hence, to start courting)

awmas All Souls Mass (the festival of All Souls' Day, 2nd November)

B

back-cut *ginnel* (qv) or alleyway behind houses (cf *entry*, *weind*)

back end later part of the year — autumn and the first half of winter

back kitchen scullery or small room behind the house, used for wet and dirty tasks; originally the **back kitchen** did not have a fire, since the cooking and heating was done using the hearth or range in the **living room** (qv) (cf **front room**)

backside yard or garden behind a house. The phrase was in general use until the early years of the twentieth century, but has since (perhaps for misplaced reasons of propriety?) become largely obsolete. Overlapping and eventually superseding it was the shorter word *back*, which can mean either the yard or the entry or alley behind the house.

back-slamming means (presumably now obsolete) of inflicting punishment for minor crimes without recourse to law: the alleged offender was seized and held by the arms and legs, and his head was then rammed into a door or wall. This was noted by Harland in the 1870s as though it was still performed in his day. (cf *buck-thanging*)

backstone (bake-stone) smooth flat slab of stone, or iron plate (**griddle**), on which oatcakes were baked. The stone or plate was heated up over the fire, and the oatcake batter poured or spread on it. *Backstones* were an essential item of household equipment for centuries, for oatcakes were a staple food. Stone which formed naturally smooth slabs, and could withstand constant heating without flaking, was highly valued: the quarrying of such stone gave rise to place-names such as Baxenden (*bakestone-dale*) near Accrington.

back-to-back houses *Back-to-backs* are those in which the rear wall of a row of houses backs directly onto another row, with no space in between (therefore, no backyard). Such houses, unless at the end of a terrace, would have windows and light only at the front, and were poorly ventilated. They were comparatively

Back-slamming.

uncommon in Lancashire, where they were only built in significant numbers between about 1800 and 1850, and were then superseded by the conventional terraced house, many tens of thousands of which were constructed in the next eighty years. The typical Lancashire terraced house is often, quite wrongly, referred to as a **back-to-back**.

bad short, thick piece of wood (see *tipcat*)

badger dealer in small provisions, or a petty trader. *Badgers* were commonly seen on market days and fair days, selling all manner of odds and ends, essential items and small luxuries. In the nineteenth-century towns, *badger* was an alternative name for a grocer.

badger-baiting (see **bull-baiting**)

badging to trim vegetation, such as the growth at the base of hedgerows, or the grasses and small saplings on a field bank or roadside verge, with a *badgin' hook*, a form of sickle

badly seriously ill, the situation being more acute than when someone was merely *poorly*: *"is doin' badly, Ah'm afeart'*

baggin' food, a meal (especially used of teatime or a mid-afternoon snack and drink); originally, the food which a labourer carried from home in a bag (cf *drinkings*)

bagpipes As in other parts of northern Britain such as Scotland and Northumberland, the **bagpipes** were a traditional musical instrument in Lancashire. They were less elaborate and complex than modern Scottish pipes, but probably made a comparably distinctive noise. Then, as now, the music of the **pipes** provoked strong enthusiasms and equally strong loathing. When Ralph Thoresby, the Yorkshire antiquarian, visited the **Preston Guild** (qv) in 1702, he recorded that he was kept awake all night by the playing of the **Lancashire pipes** in the street outside. In 1634 John Court, a Catholic, was prosecuted because he persistently played the **pipes** outside the Anglican church at Croston on Sundays, thereby disrupting services.

bag pudding Lancashire equivalent of haggis. It could be sweet (often made with suet, oatmeal, currants, and treacle), or savoury (with chopped offal of any sort, onions, herbs, suet and meal). The ingredients were mixed together, and then stuffed into a cloth or a sheep's stomach and boiled. (See also *clout pudding*.)

baited to have wages reduced, for coming to work late or other reasons (from 'bate' or 'abate', to lessen or reduce)

Baker, Hylda Hylda Baker was born in Farnworth near Bolton in 1908, the daughter of a comedian. She became a stage comedienne herself, her act being characterised by sharp and witty observation, and parodying a talkative Lancashire woman with constant use of catchphrases: *'She knows y' know'*. She appeared in several films and television series, but died comparatively forgotten in 1986. Recently, however, she has been the subject of Jean Fergusson's one-woman stage play *She Knows You Know*, and Fergusson has also published a biography of

Hylda Baker with the same title. Baker's papers are in the Lancashire Record Office in Preston.

bally ann meal put together of anything that can be found in the pantry; *'It's a bally ann day*

Baggin'.

A bally ann day.

today' was usually said of the day before pay-day. The derivation is probably from the initials, because there was b***** a** in the cupboard.

Bamford, Samuel Samuel Bamford was born at Middleton in 1788, and is now regarded as the most illustrious son of that town. In his youth he became a passionate Radical, was present at **Peterloo** (qv) and left us the best eyewitness account of that terrible day, and for over a year was on the run or in prison. He eventually settled into a comfortable and conservative old age — he did not die until 1872, by which time he had become a legend in his own lifetime. He wrote extensively, and his autobiographical volumes are a key source for the social and political history of the early nineteenth century, while his recollections of boyhood include vivid accounts of the traditions and customs of south Lancashire in the 1790s. Bamford also wrote in dialect, and his collections of local words and phrases are of special importance because he was born two generations before the great dialect poets of the 1860s — he **warbled when Waugh wur a fledglin' i' th' nest**.

band (bant) string

bandy-ball rudimentary form of golf, once popular in parts of south Lancashire, in which a wooden ball was hit with a stout wooden bat, the object being to drive it across a given line

bangle to loiter, lounge around, waste time

banksman, bonksman worker at the mouth or shaft-top of a coalpit

bannock (see *bunnock*)

bant[1] to beat, in the sense of 'get the better of', as in a financial transaction or a business dealing

bant[2] substandard cloth, defectively woven (for example, too slack or irregularly patterned). It could also mean the feel or quality of cloth, which either had or had not got *bant*: *'If it had bant you bought, if not you didn't'*. The extension of this meaning was that anything without **bant** was ineffectual or lacking. Of food it might be said that it had **not got much bant about it**, meaning that it didn't fill you up.

bant³ string (see also *sneck*)

bantlin' baby or small child

bantling small sweet cake eaten on fair days. Whittle, in 1852, refers to *Brindle Bantlings*, which were eaten at the *wakes* (qv) in that village, 'made by the old housewives a month before the wakes commenced'.

Barcroft The Barcroft family of Barcroft Hall, a mile (1.5km) up the valley from Towneley Hall in Burnley, is said to have been cursed by an heir who, suffering from insanity or imbecility, was chained in the cellar and starved to death. In a lucid moment, he foretold that the family would perish and the house would pass into other hands. Harland notes that the last male generation, which died out in the 1640s, included a 'lunatic', the possible origin of the legend — but comparable stories of monsters and curses are told of houses all over the British Isles. The other version of the tale is that Barcroft had a *boggart* (qv) called *Hob o' th' Hurst*, who began as a friendly and helpful spirit until (inexplicably) given a pair of clogs by a visitor, at which point it became more malevolent, since any gift to a witch or ghost would make it harmful.

barguist fearsome apparition, in the form (somewhat oddly?) of a cow or (more conventionally) a horse or a big black dog, which was said to leap onto the shoulders of travellers on dark roads in the darkest nights (See also *Bezza Shriker, Radcliffe Shag.*)

barley children's truce word, still in general use in many parts of Lancashire. The terms which children use when calling a truce in games were among the first subjects studied by national investigators into dialect speech, in the 1930s. They show very strong regional and local variations.

Barley — a children's truce word.

Barley Time The years around 1800 were often known later as **Barley Time**, because the weather was so bad and the harvests so poor that on occasion even the oat crop failed. People were reduced to eating barley, the least palatable of the grain crops. In these conditions of acute deprivation, made worse by the effects of the Napoleonic Wars, there was a very real threat of famine and starvation in the county.

barm (berm) yeast. Until the late nineteenth century, brewer's yeast,

A barguist attacking an unsuspecting victim.

the frothy head and yeasty lees from fermenting liquor, was the most widely used, so yeast was bought in liquid form. The frothiness of this gave rise to more-or-less affectionate terms such as *berm yed* (head) and *barmpot* to describe people who were daft or had little solid sense in their heads, while the modern word **barmy** (often now misspelled 'balmy') is from the same source.

barmskin   apron made of leather (cf *brat*)

Baron, John Thomas   Known as *Jack o' Anns*, Baron (1856-1922) was a prolific dialect writer who wrote over 1,700 poems published consecutively in the *Blackburn Times* between 1886 and 1919.

Baron, Joseph   Born at Rishton in 1859, Joseph Baron was, like many of the dialect writers and poets, a journalist, although he began working life as a solicitor. He compiled the *Blegburn Dickshonary*, which was later republished as the *Lankisher Dickshonary*, and wrote extensively on local history and scenery, as well as literary and poetical works — his *Th' Dule upo' Dun,* telling the story of how the Devil appeared in the cottage of a tailor at Brungerley near Clitheroe, is one of the longest of all the many Lancashire dialect poems written in the years around 1900. Baron's view of Lancashire speech is summed up by part of the dedication of the *Dickshonary*:

> *Th' owd lingo talked bi gradely fooak*

> *Th' owd lingo as eawr faythers spoooak*
> *Th' owd lingo as we hooap'll leaven*
> *Th' whul lot o' Babel tongues i' Heaven!*

b'art   (see *beart*)

basket making   In several parts of the county where low-lying marshy ground favoured the growth of willows and osiers, **basket making** was until recently an important craft. The trade was greatly encouraged in south Lancashire by the development of market-gardening and poultry-rearing in the late eighteenth century, which produced a large demand for specialised items such as *potato wiskets* and **egg baskets**. The most important centres were Arkholme, in the Lune Valley, and the area around Mawdesley, Bispham and Parbold, on the lowlands of the River Douglas, where the trade survived until the 1950s.

bass   impure coal; the shale and other material which was left unburned at the end of the fire, and which had to be raked out with the ashes

batter   person who beat raw cotton fibres as part of the cleaning process

beacons   Prominent hills in Lancashire were often used in the past as the sites of beacons, which lit on occasions of emergency or celebration (the threatened invasion by the Spaniards in 1588 being perhaps the best-known instance). Examples include

A beacon, lit on occasions of emergency or celebration.

Beacon Fell near Preston and Ashurst Beacon above Skelmersdale.

beamer in the cotton industry, the operative who wound the warp from the bobbins onto the beam of the loom, in readiness for weaving

bear-baiting (see bull-baiting)

beawt without; *b'art* in southwest Lancashire

beck stream. The terms used for minor watercourses are of special interest because they reflect, even at the end of the twentieth century, cultural patterns which are over

1000 years old. *Beck*, which is a Norse word, is commonly associated with the Lake District, but it is found in Lancashire as far south as the northern side of the Ribble Valley and in the Colne area. South of the Ribble the word *brook*, with its Anglo-Saxon derivation, is standard. The linguistic boundary at the Ribble, reflecting the respective cultural influence of the Scandinavian settlement (north of the river) and the Anglo-Saxons (to the south), is of major historical significance.

bed used figuratively, so that *to get her bed* meant that a woman was going into labour; could also mean 'to sleep' *Aw've 'ad no bed for three neets*

Beechams Pills Thomas Beecham, an Oxfordshire shepherd, moved to Lancashire and in 1859 settled in St Helens, where he became a grocer and druggist. He marketed his patent pills very effectively and made his fortune. The Beecham family played a dominant role in the life of the borough in the forty years before the First World War, while the firm which Thomas founded became one of the world's great pharmaceutical companies. Thomas' grandson was the great conductor Sir Thomas Beecham.

Beef Night A communal event when, after a farmer decided to kill one of his beef herd, neighbours and others agreed to buy portions of the meat; the purchasers gathered, celebrated and were entertained. In February 1835, for example, seventy-two buyers congregated at a beef night in Samlesbury.

beest(ings) first milk of a cow after it had calved — rich, thick and full-flavoured, it was regarded as a special delicacy; *beesting custards* were particularly esteemed (cf *afterings*)

Belle Vue For generations of Manchester people, a day out meant **Belle Vue**. The entertainment complex was opened by John Jennison as a zoological gardens and pleasure ground in 1836, and included a boating lake, floral displays, tea rooms, ornamental walks and later a funfair, as well as the zoo itself. Situated at the junction of Hyde Road and Kirkmanshulme Lane, and eventually covering eighty acres (32ha), Belle Vue was on several major tram routes, and until the 1950s was a byword for fun and pleasure. It then began to deteriorate and, in the brave new world of redevelopment and renewal which was Manchester in the 1970s, it closed. Today it is hardly possible, from the ground, to tell that Belle Vue ever existed.

bellin' to cry out, to make a lot of noise (from the same root as 'bellowing'); though with an apparently unrelated origin, **belly achin'** is similar in sense — making a lot of fuss

bell-tinker in some parts of east Lancashire, to thrash or to beat; but in the Liverpool area, this term was used to indicate something good or enjoyable

The Bezza Skriker, a terrifying type of barguist.

Bezza Skriker fearsome apparition which lived at Bezza, near the Ribble in Samlesbury parish. A type of *barguist* (qv), it was a huge shaggy dog, with great feet, long hanging ears and fiery eyes as big as saucers, and it crept up quietly behind people. When confronted it retreated, eyes blazing, and led the wayfarer unwittingly towards a deep pit or puddle. *Skriker* disappeared in the water and the traveller usually fell in. Perhaps the victim's presence earlier in the evening at the beerhouse was not unconnected with these terrifying apparitions. (See also *boggart*, *Radcliffe Shag*)

berm see *barm*

best better *tha'd best get on wi' it*

bidding invitation to a funeral

bilberry Also known as *whinberry* or *whimberry*, the **bilberry**, which grows in abundance on the moors and hillsides of Lancashire, was in the past was one of the most important free foods. It is still picked by people like me, to whom its delicious fruit is sufficient compensation for rivers of sweat, backbreaking toil, the bites of innumerable gnats and flies, and the tell-tale bright-purple staining of hands and mouth.

Bilberry.

billet game played in east Lancashire, whereby a five-inch (13cm) wooden peg was placed on the flattened end of a wooden club, thrown into the air and then hit with the club as hard as possible.

An effigy is paraded through the streets of Ashton-under-Lyne during Black Lad Monday.

The winner was the man who hit the billet furthest. In Liverpool the same game was usually known as *peggy*. (See also *buck-out-of-the-wood, knur and spell, tipcat, trippet*).

billy In the cotton industry, the *slub* (a long thread of slightly-twisted cotton yarn) is reduced to a thinner, finer thread on a *billy*, generally known as a *roving billy*. This process made it more even and regular, and twisted it further, so it was ready to go onto the spinning frame.

bing to go sour or spoil, as with butter, cream or cheese (especially if spoiled in the churning or pressing)

Bird and Baby traditional humorous nickname for pubs called the **Eagle and Child** (qv); in the nineteenth century, the dialect version *Brid an' Bantlin'* was common

bit a little while *Ah'll be along in a bit*

blackclock, blackjack cockroach or large black beetle (cf *twitchclock*)

Black Lad Monday An ancient ceremony at Ashton-under-Lyne, in which (originally on Easter Monday but subsequently in the early summer) an effigy of the *Black Lad* was paraded through the streets. It was said to represent a particularly evil and oppressive lord of the manor, Sir Ralph Assheton, who in the 1480s had exploited and ill-used his tenants. Winifred Bowman, Ashton's great historian, in a detailed account of the custom, points out the impossibility of this being the true origin, and attributes it to a much older tradition — the explanation for which is lost — which may be associated with **beating the bounds** and with the driving out of the darkness of winter.

Blackpool landlady The proprietress of a boarding house or 'hotel', a formidable, brawny figure of dominating and oppressive personality, ruthlessly enforcing the strictest rules and greatest parsimony, cramming in the visitors, charging for every conceivable extra (including the notorious *sixpence for the use of the cruet*) and tyrannising them and her small and henpecked husband ... the Blackpool landlady was a semi-legendary figure beloved of the postcard artist and the music-hall comedian. Do they still exist? Were they ever so terrifying? Some certainly were: read John Walton's book (see bibliography) to find out more.

blackmail In many parts of Lancashire, it was customary at weddings to tie a rope across the road from the church, symbolically preventing the departure of the couple until they had paid a forfeit or *blackmail*.

black pudding Lancashire speciality, the best of which are traditionally made in Bury and sold on the market there. Innumerable variations of the basic recipe survive and many are still made, though the important ingredients, pig's blood and a cereal filling of some sort, remain standard in almost all versions. **Black pudding** was once made everywhere in England, because pigs were kept by almost all cottagers and farmers. Nothing was wasted, and the blood was used in this savoury and tasty way. But, as with many other traditional foods, what was once commonplace has now become a rarity, a local speciality surviving in a culturally conservative area such as Lancashire while dying out elsewhere. Fortunately, the recent revival of interest in traditional foods has provided the **Lancashire black pudding** with a new market, and its future seems secure.

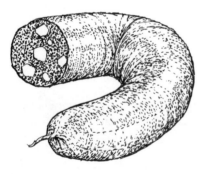

Black pudding.

Blackstone Edge The old paved road over Blackstone Edge behind Littleborough has been the subject of fierce controversy for 300 years. It has long been considered by many to be Roman, and many archaeologists have considered it

to be the best-preserved example in Britain. Others, more warily, have concluded that it is a pack-horse road of the seventeenth or early eighteenth centuries. The current balance of opinion is that the latter explanation is much more likely, and that unfortunately a Roman origin seems improbable. Blackstone Edge itself was notorious to trans-Pennine travellers because it was so steep and exposed. Daniel Defoe records crossing from Rochdale to Halifax in the early eighteenth century during a blizzard — in August!

blackthorn once-popular Lancashire children's game, in which one child, a *catcher*, stood at a mark or on a line and faced a line of other players; at a given signal (such as the chanting of a rhyme) the players ran to each other's lines. The *catcher* had to try to pick up an opponent and carry him or her to the opposite line, at which point they would both become *catchers*. The game continued *till all be caught*. An alternative name was *sheep, sheep, come over*.

Blakeley Blackley, near Manchester

blame fault, as in *generous to a blame*

blather (see *blether-yed*)

bleeding Roger Lowe of Ashton-in-Makerfield, a young shopkeeper who kept a diary in the 1660s, recorded the following incantation for staunching the flow of blood from a wound. It was, he said, 'privately used among country persons and not publicly known'

Is the paved road over Blackstone Edge of Roman origin, or a packhorse route?

and the words were 'to be seriously said three times together':

> *'There was a babe in Beth'lem born*
> *And christened in the water of flumen* [river] *Jordan*
> *The water it was both wild and wood*
> *The child it was both meek and good*
> *Staunch blood in God's name'*

blethur-yed someone with nothing between the ears, a head full of air and talk, but no sense. Nineteenth-century dictionaries suggest a derivation from *bladder head* (since bladders were full of air), but the true origin is the ON *blathra*, to talk nonsense: to *blather* or *blether* is therefore 'to say a great deal about nothing at all'.

blind scouse (see *scouse*)

blowing room section of a cotton spinning mill where the *blowers* drove cotton fibre through the *scutching* (qv) machinery by means of large fans

blue milk skimmed milk, so called from its pale watery-blue colour

bo' the word is *ball*, which was also used in the past to mean a dumpling or boiled pudding; hence *aister-bo*, an Easter dumpling

bobber and kibs girls' pavement game, also known as *alley and jackstones*. The *bobber* was a large marble (usually white) and the *kibs* were four earthenware cubes in different colours. They were placed at the four corners of an imaginary square. She had to bounce the marble and, before it landed, catch it and pick up a *kib*

Bobbers.

as well. This was done with each *kib* in turn, but on the last occasion the player had to pick up all four *kibs* in one sweep of the hand.

bobbing The *bobber* was the individual who had to wake people who fell asleep during church services. At Prestwich in the 1730s the bobber was George Grimshaw, whose other duties included whipping dogs out of church, keeping children quiet and cleaning the pulpit. The Grimshaw family were hereditary bobbers of Prestwich for over 200 years until the 1850s. *Bobbing* was accomplished by the use of a long stick like a fishing rod, on the end of which was fixed a *bob*, or wooden block, which was pressed against the slumbering worshipper.

bobbins An essential item in the cotton trade, **bobbins** were wooden spools for holding yarn at various stages of the spinning process and in the preparatory stages of weaving. **Bobbin mills**,

A bobber at work.

often situated in rural areas, used local timber supplies and were generally water-powered.

bog   outdoor toilet. In recent decades the word has become unacceptable in polite society, but it was formerly an everyday term in Lancashire. Thirty years ago, a very respectable relative of mine in the south of England would unselfconsciously refer to the *bog* and thus betray Northern origins, for no well-bred Southerner would ever contemplate using the word. To them, even a peat bog might be called a marsh, because that sounded more genteel. (cf *little house*)

bog-brast   (see *brast*)

bog-eyed   weary or exhausted, in the sense of 'ready to fall asleep'

boggart   ghost, sprite, evil spirit or *feeorin* (qv). The word has now largely fallen out of use, but it survives in, for example, the place-name **Boggart Hole Clough**, a steep-sided valley which is now a public park at Blackley on the northern outskirts of Manchester. Until recently *boggarts* were common in the folklore of many parts of the county, and there was scarcely an old house or a lonely valley which did not have its terrifying tales of creatures which roamed, shrieked and caused havoc — though most do not appear to have been especially malevolent, and some were just a nuisance. The *Trash*, though, was a terrifying *boggart* which resided in Godley Lane near the church at Burnley, where it appeared as

a *barguist* (qv) or huge dog with saucer-like eyes, shaggy hair and great broad feet, shrieking and making a splashing sound. Much more horrible was the *Bee Hole Boggart* of Brunshaw, which was said to have carried off an elderly woman ('Old Bet') and left her skin on a thorn bush as a memento. (See also *Bezza Shriker*, *Hairy Ghost*, *Radcliffe Shag*, *Tong Boggart*)

boggies   headlice

bonksman   (see *banksman*)

Bonnie Prince Charlie   In 1745, during the second Jacobite rising, Bonnie Prince Charlie (Prince Charles Edward Stewart, the Young Pretender) came south through Lancashire with his army. He stopped at Lancaster, Preston and

Bonnie Prince Charlie.

Manchester, proclaiming his father as James III, and a fortnight later his armies came back, fleeing the government forces on the long route which led to Culloden. In Lancashire, many legends and tales surround this highly romantic but disastrously incompetent figure. Families treasured the keepsakes and souvenir gifts which he distributed to attractive young ladies, while pubs and other historic buildings like to claim that he was an overnight guest: 'Bonnie Prince Charlie slept here'. The least romantic and perhaps least plausible claim was that, until recently, a privy which he used could be seen in the backyard of a house in Nether Kellet.

bonny　fine, beautiful (in the sense of young women, children, and sometimes scenery); also sometimes used to mean very or exceedingly; a common alternative meaning is plump or healthy-looking

boose, boost, bouse　cow's stall or bed in a *shippon* (qv) (see also *boskins*)

boot, bought　bend, as in an elbow or the bend of a river; for example, Boat Farm near Alston, on the Ribble, was formerly **Booght Farm**

booths　The names of hamlets in the forest areas of the Pennines often included the word *booth* in their name, and examples of such place-names survive in Rossendale (eg **Crawshawbooth**) and Pendle (**Old Laund Booth** and several others). *Booths* were originally

cattle shelters or herdsman's huts, and thus they were temporary buildings high on the moors and in more remote valleys. Most of these districts remained very thinly populated until the later sixteenth century.

boskins　divisions between the stalls in a *shippon* or cowshed (see also *boose*)

bought　(see *boot*)

bound up　constipated

bouse　(see *boose*)

box　At country funerals in many parts of Lancashire (and elsewhere in the North), sprigs of the box shrub were formerly placed in a dish at the church or the home of the deceased. Each mourner would take a sprig and cast it upon the coffin as it was lowered into the ground. Alternative herbs were rosemary or lavender.

A sprig of box.

Box Harry Week Rossendale expression, recorded in the nineteenth century but of unknown derivation. When wages were paid (in cash of course) once a month, this was the fourth week, when the money had run out and there was nothing to live on.

br- In traditional Lancashire pronunciation, especially in the east of the county, 'br-' was often used instead of the 'bi-' or 'bu-' at the beginning of certain Standard English words. Thus the older spelling and pronunciation of Burnley was *Brunla'* and 'burst' became *brast*. The form was less common in the south-west of the county, though in the St Helens area, 'burnt' was pronounced *brunt*. This changed order of letters was not unique to Lancashire: the nickname 'Brummie' for someone from Birmingham derives from the older pronunciation *Brummagem*.

brade flake, bread flake, fleak wooden frame or rack, hung from the ceiling on cords so that vermin could not reach it, on which **oatcakes** were placed to dry and harden for keeping or for toasting; often pronounced, and spelled by dialect writers, as *brade fleigh*. These were common items of household equipment, especially in Pennine Lancashire, well into the twentieth century.

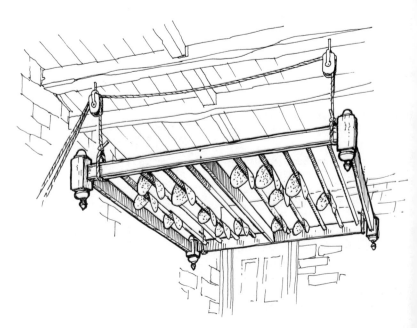

A brade flake, with oatcakes hanging to dry.

braggot drink for celebration days, based on ale (preferably newly-brewed) which was sweetened with honey or sugar and heavily spiced, then drunk either cold or hot as a form of mulled ale. In common variants, eggs were beaten and then stirred into the hot spiced ale (not so hot as to curdle them) so that the drink thickened. This was regarded as particularly fortifying and nutritious, and was especially associated with Mid-Lent or Mothering Sunday, which in some parts of Lancashire was known as *Braggot Sunday*. At Altcar, for example, 'every labourer expected four eggs from his employer, with which he repaired to the alehouse, where the eggs, with spices, were drunk in hot ale'. (See also *Simblin' Sunday*)

brandreth three-legged cast-iron trivet for use in cooking. The *brandreth* was more substantial than a modern trivet (which is used to put hot dishes on) since it stood over the hearth or fire, and flat-bottomed pots and pans would be stood on it for boiling. The term was once used throughout the North-West, although latterly it has been confined to the area north of Morecambe Bay. (ON *brandreith*, a grate)

brass money, wealth; another of the terms by which Northern speech (especially that of Lancashire and Yorkshire) is commonly signified in the media, and well known in the Yorkshire phrase *'Weer ther's muck there's brass'*. It has a long ancestry and was used by Tim Bobbin (**John Collier**, qv) in the 1750s.

brast to burst. It could be used in any sense appropriate (with variations, as in *brast-off*, to begin); a specialised meaning was a *bog-brast*, when, in certain rare circumstances, the layers of peat on a moorland become so saturated with water that they turn into a semi-liquid and start to burst, or flow, down the hillside, carrying with them rocks, walls and trees. On **Pendle** (qv), for example, destructive *brasts* are known to have occurred in 1580, 1669 and 1870.

brat apron (cf *barmskin*)

brawsen overfed, stuffed (hence, gross or bloated people)

bread and cheese commonly-used country name for the buds of the hawthorn, which were eaten as a salad or by children from the hedgerows as they passed

bread flake (see *brade flake*)

braid, breid section of the working face in a colliery

A brandreth.

29

A clapper bridge at Wycoller.

brett brill, a fish eaten a great deal in the eighteenth century but which became much less common on Lancashire markets by 1850

breck slope or hillside; found in numerous place-names throughout the north and west of the county, and in dialect use until recent times. Examples include **Norbreck** ('north hill') and **Warbreck** ('ward or look-out hill') in Blackpool. (ON *brekka*, a slope)

brew when used as a noun rather than a verb, very common in Lancashire **let's have a brew** (a drink of tea), **I stopped for a brew**

brewis oatcake toasted and then broken or crumbled into liquid — often warm ale, broth or thin stew — and eaten with a spoon. It formed a superior type of *pobs* (qv) and was standard fare in

poor families all over the county. In the Rochdale area, among other places, the oatcake-and-broth mixture was supplemented by the skimmings of fat and the wrinkling skin which forms on top of a pot of simmering meat.

bridges Lancashire has comparatively few older bridges, because so many have been rebuilt in the past 200 years to cope with heavy industrial and general traffic. Among the best medieval bridges is that over the Lune between Hornby and Gressingham, and quite a few **packhorse bridges** survive from the seventeenth and eighteenth centuries. Perhaps the oldest bridges — in style, at least, since they are undatable — are the **clapper bridges**, great rough slabs of stone, which span the beck at Wycoller.

Brierley, Ben The son of a handloom weaver, Ben Brierley was born at Failsworth in 1825 and received his formal education at Sunday school, before becoming a handloom weaver himself. However, he later became a journalist and from 1863 worked on the *Oldham Times*. In the late 1860s, with Edwin Waugh, he was a founder-member of the circle of writers and poets who revived the study of the dialect of south Lancashire, and who wrote contemporary verse and prose in dialect. Brierley himself wrote some poetry, but his literary talents lay in short sketches and anecdotal writings in dialect, which were immensely popular in his day and have retained their importance ever since. He died in 1896 and was buried at Harpurhey Cemetery.

Brief Encounter The meetings between the lovers, played by Trevor Howard and Celia Johnson, in the much-loved 1940s romantic film *Brief Encounter* were filmed in the railway station refreshment room at Carnforth. The station has recently, on the strength of this, been marketed as a somewhat modest tourist attraction.

Britannia Coconutters Every Easter Saturday the **Coconutters** dance through the streets of Bacup, covering a route of many miles and wearing out a set of **clog irons** (qv). Several groups of dancers were formed at mills in the Bacup area in the mid-nineteenth century, of which one, the

Ben Brierley.

Lee Mill dancers, moved to Britannia in 1903 and formed the **Britannia Coconutters**. In the early twentieth century there were at least four troupes of **coconutters** in the valley, but only the Britannia group survived. Their costume is clogs, black jerseys, red and white kilts, white stockings and blackened faces (which traditionally is held to indicate a Moorish origin), and their dances were allegedly brought to the area by Cornish miners in the early 1800s. The name derives from the wooden discs, fastened to hands, waists and knees, which make sounds like those associated with the clattering of half-coconut shells. The **nutters** are among the best-known and, at national and international folk and dance competitions, the most successful of all British folk-dance groups.

broadcloths   (see *flying shuttle*)

brobs   branches, sticks and other markers which are stuck in the sand to mark the channels and routes on a **sands crossing** (qv) across Morecambe Bay

brock   badger; used as the name of the animal, the word is falling into disuse, but it survives in numerous place-names in the county, such as **Brockholes** in Preston

brood   young salmon, one to two years in age and about the size of a trout. They were formerly taken in large numbers from the Mersey, Ribble and other south Lancashire rivers, and were particularly prized for their delicate flesh.

brook   (see *beck*)

Brookside   Celebrated for having a death rate many times the national average, and with violent demise and unexplained disappearance an occupational hazard of the residents, *Brookside* is Liverpool's answer to *Coronation Street*. In contrast to the older Mancunian product, it attempts to portray life in the new suburbs of the 1980s and '90s, rather than a version of the traditional terraced

A brock.

house view of Lancashire. Whether it is any more successful, and whether it will ever share the same special place which *Coronation Street* now occupies in television's roll of honour is, fortunately, a matter for individual opinion.

brow (broo) hill or slope, often on a street or road (for example, **Pin Mill Brow** in Ancoats, Manchester)

brown George (see *ran dan*)

bruart to spring up or to rise; for example, the first shoots of a crop, or the upturned brim of a hat. The word has many variant spellings, including *brewert*, *brewit* and *browart*.

bucko rough, fighting man (used especially in Liverpool, and probably derived from the Spanish *vaquero*, via *buckeroo*)

buck-out-of-the-wood one of a large group of very similar games which were very popular in east and south Lancashire. A short, thick, wooden peg was placed in a socket in a wooden board on the ground. On being struck with a club, the peg shot into the air, making a whirring sound. The winner was the person whose peg travelled the greatest distance from the board. (See also *billet*, *knur and spell*, *tipcat*, *trippet*)

buck-thanging According to Harland, writing in the 1870s, this was a 'Lancashire punishment still practised by schoolboys', in which the victim was laid on his back and four boys each held an arm or leg. They tossed him in the air and let him fall back to the ground

with a violent thud. This is clearly a more savage predecessor of the modern practise of 'bumping', whereby the victim (often someone celebrating a birthday) is tossed up, but now the perpetrators retain hold of the limbs and so the descent is slightly less hazardous. (cf *back-slamming*)

bule handle of a pot, kettle, bucket or other vessel

bull-baiting Bull-baiting was a very popular entertainment for centuries, a highlight of many a Lancashire *wakes[1]* (qv) celebration; for example at Eccles in 1819, when 'the day's sport [was] to conclude with baiting the bull "Fury"', the prize being 'a superior dog-chain'. In Rochdale in 1820, several young men were killed when a wall collapsed because of the press of the crowd during a **bull-baiting**. The 'sport' died out soon after this, the victim of a more enlightened attitude to the treatment of animals. **Bear baiting** was also enjoyed in Lancashire before the 1840s. Langton, in his history of Flixton written in 1898, records that an old man who died that year had told him of seeing a **bear-baiting** in the village when he was young; while Nicholls states that the last **bull-baiting** in Radcliffe was in September 1838. **Badger-baiting**, on the other hand, has never fully died out, and local newspapers from time to time report cases of this appalling practice even in the 1990s. In the 1870s, **badger-baiting** was still going on in yards

Bull-baiting.

and inn courts (even one in Deansgate in Manchester) to entertain the drinkers of south Lancashire.

bullock to cheat, deceive or bully

bullockin' time period of about five minutes after the end of official working hours when the machinery of a cotton mill continued running. No extra pay was given, and the workforce considered, rightly enough, that they were *bullocked* as a result.

bull-scutter Taylor (1901) says 'literally the excrement of the bull;

nonsense; bragging; loose talk'; the term is more familiar a century later as what is usually assumed to be a purely transatlantic import — 'bullshit' — but it clearly has authentic home-grown origins

bump bankrupt *goin' bump*

bunnock oat bun or cake which, unlike the usual oatcake which was very thin, flat and large, was two to four inches (5-10cm) across and more solid (the oatmeal was often mixed with treacle and a little water to give cohesion). *Bunnock* became a term of friendly derision to imply a fool or a somewhat simple-minded person; the people of Penwortham, for example, were widely known as *bunnocks*. (var of *bannock*)

burgy[1] inferior, poor quality (used of coal, or of bad ale)

burgy[2] In the St Helens area, the word *burgy* came to mean the waste material from the glass industry — the discarded sand and used rouge which had been employed in the grinding and polishing processes. *Burgy* was dumped alongside the St Helens Canal, particularly around Gerards Bridge and Cowley Hill, forming great mounds and ridges by the end of the nineteenth century. They are still there, although now colonised by trees and grass, a process which happened more or less naturally; in the 1950s and early '60s, Pilkingtons spent a great deal of money on the deliberate planting of trees and grass, almost all of which immediately died.

burl knot or lump, as in a thread or piece of cloth

burning wells In the Wigan coalfield there were a number of **burning wells**, places where the methane and other gases from the coal measures escaped through fissures. The most famous, a tourist attraction in the seventeenth and eighteenth centuries, was the **Burning Well** at Derby Lane in Hindley, where the 'vent' was several inches across. A turf would be placed across the hole to extinguish the flame, and when the visitors were assembled, the gas would be reignited with a spill. It burned with the familiar blue gas flame which, to those accustomed only to the red or yellow flames of wood fires and candles, seemed deeply mysterious. Celia Fiennes described her visit in 1695:

'2 miles off Wigon towards
Warrington ... is the Burning
Well which burns like brandy;
its a little sorry hole in one of the
grounds 100 yards from the road
that comes from Warrington to
Wiggon, just by a hedge or banck,
its full of dirt and mud almost but
the water continually bubbles up
as if it were a pott boyling which is
the spring ... nevertheles I felt the
water and it was a cold Spring; the
man which shewed it me with a
dish tooke out a good quantety of
the water and then with a piece of
rush he lighted by a candle he set
the water in the well on fire, and it
burn'd blewish just like spirits and
continued a good while.'

Other descriptions of that well suggest that the flame formed a cone about two feet (0.6m) across at the base, and that there was a pool of tar in the bottom of the hole. The well was lost under rubbish and debris in the 1840s, by which time gas was no longer a novelty.

bury my old wife humorous term used by eighteenth-century apprentices to refer to the long-awaited time when they came to the end of their seven-year term and were released from their indentures

Bury simnels The **Bury simnel**, a cross between a fruitcake and a biscuit, was one of the traditional dishes of the county. It was very solid, dry and durable, and some recipes suggest that a **simnel** might be well over a foot (30cm) in diameter. It was first recorded in the late eighteenth century, but is almost certainly of medieval origin. **Simnels** were eaten on **Simnel** or Mid-Lent **Sunday** (now known generally as Mothering Sunday), and were a speciality of Bury and neighbouring villages. During the nineteenth century the town held a special feast day, when the cakes were eaten with spiced ale, and when Bury people who had gone to live elsewhere returned to meet family and

friends. The making of **simnels** had more or less died out by the late 1970s, but recently a firm of bakers in the town has begun to make small versions of **simnels** once more. **Bury simnels** bear no resemblance to the marzipan-covered fruitcakes, decorated with marzipan balls and fluffy chickens, which are today called simnel cakes.

butter cake slice of bread and butter, *cake* being used here in the old sense of 'piece or slice, or lump' (cf *cake of soap*). The tendency to use it solely to mean a sweet, baked cake is more recent.

butty sandwich. In the nineteenth century the word was used to describe a slice of bread and butter, a variant upon **butter cake** or **butty cake** *'Thi' mother ga' mo a traycle butter-cake an a' hawpn'y when aw geet tha whoam'* (Edwin Waugh)

butty shop shop which was owned by the overlooker or owner of a mill or mine, where workers were paid on credit for goods and the amount deducted from their wages at the end of the week. The system was open to a wide variety of abuses and offered opportunities for exploitation of the workers, which led to its being made illegal (officially at least) in the 1870s. (See also *truck*)

C

cack excrement; a child's nappy might be described as *cacky*

cack-handed left-handed; clumsy (cf *keck-handed*, *keigh-paw*)

cackle-berries eggs

caddow thin quilt or coverlet; in the nineteenth century this was usually thick unbleached cotton wadding, but the term (and the item of bedding) can be traced back to at least the sixteenth century

cady man's flat straw hat

cake We now use the word almost exclusively for a sweet baked cake, but in Lancashire dialect the term meant any baked bread, cake or biscuit, such as a **breadcake, Bury Simnel** (qv), **Chorley cake** (qv) or **Eccles cake** (qv)

cale (see *kail*)

cally calico; lengths of cloth smaller than the standard width were often known as *narrow callies*, and the weaver of calico was a *cally weighver*

cam crooked, awry; and, by association, ill-natured, quarrelsome

Camelot name of a theme park near Chorley with no obvious Lancashire connections, but also of King Arthur's court. Over the past two centuries, right up to the present day, various writers and 'historians' have suggested that the Arthurian Camelot may have been located somewhere in Lancashire. We may disregard them.

campin' going to somebody else's house and making yourself comfortable there

Canaan nickname given to districts in various Lancashire towns (eg Higherford at Barrowford) which had an unusual number of Nonconformist chapels

can general name for any tin or other metal receptacle, and also used more widely as a term for a container for drink. In a cotton-spinning mill, a *can* was a tall cylindrical metal container into which the thick, soft *sliver* (qv) was collected. Once full the can had to be lifted clear, and it is often alleged that this is the origin of the phrase *carrying the can*.

can-lad apprentice, especially in engineering, and particularly in the Liverpool area; the youngest or most recent employee, whose job it was to make the *cans* of tea,

The carding room.

and hence anyone who did menial tasks *don't ask me, I'm only th' can-lad*

cannel form of coal which is hard in texture and burns with a bright, clear flame (the name derives from 'candle'). It was found extensively in the Wigan coalfield, where it was mined on a large scale from the Middle Ages onwards. Early travellers frequently commented on the **cannel mines** in the neighbourhood.

cant lively, cheerful, in good health, going on well; often applied to those who might not be expected to be in that condition, such as pregnant women or old people

carding action of straightening and separating the unspun fibres of raw cotton or wool. The work was originally done with wooden bats, the surfaces of which were covered with numerous pins. The fibres were placed on one bat and drawn down onto the other, and as this operation was repeated, the pins arranged the fibres as required. Subsequently **carding engines** were developed, where the pins were replaced by projecting pieces of wire mounted onto a large metal drum or cylinder, and the same process was effected as the cylinder revolved. **Carding** was a vital part of the textile process, and young children and girls were often put in the **carding room** as their first job.

Carling Sunday fifth Sunday in Lent when, in Lancashire villages, parched peas (*carlins*) were eaten in the afternoon, having been boiled until soft during the morning and then fried in butter. In some places, vinegar and sugar were added. Similar customs were traditional elsewhere in Northern England, such as Tyneside. In the 1830s, baked peas known as *carls* were sold in the streets of Liverpool by vendors who sang the following unambitious rhyme:

Carl, carl, carl away
Palm Sunday, Easter Day

cart-arse (see *arse-board*)

cartlone back lane or 'cart lane'

carr overgrown wetland. Although largely obsolete as a term of everyday speech, this word is still in general use among historians, ecologists and natural historians to describe the distinctive land-scape of these areas, while it is an extremely common element in minor place-names, farm names and field names throughout the county. (Old Norse *kjarr*)

cast[1] resemblance *she's a cast of 'er mam about 'er*

cast[2] squint

cattle historically this meant all live beasts, including horses and sheep, and was used as such in seventeenth and eighteenth-century legal documents (invent-ories often referred to 'cattles and chattells', for example)

ceawr to squat

chaff to tease, poke fun at

chairs *'e's got all his chairs at home* — he's very successful

chamber lye (see *lant*)

champion grand, or (in **Taylor's** (qv) words) 'anything superlatively great or good'

'Change the Manchester cotton exchange, better known as the **Royal Exchange**. Beneath its great domed roof, the huge Lancashire cotton industry had its focal point, cotton was bought and sold, and fortunes were made and lost. To have a place on the *'Change* was confirmation that a man had made his mark in the world, and with a house in St Annes and a season ticket on a club train, it defined success. On the closure of the cotton exchange in 1962, the building was converted into the famous Royal Exchange Theatre, the theatre 'module' being built inside the vast central space of the floor of the exchange. It was badly damaged by the IRA bomb of 1996, but now, fully restored, it is a central feature of the redesign-ed city centre.

chap Although this has the usual general meaning of a man, it can also specifically mean sweetheart, as in the famous poem by Sam Fitton, *Eawr Sarah's getten a chap*; hence, courting could be referred to as *chappin'*

chat, chit[1] small potato, too little to be sold, and so either eaten by the family or used as a major ingredient of pig food.

chat, chit[2] small twigs gathered for kindling or as a makeshift strainer

cheese The true **Lancashire cheese** (not the pale, acid travesty usually marketed under that name in supermarkets) is now only made in the Longridge and Goosnargh area, north-east of Preston, where several farms still specialise in its production. It has recently emerged from the shadows to be recognised as one of the greatest of all the cheeses of England — indeed, of Europe. Cheese was formerly made all over south Lancashire, and the cheeses of the Leigh area, which resembled those of Cheshire, were held by many to be even finer than the best produced in the neighbouring county. On the other hand, the cheese produced in north Lancashire and Westmorland was said to be so hard and resistant that it could be used to mend clogs!

cheese press One stage in the cheese-making process involved pressing the partly-formed cheese between solid boards, so that the liquid whey was driven off, and the cheese became firm and took on its characteristic shape. Traditionally this was done by slowly lowering onto it a great block of stone (usually more or less a cube)

by means of a screw mechanism or supporting wooden frame. These stone blocks, with their characteristic shape (they normally have a channel cut in each side, into which the frame slotted), can be seen in farmyards and country gardens all over the county. Because of their size, they have usually not been moved very far, and they may serve as garden ornaments or gate-stops, or simply stand overgrown beneath a hedge.

cheggie conker

Humphrey Chetham.

Chetham Society The oldest local history society in north-west England, the Chetham Society was founded in 1843 and has since published almost 270 volumes of 'remains historical and literary pertaining to the counties palatine of Lancaster and Chester', to use its esoteric Victorian title. It is named after **Humphrey Chetham**, Lancashire's first self-made

Cheese presses.

businessman and a multi millionaire by seventeenth-century standards. On his death in 1653, Chetham left much of his fortune to educational and philanthropic causes, including Chethams Library in Manchester.

child labour   Among the traditions of which Lancashire has least cause to be proud is that of child labour. The county was notorious in the early nineteenth century for the harsh and inhuman exploitation of child workers in industries such as coal and cotton, although they were also extensively employed in brickworks and trades such as *cockling* (qv), where children of seven or eight worked full-time on the sands. The county's poor record was highlighted by the parliamentary reports into the problem produced in the 1830s and 1840s: the 1833 Factories Inquiry, for example, described the five and six year olds working underground in the Duke of Bridgewater's collieries at Worsley. Although the worst abuses were removed as a result, in 1871 Lancashire still had the largest proportion of under-fourteens at work of any English county.

chincough   whooping cough or *chink-cough*, so called for the harsh catching sound made during the illness; to *chink* was to lose one's breath with laughing and then to catch the breath. Although originally specific, the word eventually became a general term for many vague illnesses, including this example from St Helens: ***Don't sit there*** [on somewhere wet or cold], ***you'll get chincough in yer bum***.

Chingle Hall   Chingle Hall near Goosnargh, a small late medieval and sixteenth-century manor house, has acquired a reputation (as 'the most haunted house in England'. On what grounds such a claim can be made is unclear, but in the 1980s a new pastime developed in the Preston area: to 'dare to spend a night at Chingle Hall' was a good way of raising sponsorship money, and an excellent method of getting your picture in the local papers (usually with a scared expression and a sheet held up in the background of the photograph).

chit   (see *chat*)

chitty   young girl who stood and assisted a powerloom weaver in the cotton industry; a weaver would have to attend many looms, and a *chitty* was a very important 'extra pair of arms and legs'

chuzzeauw   There are many spellings of this dialect term, which has other variants. **Taylor** (qv) gives the following:

choose-heaw	anyhow, however
choose-hooa	whoever
choose-what	whatever
choose-wheer	wherever
choose-when	whenever

Chorley cakes   Chorley cakes are one of the best-known traditional foods of the county, and are close relatives of other sweet fruit cakes and biscuits such as **Eccles cakes** (qv). They are flat pastry cakes, shaped like a large biscuit, with currants mixed in the pastry and sugar sprinkled on top. They have been made for at least 200 years and are probably much older than that, and from them Chorley people derived their old nickname of *Chorlah-currans*.

Christ's Croft An ancient rhyme claims a special status for south Lancashire:

'When all England is aloft [in peril]
Safe are they that are in Christ's Croft
And where should Christ's Croft be
But between the Ribble and the Mersey'

The idea that this land should be secure and safe probably derives from its comparative remoteness,

Child labour: boy navvies on the Manchester Ship Canal in 1892.

remembering that, even in the eighteenth century, real danger could come from the north as well as from the south — Cumberland and Westmorland were too near Scotland to be secure; but we may also detect a note of Lancastrian pride that here was God's chosen land. Unfortunately a very similar rhyme was also told concerning Hallamshire, the Sheffield area of Yorkshire!

chuck   Probably derived from the widespread word *chuck* or *chuck-ies*, meaning chickens, this is another of the terms (with its variant, *chucky*) which has become a hallmark of Lancashire speech according to the perceptions of the media and hence the outside world. It has long been used as a term of endearment, though nineteenth-century sources suggest that it was applied specifically to children and women. However, it has recently become a more general form of address, and — depending on the tone of voice — can also have less affectionate implications: *'Don't give me that, chuck, or I'll ...'*

chunner   to mutter

church ales   The distant, and rather more rowdy, ancestor of the church fête or flower festival, church ales were feast days sponsored by the medieval Church, incorporating sports and games, dancing, entertainments and — as the name suggests — large-scale drinking, for which ale would be specially brewed. The custom survived into the seventeenth century, but was much frowned upon by puritan elements, and most **church ales** did not last beyond the Civil War and the Commonwealth period. However, in Lancashire there was a tradition of such celebrations which seems to have been more resilient than most, and it is likely that many of the county's eighteenth-century *wakes[1]* (qv), holidays and festivals were in fact **church ales** under a different name.

Chylde of Hale   John Middleton, the **Chylde of Hale**, was born in 1578 and buried at Hale in 1623. He is said to have been nine feet three inches (2.8m) tall, and a wealth of extravagant stories sprang up around his legend and reputation as the tallest man in England. For example, one tale states that he was so strong that, when ill, he had to be chained to the bed; and one of the chains was later used to capture Satan. His bones were apparently exhumed in the late eighteenth century and then conveniently lost, so that the real height of one who was undoubtedly an exceptionally tall man cannot be confirmed.

cinder tea   traditional folk remedy for relieving children of wind, preventing or curing indigestion, and generally helping the insides: a red-hot cinder was dropped in liquid (either tea, weak ale, plain water or a herbal concoction) and the resultant fluid was drunk

cinder toffee   honeycomb toffee made with vinegar, of the sort now found in Crunchie bars; formerly made and sold in irregular lumps which resembled cinders (see also **Dolly Varden**)

claggy   sticky, as in wet clay or dough which is too wet

clapbread   oatcake. The name relates to the clapping, or placing of the oatmeal batter on the *backstone* (qv) and it is recorded as early as 1695 when the traveller Celia Fiennes described the production of *clapbread* in the Garstang area.

Clarke, Allan   Using the name Teddy Ashton as his pseudonym, Allan Clarke (born in 1863 at Bolton) became perhaps the best-known of all the late Victorian and Edwardian writers on Lancashire dialect and tradition. He began working in a cotton mill, but then became a pupil teacher and subsequently a journalist, exploiting his talents as a writer, and using his flair for popularising the subject and capitalising upon the strong sense of county identity already apparent in Lancashire. Thus, his *Lancashire Annual*, which appeared each Christmas from 1893 onwards, was a favourite present for sending to expatriate Lancastrians. He wrote extensively for local newspapers, published volumes of verse and prose, and among his works were the book *Windmill Land*, describing the Fylde where he had made his home, and his serious social investigation, *The Effects of the Factory System*. His dialect poems are, in keeping with the genre — short, down-to-earth and effective:

> *'Th' bonniest lass i' th'world*
>   *to me*
> *Is a lass that comes fro'*
>   *Chorlah'*

— but his straight verse is often flowery and sentimental. He died in 1935, and is buried at Marton in Blackpool.

clarty   filthy, muddy, sticky, referring particularly to, for example, clothes and feet, or to ground which is a mess of mud; **to clart** means to plaster on thickly — food might be **clarted wi' butter**, for instance

cleck, click   door latch

cleek   to snatch

Clegg Hall   An early ballad, later embroidered and elaborated into a series of legends, told how at Clegg Hall, near Rochdale, two orphan children — heirs to the estate — were murdered by their wicked uncle who threw them from a balcony into the moat. Ever after the place was haunted by the restless ghost of the evil uncle, who could not lie in peace. The event, which has no historical foundation, was said to have happened in the thirteenth or fourteenth centuries. This story is another of those tales of antique (and especially medieval) terror which so delighted the Victorian romantics. The legend was so well known that a local saying for someone who wouldn't go away was **'e's 'ere agen, like t' Clegg Hall boggart** (qv)'.

Clegg, John Trafford   dialect poet, known as **th' Owd Weighver** born at Milnrow in 1857 and author of many poems and short stories in the dialect of the Rochdale area. He died of consumption at Bournemouth in 1895. His best-known verse is *Rachda' Wakes* (1890), a lively recitation of the fun of the fair and the courtship there:

> *An' when it's o'er aw'll link*
> *thee wom*
> *Through quiet fielt an' lone*
> *An' afore another Wakes con*
> *come*
> *Wi cwortin we'll ha' done*

clemmed starving with hunger (*starved*, in Lancashire dialect, meaning 'frozen with cold')

Clifton Junction The battle of Clifton Junction took place in 1848. Two rival railway companies, the East Lancashire and the Lancashire & Yorkshire, blockaded each other's trains at the junction where the line from Bolton to Manchester was joined by the ELR route from Bury and Radcliffe. The dispute, conducted with no regard at all for the hapless passengers, was concerned with rights of access by the ELR into Manchester on the L&YR line. Eventually it was resolved, and shortly afterwards the two companies amalgamated.

climate It was an article of faith that Lancashire's damp climate was peculiarly suited to the spinning and weaving of cotton, and generations of schoolchildren were taught this in their litany of industrial facts. In reality the climate was often not damp enough, hence the need for steaming (qv) and for flooding mill cellars. In the late nineteenth and early twentieth centuries, it was fondly believed that nowhere else in the world had the special climatic conditions which would allow cotton pieces to be woven, so that Lancashire's industry was totally secure. Time soon showed how wrong that view was.

clitter (see *clutter*)

clogs The standard footwear of urban and industrial Lancashire until the early twentieth century, when the advent of mass produced leather shoes made rapid inroads into the dominance of the wooden-soled **clog**. Changing working conditions and improvements in street paving may have played a part in the decline of the **clog**, but fashion was undoubtedly the key factor. Many myths claim that **clogs** were introduced by **Flemish weavers** (qv), but we don't need to take these too seriously — all such stories imply

A clog.

that Lancashire people in the Middle Ages were incapable of producing commonsense and straightforward commodities such as **clogs** and *havercakes* (qv) themselves. Clogs were an eminently practical and comfortable item of footwear, and the making of wooden shoes of this sort, with leather uppers and with or without iron toecaps and runners, was an essential craft industry in the county — and, of course, in many other parts of England, for **clogs** were by no means confined to the North-West. **Clogs** could be boot-like (**pit clogs**) or resembling a shoe, with different versions for men and women, but, with the exception of children's **clogs**, the colour was almost universally black.

clogs back to clogs rags to riches and back again (*from clogs to clogs in three generations*)

clogs won't have her vivid phrase for somebody who is particularly choosy and fussy, especially about finding a girlfriend or boyfriend: *'She'll look for shoes till clogs won't have her'*

clough cleft or deep, steep-sided valley, tributary to a larger valley; the term is very widespread across northern England

clout pudding pudding boiled in a floured cloth or *clout*; often a savoury mixture based on suet and flour, made into a dough with milk or water, and flavoured with onions and herbs. It was boiled in water or broth, or in a stew, until soft but firm, and eaten with the broth or stew, or on its own if boiled in water. Puddings such as these were filling stodgy fare, of the sort which was an everyday food for many Lancashire people in the nineteenth century, but they were only dreamed of by the very poor. (see also *bag pudding*)

club days An annual event in a number of Lancashire towns, such as Lytham, **club days** are an occasion for civic and community celebration, with processions of floats and tableaux, bands and musicians, and marching groups of people for all manner of local societies and organisations, schools, churches and civic representatives. There is in the county a powerful tradition of such occasions, as in *wakes* (qv), galas and **Whit Walks** (qv). **Club days** originated in the yearly entertainments and processions organised by friendly societies such as the Foresters and the Oddfellows.

club houses Lancashire was one of the cradles of the building society movement. Many local societies originated in schemes whereby skilled workers or craftsmen with some spare cash pooled resources on a profit-sharing basis to build speculative housing for other workers. Less frequently, workers themselves co-operated in such ventures to build houses for themselves. Schemes such as these were often known as **club houses**. A fine example is Newtown at Longridge, parts of which (Club Row and King Street) were built

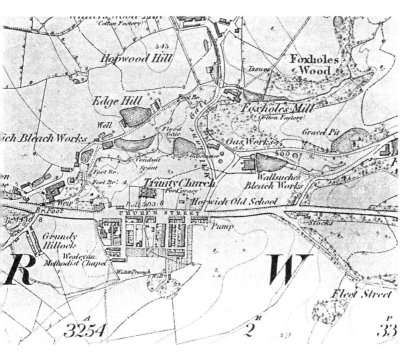

The club houses in Church Street, Horwich, in 1844.

under separate small schemes in 1793-5 and 1800-14 respectively — the former was one of the earliest building societies in the country. Another excellent survivor is **Club Houses** at Horwich, where a 'colony' of over fifty dwellings dating from the early nineteenth century is to be seen on the south side of Church Street.

Club Trains exclusive commuter services to Manchester which the Lancashire & Yorkshire Railway ran for prosperous merchants and businessmen (especially those in the cotton trade). Carriages were reserved for first-class ticket holders, who

also paid a membership fee (hence the title). The first such service, from Blackpool Central via St Annes and Lytham, ran in 1895, and a similar train was later operated from Blackpool to Rose Grove and Burnley for the many east Lancashire businessmen who had moved to the fresh air of the Fylde coast. A Manchester to Southport service was also known as 'the club train', although it did not have the special reservation and membership of the Fylde routes.

clutter As well as its basic implication of untidiness, *clutter* in

Lancashire had associated meanings such as loose and unstable, crowded together, and 'piled in a heap'. A connected word was *clitter*, meaning scree or loose stone and debris.

cluttermuck someone who was clumsy, uncoordinated, always dropping things

coaken to heave and strain, before vomiting

cob¹ lump of coal or earth. Edwin Waugh's celebrated poem, *Come whoam to thy childer an' me*, begins

Aw've just mended th'fire wi' a cob; an extension of the same meaning is seen in the forthright phrase *Ah'm swettin' cobs*

cob² strange, different, curious, uncommon, odd

cob³ bad mood, sullenness *e's got a cob on* (S Lancs)

cobbles rounded stones or pebbles, owing their shape to erosion by water or glacial action, picked from the beaches or from fields and used for building in areas such as the Fylde, which lacked

Cock-fighting.

48

local stone. **Cobble walls** were made of such stones, plastered together with mud and clay, and then thickly whitewashed so that the outside was protected from the rain. Walls were also made of **cobbles** set in mortar, and streets were **cobbled** with such cheap and easily-obtained stones as well. These (with rounded profile) produced true cobbled streets. (see also **setts**)

cock-fighting This was a popular pursuit and fashionable until the early nineteenth century; very large sums were gambled on the results and many of the county's gentry were passionate enthusiasts. The earls of Derby owned cockpits at Preston which they and their friends regularly attended, while at a fight in Liverpool in 1810 between birds owned by Thomas Townley Parker of Cuerden and Thomas Clifton of Lytham, the main prize was 200 guineas (£210, or well over £10,000 in 1990s values). By the 1860s, cockfighting was enjoyed mainly by

the lower orders. Edwin Waugh wrote in 1867 of a group of colliers from Rochdale, 'a lot of raw-boned young fellows ... talking with rude emphasis about the exploits of a fighting-cock of great local renown, known [as] "Crash-Bwons".' Thomas Middleton describes a cockfight held in a hayloft at Denton in 1888, attended by over 100 people, which was broken up by the police because by then it was illegal.

cockling For centuries a major occupation on most of the Lancashire coast, *cockling* is still carried on commercially in several places from Formby northwards to Morecambe Bay, although the scale of operations has been much reduced since the Second World War. The extensive sandy flats of the coast are particularly suitable for cockles, which traditionally were taken by 'paddling' the wet sand, either with the feet or with a *jumbo* (qv). The vibrations brought the cockles to the surface, and they could then be raked from the sand with a *craam* (qv), riddled and rinsed, and collected in large sacks or *pokes* (qv). Today the method is not dissimilar, but instead of men's backs or horse-drawn carts, the cocklers use tractors and trailers to go out onto the sands and to carry the shellfish. Local cockles were a prized delicacy in industrial Lancashire and large quantities were taken, with the shrimps gathered in the same locations, to markets in towns such as Preston,

Cockles.

Blackburn and Bolton. Recently there have been instances of large-scale illegal poaching of the shell-fish by gangs supplying restaurants in London and the Continent. (See also **shrimping**)

Coketown In Charles Dickens' novel *Hard Times*, the nightmarish industrial centre of Coketown was modelled on Preston, which Dickens several times visited and which, ironically, was the only major south or mid-Lancashire industrial town where there was no coal-mining and hence no coke.

cock o' t' midden less decorous phrase for what was later, and more politely, known as **king of the castle**

Collier, John under the pseudonym **Tim Bobbin**, John Collier was the first great Lancashire dialect writer. He was born in 1708 at Urmston, the son of the curate, became schoolmaster at Milnrow when he was twenty-one, and stayed there for the rest of his life, producing extensive verse and prose writing in the dialect speech of south Lancashire. The prose works are perhaps the most celebrated, and his dialogue *Tummus and Meary* (qv) published in 1746, was particularly highly-regarded by the mid-Victorian school of dialect writers, to whom Collier was a revered founding father. Several writers, including Samuel Bamford, wrote rather maudlin poems about Collier's grave. Collier's collected verses, published as *The Lancashire Dialect*, went into over twenty editions.

John Collier, or 'Tim Bobbin'.

The book was a bestseller by eighteenth-century standards, and some of his works have never been out of print. He died in 1786 and was buried in the churchyard of Rochdale St Chad: 'It is here, where his dust perished, that his memory is most cherished'.

collock large wooden pail with an upright handle

collop slice (as in meat): for example, *eggs and collops* (Edwin Waugh: *There's some nice bacon-collops o'th' hob*)

Collop Monday The day before Shrove Tuesday, when all the meat was eaten up in readiness for the abstinence of Lent. This feast was celebrated very widely in Lancashire before the mid-nineteenth century and, with Shrove Tuesday and Ash Wednesday, formed a half-week of religious and social observances.

comer outcomer — one who lives in a place but is not of that place, not a native; usually used in a derogatory sense, of an interloper or, especially today, one who arrives and then begins to throw his or weight around and voice opinions (*o' course, he's a comer*). It is questionable whether any non-native can ever be regarded as anything but a *comer*, no matter how long his or her length of residence and extent of community involvement.

comfrey The soothing and healing properties of comfrey, long known from folk remedies, have now been confirmed by scientific analysis (one of its folk names is knitbone). Leaves of the plant were formerly sold on Lancashire markets, and were used by weavers and spinners to line clogs to ease tired and aching feet.

cooey narrow back lane, in areas such as Liverpool and Huyton

Co-operative movement Although there had been earlier forms of mutual assistance, the modern Co-operative Movement was born in 1844 when the Rochdale Pioneers set up their first shop in Toad Lane. It quickly established an important place in the working class life of Lancashire, and the *corp* or *cworp* became a familiar everyday element for hundreds of thousands of people. There were Co-operative Societies in every town, but today almost all have either gone, or have been altered entirely beyond recognition. Nevertheless, the role played by the Co-op in raising living standards and widening the opportunities available to its customers cannot be overestimated.

cop¹, cowp bank or small ridge; often used in descriptions or names of landscape features, such as seawalls and banks (**the seacop**) or ridges. Examples include **Cop Lane** in Penwortham and **Meols Cop** in Southport.

cop² to catch; *cop 'old o' this* or *if 'e sees thi, tha'll cop it*

cop³ cone shape of spun yarn which was used for loading shuttles in the cotton industry. By the early twentieth century, looms had been developed which incorporated *cop-changing* machines, whereby the empty *cop* was ejected and a new one inserted and threaded into the shuttle eye without halting the machinery of the loom. This represented a major saving in time and interruption, and greatly accelerated the output of the most up-to-date mills.

copster spinner (cf *attercop*, a spider; *cop* as in cobweb)

corn-shutting (see *kurn-shuttin'*)

Coronation Street For almost forty years the world has been given an insight into what it thinks Lancashire and its people are like, as *Coronation Street* has charted the progress of dozens of warm-hearted barmaids, irascible elderly ladies, lovable rogues and detestable villains, dotty spinsters and tarty young things, many of whom have not only become household names but have remained so long after dramatic death or sudden

The shop in Toad Lane, Rochdale, which was the birthplace of the Co-operative movement.

departure have taken them on to pastures new eg *She's a real Ena Sharples*. The script, like the good old music-hall routine which (as more than one commentator has noticed) the programme really is, remains sharp and lively, exaggerated for dramatic effect but based on acute observation. For millions of people *Corrie* (a very recent name bestowed by the media, presumably because the full title occupies too much space in a headline) is the real Lancashire. Well, maybe — though not, of course, if you live in Liverpool (see *Brookside*).

Cotton Famine The most traumatic of the several major crises which hit the cotton industry in the nineteenth century, the great **Cotton Famine** (1861-65) was caused by a cyclical depression in the industry which was exacerbated by the effects of the American Civil War, since most of the raw cotton used in Lancashire came from the Confederate States. There was mass unemployment, widespread destitution, near starvation, and immense personal and community distress. The **Famine** stirred the conscience of the nation, while in Lancashire the pitiful distress among the poor prompted some of the finest and most perceptive writing from the dialect poets and authors. It became engraved on the folk memory, not only of that generation but also of those which followed.

Cotton Factory Times operatives' newspaper which provided a vehicle for much of the literary and artistic output of **Sam Fitton** (qv), and also campaigned in the interests of the millworkers on a wide range of social and employment issues. It was founded in 1885 as the publishing voice of the unions in the industry, although it was owned by the Andrews family who also ran the *Ashton Reporter*. The newspaper is a valuable source for the day-to-day activities, attitudes and concerns of the 'shopfloor' in the industry. The humour columns are particularly rich in *overlooker* (or *tackler*) jokes.

cotton men term sometimes used to describe the wealthy merchants on the Manchester Exchange who had made their fortunes out of cotton trading; the alternative, **cotton lords**, referred to the owners of mills and was frequently used in a somewhat derogatory or cynical sense.

coulter, cooter iron blade of a ploughshare; the term was in general use in the county until the 1850s, when larger mechanised ploughs began to push out the older forms

council weed recent folk-name (recorded in, for example, Bickerstaffe and Melling) for mugwort (*Asteraceae vulgaris*), which springs up on cleared land and roadside verges, and is held to grow 'when the council have been along'

counts The count is a means of numbering the quality and character of yarns. The system was based on a calculation of 840 yards (768m) of yarn to a hank, and the number of hanks which equalled one pound (0.45kg) in weight was the 'count': thus a count of 8 meant that there were 8 x 840 = 6,920 yards per pound, whereas a count of 10 meant 10 x 840 = 8,400 yards per pound, a thinner and lighter thread.

County Palatine The term County Palatine is now often used to refer to Lancashire within its pre-1974 boundaries, including areas such as Furness, Manchester, Liverpool and St Helens, but excluding Saddleworth and the Slaidburn-Earby area which were formerly in the West Riding. **Palatine** status was granted to the county in the 1350s by Edward III, an honour it shared with Cheshire and Durham. It meant that, within the bounds of these counties, the king's writ was exercised by another individual on his behalf — the bishops of Durham, the earls of Chester and, in Lancashire, the dukes of Lancaster. Local courts and the legal system operated in their name, rather than that of the king. The duke of Lancaster until 1399 was **John of Gaunt** (qv), but on his death his nephew Richard II took the **palatinate** powers back into the hands of the Crown. This provoked an uprising by Gaunt's son, Henry of Bolingbroke, who in 1399 overthrew his cousin the king and seized the throne as Henry IV. Thenceforth the **palatinate** status was exercised on behalf of the Crown in a nominally separate fashion. The legal jurisdiction of the **palatinate** was finally abolished only at beginning of Victoria's reign, and the palatinate retained its own courts and legal powers until that date.

courts Court housing was extremely common in Liverpool and was also found in most other major Lancashire towns. Single-storey or two-storey hovels were crammed into blind courtyards (that is, yards with only one entrance) which were often approached by narrow tunnels or passageways only two to three feet wide. The courts usually had no water supplies, a single bucket privy shared among all the inhabitants, no sewerage or drainage, no refuse disposal and inadequate ventilation. As a result they were exceptionally squalid and unhealthy, and the death rate among the occupants was correspondingly high. Although court dwellings were forbidden by legislation form the 1870s onwards, thousands of people in Liverpool were still living in such conditions in the 1920s.

cow-slavver cow dung; *slavver* meant dribble, or something liquid that squirts or trickles out from somewhere — a perfect term, considering the qualities of cow manure. Equivalent terms included *cow-patch*, *cow-clap* and *sharn-clap*.

craam three-pronged rake which was used on the shores of north and west Lancashire for collecting shellfish clinging to the rocks. A *mussel craam* had prongs 3-4 inches (7.5-10cm) long, while *cockle craams* had long handles, sometimes up to 30 inches (75cm) long but usually about a foot (30cm), with three curved prongs 'like the talons of a hawk'. (see **cockling**)

crack talk, conversation, gossip. Today the word is generally thought to be characteristically Irish, but it was in widespread use (perhaps because of the influence of Irish immigration) in late nineteenth-century Lancashire.

Cracknel Friday In Rochdale before the 1850s, Good Friday was known by this name. It was customary to eat *cracknel cakes*, small, thin loaves in which quantities of *cracknels* (see *cratchins*) had been baked.

cratchins scraps of brown solids left over after lard has been melted down and rendered. *Cratchins* (also known as *cracknels* or, unfortunately to modern ears, *craps*) were a delicacy which was often eaten on its own, or mixed with dough or oatmeal and baked into savoury cakes or breads.

cratchy grumpy, irritable, crotchety

cripple hole small openings in drystone walls which allow sheep and small animals to pass from one field to another, but prevent the straying of cattle and larger beasts

croft in a rural area, the land belonging to, and usually behind, a house or cottage (larger than a backyard or garden, and resembling a smallholding); in an urban context, a piece of waste ground, such as the open space often lying at the rear of streets of terraced housing; also, open ground used for industrial purposes, such as a *brickcroft* or *bleachcroft*

Cromwell, Oliver In August 1648 the second Civil War ended with **Cromwell's** victory over a royalist and Scottish army at Preston, one of the most significant battles in English history. **Cromwell** advanced from Yorkshire along the Ribble Valley into Lancashire. A number of legends are attached to his exploits on this occasion. Stepback near Darwen was said in the nineteenth century to have acquired its name because **Cromwell** said to his men, assembled there, 'Step Back! Go no further' — a manifestly impossible tale. The sixteenth-century packhorse bridge at Mitton, the old Lower

A cripple hole, used for the control of farming livestock.

Cromwells Bridge — the Lower Hodder Bridge.

Hodder Bridge, is now usually known as **Cromwells Bridge** because he used it to cross the River Hodder, and before doing so held

Oliver Cromwell.

a council of war at the spot, at which it was decided to press on westwards. He stayed the night of the 16th August at Stonyhurst, where he is said to have slept on a table, and then moved on towards Preston. According to a wildly improbable legend, he watched the course of the battle from **Chingle Hall** (qv) where he climbed up the chimney to get a better view, but **Cromwells Mound** near Sherwood has a much better claim to be his observation post. After the battle he is said to have gone to Astley Hall, where carelessly he left his boots behind, but the most recent historian of the battle, Stephen Bull, argues that 'given the whirlwind pace of events he cannot have stopped for much time anywhere'.

crosses Wayside crosses were very numerous in Lancashire, and many were probably not of Christian

A cuckstool, or cuckold's stool, in use.

origin, but had a pre-Christian ancestry and were later claimed as 'holy' crosses by the Church as it assimilated older practices into its own traditions. Some **crosses** held more than usually sacred powers. At Kirkland near Garstang, for example, there was a **cross base**, a hollowed stone socket which had once held an upright. The rainwater which collected in the basin was alleged to cure warts. The sufferer had simply to wash his or her hands in the basin, hold them up and exclaim 'Go away', and the warts would gradually disappear. This, and other **crosses** in the area, were used as stopping places for funeral processions until well into the seventeenth century, despite official intolerance of such 'Popish' goings-on: in 1624, several local men were prosecuted because they did this and spoke prayers for the souls of the dead at each place.

crossin'-off time time when a weaver reckoned up the length and type of cloth which he or she had woven, if paid by the piece

crow As elsewhere, the **crow** was held to be a bird of evil omen, and many superstitions were attached to them (and to any other large black bird). At Rakehead near Bacup, in the time of the Second World War, the **doom crow**, a single rook or crow in flight, was indicative of bad luck or an omen of disaster. If you were alone when you saw it, you were supposed to turn back at once; if with a companion, you had to make the sign of the cross in spit on a stone to ward off the evil.

cruds curds, as in *crud cheese*; from the verb *to cruddle*, which in a broader sense meant to curdle or to separate; hence a curdled liquid was *crudded*

cuckstools Ducking was a common punishment for women and, though much less frequently, men who were convicted of minor offences. Proverbially, it was those women who had nagged and scolded their husbands who were ducked, but this view perhaps owes something to Victorian sensitivities, for the usual term was *cuckstool*, that is **cuckold's stool** — a place where women who had been unfaithful to their husbands were plunged into filthy cold water. Most towns and villages had a *cuckstool*, and a field on the edge was often designated **Cuckstool Meadow**. According to Thornber, the *cuckstool* at Carleton in the Fylde was still in use in the late eighteenth century, while he claims that Poulton (perhaps a particularly immoral place?) had no fewer than than three *cuckstools*.

cuddy left-handed

curly-burly game played by children at night, using a burning stick which was waved in circles in the air and passed on from one child to another, to a song commencing *'Curly, burly, limber, lock'*. The child wrote his or her name in the air, just as we do with sparklers on Bonfire Night to this day.

Enjoying a game of curly-burly.

custom of the province of York
old tradition in customary law,
operative (though without clear
legal validity) until the nineteenth
century, which stated that, on the
death of a man, his wife should
have one third of his estate (the
widow's portion); his children should
have, between them, another third
(the child's portion); and he himself could dispose of the remaining
third in whatever way he wished.

This custom was found all over Northern England, and was in marked and enlightened contrast to the situation which prevailed in the Southern and Midland counties, where the woman had no rights at all. References to the division on these lines are extremely frequent in probate records before the 1850s.

cut[1] canal (because it was cut by excavation, in contrast to any natural watercourse)

cut[2] standard length of warp for cloth weaving, variable according to the weight of the cloth: 50 yards (45m) for heavy goods and 100 yards (90m) for light. A cut (or *lea*) of linen yarn was 300 yards (275m).

cycling clubs The fashion or passion for **cycling** reached Lancashire in the late 1870s, and in the industrial towns and cities it quickly became one of the main leisure activities for thousands of young men and a few intrepid young women. **Cycling clubs** sprang up in every place of importance, and bands of people spent their Saturday or Sunday afternoons, occasional holidays and summer evenings riding out into the countryside, up into the hills

Members of a cycling club.

and down the still-rural stretches of river valleys. In this way many urban workers were introduced to the delights of the open air, and many others were introduced to fiercely competitive sports, for **cycle races** were adopted with equal enthusiasm. Perhaps the best-known organisation was the **Clarion Cycling Club**, in which the sport was closely associated with socialism and the campaign for female suffrage.

D

-d In west Lancashire and the Fylde, a final 'd' in many words has historically been pronounced 'th'. This means that in place-names the word 'ford' has often become 'forth', as in Carnforth, Catforth and Hollowforth. Rufford was very often written, and usually pronounced, *Rufforth* until about a century ago.

Daisy Nook small hamlet in the Medlock Valley between Ashton and Failsworth, famed far and wide for its Good Friday Fair, which was popular for its dancing and other entertainments, and notorious for the vast amount of drinking which went on

dandy small version of a hand-loom, used for weaving small lengths and widths or very fine fabrics; for example, handkerchief cloth

Danes Before history became an academic discipline, the origin of many of our most famous monuments was uncertain. Their builders were often referred to as 'Caesar' or 'the Danes', although the Devil was also thought to have been an active civil engineer. In Lancashire the word *dean* or *dene*, a valley, was pronounced *dane*, which often led to misunderstanding, while perhaps distant folk memories of Scandinavian ancestry contributed to the assumption that the **Danes** built, for example, the prehistoric and Roman trackway in the Fylde known as **Danes Pad**, or the great **Nico Ditch**, an ancient earthwork in the Reddish area.

Darwen Tower Looking as though it is Darwen's early attempt to enter the space race, this rocket-shaped stone tower, eighty-six feet (26m) high, was built in 1897-8 to commemorate the diamond jubilee of Queen Victoria. Today it is one of Lancashire's best-known landmarks, particularly prominent from the new M65 motorway.

dateless stupefied, foolish, disordered, insensible

datestones Architectural historians recognise that, three to four hundred years ago, there was a major change in building materials and styles, which they have termed the Great Rebuilding. In Lancashire this transformation,

Darwen Tower.

from thatch and wooden construction to slate, brick, stone and tile, took place from the late seventeenth century onwards. All over the county, but especially in those areas of the north and east where there has been less urban and industrial development, may be seen houses which have **date-stones** reflecting that rebuilding and improvement of property. Usually set above the front door or porch, the **datestones** generally include the initials of the owner and his wife, as well as the date of reconstruction or building.

dawn (see *down*)

Dead Hand The right hand of Father Edmund Arrowsmith, the Jesuit priest born at Haydock in 1585 and hanged at Lancaster in 1628, was cut off after his execution and taken to Bryn Hall (though local legends confuse this with Ince Hall), and eventually via Garswood to the Catholic church at Ashton-in-Makerfield. The relic was held to perform miracles.

death The range of euphemisms for death was wide and varied, some being sentimental and others jocular, much of course depending on whether the deceased was well-liked or was a close friend or relative. Among examples of the sentimental usage are *passed away, on* or *over*; *gone home*; *met* or *joined his maker*; *breathed* or *seen his last*; and *among the angels*. More robust phrases included *popped his clogs* and *turned up his toes*, while *gone west*

could also refer to items which had been lost or were missing. There were also many phrases to describe somebody who was dying: *not long for this world* or *on his way* contrasted with the much more direct *oo's 'ad it.*

Death Man insurance or burial club collector

deawldy miserable, gloomy, sad

Felling deawldy.

deet to make dirty, to soil; by association, this term also came to mean 'to size', as when the weaver sized the warp by brushing on a flour and water paste using a *deetin' brush*

deggin' can water-can which was used in the yard, mangle-house or outdoor lavatory

Deighn Layrocks According to Edwin Waugh (qv), the people of Dean in Rossendale in the mid-nineteenth century were renowned for their love of, and talent for, music, so that they were widely known as the ***Deighn Layrocks*** (Larks of Dean).

delph quarry or excavation (from ***delve***, to dig)

dent wire in the reeds of a loom; each wire is separated by a space, through which the warp ends pass

Derby, seventh earl of The first earl of Derby was Thomas Stanley, stepfather of Henry VII, who was given the title for his part in securing Henry the throne at Bosworth in 1485. His most famous descendant was James, the seventh earl, a leading royalist during the Civil War, who fought hard and long for the king. Among James's exploits was the near-destruction of Bolton after a prolonged siege in 1644, as a result of which perhaps half the townspeople died. When the war ended he fled to the Isle of Man (where his family were hereditary rulers),

James Stanley, the seventh earl of Derby.

but in 1651 came back to England to support Charles II's attempt to regain his throne. The earl was captured, and in the autumn was executed in the market place at Bolton, a calculated act of vengeance by the government.

devil In the textile industry, ***devils*** were machines with toothed or spiked rollers which tore open bales of cotton, or shredded woollen rags to make ***shoddy***.

Dhoul, Dule the devil, about whom numerous stories were told in Lancashire. At the old Burnley Grammar School, for example, he is said to have appeared head-first through the flagstones after some pupils had said the Lord's Prayer backwards, only disappearing when the boys beat him back down with hammer and tongs. A black mark on the flags marked the site of his emergence.

dialect writers The earliest major writer in the Lancashire **dialect** (by which almost without exception is meant south Lancashire) was **John Collier** (qv), who from the mid-1740s wrote and published under the name of Tim Bobbin. He worked largely in isolation, although his influence upon later poets and authors was profound. In the early nineteenth century, some work of lasting merit was achieved by the **Wilson family** (qv) and in the early 1840s the novelist **Elizabeth Gaskell** (qv), in her stories set in ordinary urban and industrial settings, made extensive use of a form of **dialect**. The great flowering of dialect

Dib i' th' oil.

writing came with the works of **Edwin Waugh** (qv) from 1856 onwards, who not only achieved widespread fame but also made dialect writing 'respectable'. Between the late 1850s and the First World War, a considerable number of **dialect writers** published their work, and in doing so recorded — by accident or design — pronunciations as well as vocabulary which were already in decline. Their work is not easy to read, and was often intended for reciting aloud, but was sufficiently regarded for a few poems (notably, Samuel Laycock's *Welcome, bonny brid*) to be taught in schools. The interest in **dialect** led to the formation of several societies devoted to the subject, of which the **Lancashire Authors Association** (qv) is now the most important.

dib i' th' oil standard paupers' food of the nineteenth century: a large communal bowl of mashed potato or thick oatmeal gruel, with a hole made in the centre and melted butter, bacon fat, treacle or skimmed milk poured into the hole. Each person took a spoonful of the potato or gruel, and then *dibbed* it in *th' oil* full of liquid. It was sometimes known as *dip an' bore*.

Dick Turpin According to stories firmly believed in Kearsley and Farnworth in the nineteenth

The dinner-carriers' parade.

century, the legendary highwayman once visited Lancashire and, while riding fast between Bolton and Manchester, heard pursuers behind. He hid in a cottage near the later site of the paper works at Stoneclough and thereby evaded capture.

Dicky Sam native of Liverpool; the term was very widely used in the nineteenth century by Liverpool people themselves, at a time when the city was overwhelmed by hundreds of thousands of immigrants

Diddle 'em Club informal local savings club, in which the participants put in a small sum each week to pay for the next *wakes holiday* (qv) to Blackpool. The money was shared out at the beginning of the holiday week, but the name derives from the fact that all too often somebody was tempted and had spent the money or run off with it long before.

dig duck (*digpoo'*, a duckpool or pond)

dinge dent or depression, such as that produced by pushing a finger into dough

dinner carriers At the midday break in the cotton mills, the workers had their dinner break. Almost all would have their own food, either brought with them or delivered to the mill at noon by a member of the family. Wives would bring food for husbands, sometimes husbands for wives, and children would be let out of school to bring pies, basins of

'ash (qv), tarts, hot potatoes and other food, always carefully wrapped up with a handkerchief, to the mill. Sam Fitton wrote a poem and drew an evocative cartoon of the scene:

  'Little dinner carriers
  Wi' big breawn deeshus
  Toddlin' i' dozens wi'
  The'r loaves an' feeshes
  Crook't legs, straight legs,
  Every sort 'at's made
  Trottin' wi' the'r dinners
  On the grand parade'

dip sauce (such as syrup or melted jam) served with suet and other puddings; also used of any other liquid or sauce, such as the melted fat left in the pan after bacon had been fried in which bread was soaked

dished up ruined, bankrupt, gone broke

do[1] event, a gathering and, especially, a party or social occasion: *aye, we 'ad a reet good do*

do[2] to get on, to manage, to get by

dobby loom loom in which a mechanism (operated either by punched cards or by pegs) lifts and lowers the **healds** (qv) to move the warp threads, so allowing the weaving of patterned cloth. The development of mechanised **dobby looms** was an important advance in the extension of machine weaving at the expense of the handlooms.

Dockers' Umbrella The nickname of the Liverpool Overhead Railway, which was opened in 1893 and ran the full length of the city's waterfront, from Dingle to Seaforth. For most of its route the LOR, one of Britain's earliest electrified railways, was elevated on the massively-built viaduct of iron girders and decking from which it derived its affectionate popular name. It closed in 1956, in a move which was misguidedly seen as progress.

doffer person who removes a spool or bobbin from a spinning mule: the *doffer* (as in **doffing a cap**) was a crucial operative, as this work — until the advent of automatic bobbin changing — was essential to the smooth and uninterrupted operation of the machinery

dole handout, or a portion; thus, charities might give a *dole* to eligible people (perhaps a loaf of bread on a Sunday to a poor widow), while individuals might have a *dole* of land within a common meadow or arable field. The older sense of the word goes back centuries, but in the 1930s it was transferred to the new form of handout — public assistance to the unemployed and those in dire financial need — and it has thus become an integral part of the English language.

dolly tub washing tub with a *dolly*, a stick or paddle which was lifted up and down in the tub or revolved in it to churn and beat the clothes

Dolly Varden The heroine of Dickens' *Barnaby Rudge*, Dolly Varden gave her name to a variety of products, including a type of dress,

a fancy hat and a toilet. Women who put on airs might be so called, as might people who were messing around in a silly way. In the Widnes and St Helens area, *cinder toffee* (qv) was known as *dolly varden*; while in south-east Lancashire, less agreeably, the *dolly varden cart* was the nightsoil cart.

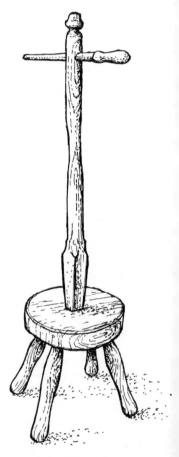

A dolly, without its tub.

EVERY HOUSEWIFE SHOULD USE

Donkey stone got its name from a proprietory brand.

donkey stone Also known as *mopstoning*, *donkey stoning* was part of the public ritual of cleaning which was an essential part of being respectable in the grimy working-class areas of industrial Lancashire. It involved rubbing the front step with soft, coloured stone, after swilling down with water, so that the step appeared bright and fresh. *Donkey stoning* had a strict protocol of its own: it could only be done at certain times of certain days, and the range of permissible shades (white, pale yellow, pale fawn) was very small. To do it at the wrong time, or to use a non-standard colour, was reprehensible, but not to *donkey stone* at all betokened a woman who was a slut of the worst sort, *'no better than she should be'*. By such disciplines, pride, respectability and cleanliness were maintained in the face of poverty and dirt. The name came from a proprietary brand, **Donkey Stone**, and the stone itself was very often obtained from the rag man in exchange for old clothes or other items. (See also *sand knocking*)

doubling process in the cotton trade whereby two separate yarns are twisted together on a **doubling frame** to make a thicker thread

Dow-days colloquial name given to the days during the **Cotton Famine** (qv) of the mid-1860s, when food or other assistance was doled out to the destitute

down (dawn) accumulated fluff and lint which settled on and around a loom, and especially on the floor beneath it, and had to be swept up frequently because it represented a major fire hazard

Dragon of Unsworth Unsworth near Bury was the home of the Lancashire version of the 'great dragon which ravaged the surrounding countryside' legend, very similar to stories found elsewhere in England. The dragon was clearly the cousin of Durham's **Lambton Worm**, for instance. Thomas Unsworth (his dates conveniently unspecified) was the local lord when a huge dragon terrorised the area, destroying property and eating women and children. The manner of the dragon's death was distinctly remarkable. Bullets had no effect, merely bouncing off its iron-hard scales, but Thomas shot the dragon by firing his dagger from his gun. The origins of the legend are inexplicable, but we might perhaps detect a reactionary late medieval view that swords and daggers would always be more effective than those new-fangled guns, which would never come to anything.

drawer-in operative who puts the warp thread through the **healds** (qv) of a weaving loom; each end of the warp is drawn separately through the **dents** (qv) of the **reed** (qv) and the eyes of the **heald**

drawing frame part of the process of spinning involved drawing together several slivers of fibre and then combining them in a single thread. This was done on a **drawing frame**, which ensured that the thread was smooth, regular and even.

dree incessant, in the sense of 'wearily continuous'; monotonous, as of work or life *'Th' rain's comin' deawn very dree'* (Edwin Waugh)

dressing various processes in the textile trade were termed **dressing**, including sizing the yarn in the cotton industry and raising the nap on woollen cloths

drinkings tea-break or snack between main meals. In farm work this might be quite substantial, with cake and pie as well as tea or ale (though many workers fared far less well), but in factory work — if given at all — a quick drink was likely to be the only refreshment permitted. A *drinking* meant that food was brought to, or given to, the worker; a *baggin'* (qv) was food or drink taken to work by the man himself.

drizzing form of harrowing in south Lancashire. A five-barred gate would be taken from its hinges and strong branches of hawthorn plaited among the bars. It would then be dragged flat over a field to tear out the old grass and scratch the surface of the soil.

The fearsome Dragon of Unsworth.

droighin' iron (see *sow*)

drop cork-legged to be completely astonished or taken aback by an event or a piece of news (similar in sense to flabbergasted) *I nearly dropped cork-legged when he told me*

Droylesden Wakes The *Droylesden Wakes Song*, among the best-known of Lancashire ballads, is of relatively recent origin. It was probably composed in the early eighteenth century and there is in fact much doubt as to whether it originally referred to Droylesden (east of Manchester) or — more plausibly — to the nearby hamlet of Woodhouses. An alternative name is the *Greenside Wakes Song*, which suggests that versions of the song were known in a number of local communities. During the Droylesden Wakes, a procession wound through the village, headed by two men, dressed as husband and wife, who spun thread and sang of domestic strife:

> *'Theaw saucy owd jade,*
> *theawd'st best howd thi tung,*
> *Or else awst be thumpin thi*
>   *'ere it be lung'*

All ends happily, but the last lines of the verse reflect the potential drudgery of everyday life in the eighteenth century:

> *'So let us unite and live free*
>   *fro' o' sin*
> *An then we shall have nowt to*
>   *think at but spin'*

drystone walls As elsewhere in northern England, **drystone walls** are a characteristic feature of the upland landscape throughout the Lancashire Pennines. Many are now in a sad state of disrepair, or have been demolished and replaced by ugly post-and-wire fencing, but thousands of miles survive in the gritstone areas. A high proportion of those across the high moorlands were built in the later eighteenth and early nineteenth centuries, but on lower slopes the walls may be several hundred years old.

duchy of Lancaster The duchy of Lancaster was created in 1351, when the earl was given the title of duke. The earldom itself, with its vast estates and considerable privileges, had been held by a succession of close relatives of the royal house — the first earl of Lancaster, Edmund Crouchback, was the younger brother of Henry III. The **duchy estates** included extensive properties outside the geographical boundaries of Lancashire, including parts of the West Riding (around Pontefract) and the honor of Tutbury in Staffordshire. It was the richest territorial inheritance in England other than that of the Crown. When Henry, *de facto* third duke of Lancaster (the son of **John of Gaunt** (qv)), overthrew his cousin Richard II and seized the throne in 1399, the **duchy estates** were for practical purposes united with those of the Crown. They remained under separate administration and have done so to the present day, even though the duke of Lancaster has without exception been the reigning monarch since that time. This

A drystone wall.

explains why in Lancashire the queen is usually referred to officially as **duke of Lancaster**. The **duchy** still includes large areas of land outside Lancashire's boundaries, while large parts of Lancashire are not included in the **duchy estate**.

ducks faggots: chopped meat with onions and herbs, cooked inside a skin (often of caul fat from around the kidneys); there are various local versions of these, with popular names including *savoury ducks* and *Yorkshire ducks*. One old lady recalled forty years ago that, on Leigh market in about 1905, 'you could get a *savoury duck* rolled up in an oatmeal cake for a few coppers, or **black pudding** (qv), with mustard on, on a tea-cake'.

duds teats of a cow; from the colloquial medieval term *ducks* or *dugs*, which referred to the breasts or teats of the female of any species

duckie stooan (see *knockdown brick*)

dunnock hedge sparrow or any other small brown bird

E

Eagle and Child One of the commonest pub names in the county, the Eagle and Child derives from the coat of arms which has been borne by the Stanley family, earls of Derby, since the fourteenth century. There are various versions of a family legend which states that Sir Thomas Lathom, last of the Lathom family, had one legitimate daughter, Isabel, and an illegitimate son by a local gentlewoman whose name is (not unexpectedly, because this is a legend) unknown. In order to provide himself with an heir, Thomas connived in a plan whereby the baby son was left at the foot of a tree, and there he and his wife stumbled upon it as though by accident. The abandoned child was claimed, somewhat implausibly, to have been carried away from somewhere else and dropped there by an eagle which nested in the tree. He was adopted by Sir Thomas as his heir, but, on his deathbed, guilty Sir Thomas repented, reinstated his legitimate daughter as chief heiress, and — through her marriage to Sir John Stanley — she therefore became ancestress of the line of the earls of Derby. Sir Thomas and his daughter Isabel were genuine historical figures, and Isabel did indeed marry Sir John Stanley, but the story of an eagle carrying away a child is many centuries older than this. Comparable tales are told in Greek mythology.

easings eaves of a house (OE *evesinge*)

eating contests Gargantuan eating contests were a popular though revolting entertainment in the nineteenth century, and large sums were wagered on the results. Chris Aspin, in his book on Haslingden, records several examples from that town. In 1827 it was reported that at the Black Dog one James Isherwood had eaten twenty raw eggs, including the shells, in seven minutes, his prize being a quart of ale. In 1866 a local man was challenged to eat 2lb (0.9kg) of mutton suet, but he abandoned the heroic attempt after three-quarters of a pound. A week later, a man volunteered to eat a 4lb (1.8kg) suet pudding with ten shillings as the stake. He gave up when 3lb had been consumed.

eawl-leet 'owl-light': twilight or dusk

Eccles Cakes The most famous of the traditional sweet cakes of Lancashire, **Eccles cakes** have been made for at least 200 years, but are probably much older than that. They are made today of flaky pastry, with a thick layer of currants in the middle and topped with crunchy sugar. The basic idea is very close to that of **Chorley cakes** (qv), but in the latter the currants are mixed in with the pastry. **Eccles cakes** have been produced commercially since the late eighteenth century, and various recipes have been claimed as the authentic version, though in reality there were probably a number of variations on the basic theme. Foods such as this, with their combination of sugar and dried fruit (both of which were much rarer and a great deal more expensive than they are today), were usually associated with feast days and festivals such as, in this instance, Eccles Wakes. (See also **Bury simnels, Chorley cakes, Goosnargh cakes**)

dderfeeder (edderbowt) a term, sadly obsolete, for a dragonfly

ddish aftergrowth; for example, the new grass (also known as *fog*) which springs up on the field after haymaking and can in good years provide a second crop

dge in Lancashire, the steep outer slope of a range of hills, usually

with a plateau or flatter summit area behind. The term is found across northern England — cf Alderley Edge in Cheshire — but local examples include **Blackstone Edge** and **Standedge**.

Edwin Waugh Dialect Society established in 1938 at Rochdale and dedicated to furthering the memory and work of the local man who was arguably the greatest and was certainly the best-known of Lancashire's Victorian dialect poets and writers (see **Waugh, Edwin**)

e'e, een eyes

egg rolling Among the traditional Easter activities in Lancashire was *pace egging* (qv), in which eggs were painted and decorated, and either taken from door to door with money being given in return, or were given out to children who called at the door. Associated with this was *egg rolling*, when the decorated and ornately-painted hard-boiled eggs were rolled down grassy slopes. This custom was found in many places in the county, and its origins are lost in the mists of time. It has survived into modern times in a few localities, most notably perhaps in Preston, where every Easter Monday *egg rolling* takes place on the slope of Avenham Park, above the Ribble just south of the town centre. At Bolton-le-Sands around 1900, the *egg rolling* was preceded by a small ceremony in which a local smallholder distributed a free egg to each child in the village.

Egg rolling, a traditional Easter pastime.

Elgin Street, Bacup Claimed to be the smallest street in Britain, this small enclosed area of backyard was formerly part of the market ground in the centre of Bacup.

elder cow's udder; a word now used mainly when it is sold as offal in the markets of towns such as Preston, where it is still regarded by some as delicacy, though by others with abhorrence

Ellen Strange A cairn high on Holcombe Moor was said in an old tradition to be the burial place of **Ellen Strange**, who lived at Ash Farm near Hawkshaw Lane and was murdered on the high moor by a pedlar who had become her sweetheart. Its stones were the subject of a particularly bad melodramatic verse written in the 1870s:

'Not picked and carted there in careless loads
From off the heather and the mountain roads
But one by one by trembling fingers laid
Down to the memory of this hapless maid'

Engels, Friedrich Engels was a prosperous German textile merchant who in the 1840s visited, and for a time lived in, Manchester. While there he observed the blatant evils which the capitalist system produced — social degradation, filthy and insanitary housing, alarmingly high mortality rates and child labour — and as a result he and his friend and collaborator Karl Marx developed their work on the principles of Communism. The window seat in Chethams Library, Manchester, where they worked and discussed their philosophies is still pointed out, though today, since the almost complete collapse of the system they promoted, the number of visitors who come to stand in reverence is minimal. Only North Koreans now adhere strictly (in principle, at least) to those ideas formulated in Manchester a century and a half ago.

England's bread In the great days of the Lancashire cotton industry, the proud boast was 'England's bread hangs by Lancashire's thread', reflecting not only the certainty that a very large part of the country's export income was derived from manufactured cotton goods, but also the confidence that the county's industrial might was secure. It proved not to be so.

entry passage or narrow lane between houses or blocks of buildings; in some Lancashire towns, such as Preston and Garstang, these would be called *weinds* (qv), while *ginnel* (qv) is another local alternative. In Manchester in the 1930s, it might be said of a bandy-legged man that he *couldn't stop a pig in an entry*. (cf *back-cut*)

esshole (see *asshole*)

Everton Toffee In the far-off days when Everton was a country village on the slopes of rural Edge Hill, it was a popular Sunday afternoon trip for Liverpool people to walk up the hill and enjoy the fresh air, and then buy **Everton**

A typical Lancashire entry.

Toffee, a local speciality. It was first commercially marketed by Molly Bushell in about 1753, using a 'secret recipe' which was jealously guarded.

ewe loaf   (see **Yule log**)

eye   in a coalpit, the mouth of the shaft or entrance to a level or adit; the adit entrance might be called the *day-eye*, as you could see light at the end of the tunnel

F

fades damaged and bruised apples, tired and weary fruit with wrinkled skins; often sold off very cheaply at the end of a Saturday night market

faff to mess, waste time *stop faffin' around and do summat useful*

faggot derisive or derogatory term for a woman, as in *th' owd faggot* for one who did something which caused outrage or annoyance

fag pie pie made with chopped, dried figs, sugar and lard, which was eaten on special occasions and was particularly associated with the Blackburn and Burnley areas, where it was the highlight of *Fag Pie Sunday* (Mid-Lent Sunday, now usually known as Mothering Sunday). The dish was alleged, somewhat implausibly, to be in commemoration of the cursing of the fig tree by Christ.

fair really, entirely, completely *Ah'm fair wore out*

Fair Ellen An ancient and peculiarly gruesome ballad (one version of a folk theme which is found all over Europe) set at Radcliffe Tower, a medieval fortified house of which the ruins still survive. *The Radcliffe Tragedy or Fair Ellen* (other versions call her Isabella) tells how Ellen, a beautiful eighteen year old girl and the apple of her father's eye, is killed on the orders of her wicked stepmother, cut up and baked in a pie, which is then served to her father:

'If now you will your daughter see
My lord, cut up that pye,
Wherein her flesh is minced small
And parched with the fire
All caused by her stepmother
Who did her death desire'

fangle whim or fancy; by association, an ornament or frippery, so that **new-fangled** was a contemptuous term for something just come into fashion

farrantly handsome, good looking, well-behaved; in some areas, such as Liverpool, it meant — in a related sense — quickly, promptly, efficiently *I'll set about it farrantly.*

fash to trouble or take pains

father (fayther) to authenticate, to be derived from; *aw con fayther*

79

She's fair wore out.

mi' tale meant that a story was true. The origin is probably the procedure by which, under the Poor Law in the seventeenth and eighteenth centuries, the mothers of illegitimate children were required to name the father to the authorities, who would then serve a filiation or bastardy order on the man. This was known as **fathering** the child.

fatherless pie (see **hotpot**)

fauce (fause) crafty, clever, sharp, quick off the mark

favour to resemble *she favours 'er Auntie Maud*

fayberry (feaberry) gooseberry

feeorins frightening or fearful things; ghosts or *boggarts* (qv), evil spirits or fairies. Until they were sentimentalised in the twentieth century, fairies were far from the dainty and delicate beings which is their present image.

fell Ubiquitous in the Lake District both as a place-name and as a surviving form of dialect speech, the word is also common in north Lancashire, but there are no examples south of the Ribble — **Beacon Fell** and **Longridge Fell** are the most southerly instances. Here, as in other ways, the Ribble represents a cultural and linguistic boundary, as it has been for well over a thousand years. (ON *fjell*, a mountain or hill)

fent end of a roll of cloth, a small piece of left-over cloth. In most towns there were shops which sold nothing but *fents*, at bargain prices, and children's clothes were often made from them (to the embarrassment of the wearer, since the materials, colours and patterns were often highly undesirable to the fashion-conscious).

fettle to repair, mend; alternatively, to clean, keep tidy and polished — a slovenly housewife could be condemned as **not a fettler**

fewtrils (see *littledoms*)

fields, Gracie Born Grace Stansfield over a chip shop in Rochdale in 1898, Gracie Fields went into showbusiness via touring companies and provincial revue, until arriving in the West End in 1922 and making her first film, *Sally in our Alley*, in 1931. There followed a succession of triumphant pictures, including *Looking on the Bright Side* (1932), *Sing As We Go* (1934) and *Look Up and Laugh* (1935), and from 1936 to 1940 Gracie Fields was the top box-office attraction among British female stars. Her powerful personality and unashamed glorying in her working-class Lancashire origins (strong accent, lively character, forthright opinions) made her a national celebrity, and she came to personify many aspects of Lancashire and its women. Lancashire, and especially of course Rochdale, worshipped her. Her celebrity status was somewhat marred by wartime controversy over her removal to Canada and the USA, and after the war she retired to Capri, where she died in 1979.

fig pie (see *fag pie*)

fig sue dish eaten in north Lancashire on Good Friday. Chopped dried figs were simmered with ale, bread, sugar and nutmeg until the bread disintegrated and thickened the mixture, and the figs softened and swelled. The resultant dish had the texture of a cross between porridge and soup. (See also *fag pie*.)

finger games The rhymes and word games that people play with children's fingers are very numerous, with countless local variants.

Here is one from the Burnley area:

'*Tommy Thumper*
Cherry Bumper
Long Lacy
Billy Milker
and Little Top o' Town's End'

fins fishbones

fish and chips One of Lancashire's greatest gifts to the wellbeing of mankind, the **fish and chip shop** was invented in Oldham in the 1870s. Fried fish and fried potatoes had long been sold separately, on stalls and in small shops, but the idea of putting the two together — an inspiration of genius — dates from that time. The innovation was especially welcome in the cotton towns, with their large numbers of working mothers, who did not have time to cook a meal but had a

Fish and chips in their traditional newspaper wrapping.

little money to buy ready-prepared 'fast' food.

Fisherman's Friends Fleetwood's fishermen may be far fewer in number than they once were, but the hot and warming pastille which once helped to *clear the tubes* and soothe their throats is still one of the town's best-known and most distinctive products.

fishing stalls In areas such as Formby and Birkdale, before the growth of the large urban areas just behind the shore, fishing was a mainstay of the economy, and it remains locally important. Traditionally, the beach was divided into *stalls*, or areas which were marked and leased by the lord of the manor to individual fishermen.

Fitton, Sam Sam Fitton was born in Congleton in 1868. As a baby he moved with his family to Rochdale, and when he was ten went to live in Crompton. He worked as a *doffer* (qv) and a *piecer* (qv) in the cotton industry, but he had a genius for drawing cartoons and caricatures, and for the writing of witty and clever prose and verse. When in 1903 he had to give up factory work because of ill-health, he could therefore earn his living as a reporter and journalist, playwright, artist and cartoonist, illustrating his own works and writing regular columns in local papers including, most notably, the *Cotton Factory Times* (qv), in which much of his best work appeared. The best-known of his poems is *Eawr Sarah's getten a chap*. He was a champion of the Lancashire working class, emphasising in humorous drawings and words the distinctive though often hidden comedy of the cotton mills, and was largely responsible for developing the *tackler tale* (qv) as a special feature of mill humour. At the same time he highlighted injustices and harshnesses in the employment system. He died in 1923.

flashes The lakes and marshy hollows which result from mining subsidence are known as *flashes*. In Lancashire, examples include the great **Pennington Flash** at Leigh, a mile (1.6km) long and half a mile (0.8km) wide; the complex of small lakes and ponds between Wigan and Bamfurlong; and the numerous round pools between Preesall and the Wyre Estuary. The Leigh and Wigan *flashes* result from mining, those of the Wyre from salt extraction by brine pumping.

Flat Iron The main street market in Salford was popularly known as the *Flat Iron*, and the term was also used in other towns such as Chorley. It probably originated because the market grounds were roughly triangular in shape, and so resembled the old-fashioned smoothing iron. The Salford *Flat Iron* was described in several accounts of working-class life in the city and, as **Robert Roberts** (qv) notes, there was a tendency to sentimentalise what was in reality a grim and grimy place, redolent of poverty and deprivation.

A shoe-seller at work on the Salford Flat Iron, c1900.

flay to frighten; hence *flaysome* and *flayed*; and *fleycrow*, a scarecrow

fleck flea; a cat which scratches a lot could be described as *flecky*, full of fleas

fleetin' dish shallow earthenware bowl in which milk was left so that the cream rose and could be skimmed off; **fleetings** was skimmed milk

Flemish weavers Stories abound that various standard features of traditional Lancashire life, including clogs and oatcake, were 'brought over by the **Flemish weavers**' who are said to have settled in the Bolton area in the reign of Edward III. There is in fact no documentary evidence to support the story of this influx of European refugees, although the tales may hold some folk memory — they first appear in print in the eighteenth century. What is more odd is that there seems an unpatriotic desire to attribute the invention of various ordinary and everyday items to these outsiders, as though the county was a peculiarly primitive place before the **Flemish weavers** are alleged to have appeared on the scene. In reality, of course, Lancashire people were well aware of clogs and oatcake centuries before their supposed introduction by migrants from Europe who probably never existed.

Flesh Day Christmas Eve, the time when people would go to the market to buy meat for the next day's celebration — one of the

A fleycrow.

few days in the year when they might eat proper meat

fleshmeat standard nineteenth-century and older term for **butcher's meat**; since **meat** meant food of any sort, the word flesh qualified it. Of the poor handloom weavers in 1840s Blackburn, it was said 'fleshmeat they scarce ever see, let alone eat'.

flit to run away, to depart, especially with the sense of doing so furtively *doin' a moonleet*

flitch side of meat, particularly bacon

float fault in woven cloth

flukes (flooks) a species of small flatfish which was particularly abundant on the shallow sandy shores of Lancashire and was caught in huge numbers. *Flukes* were one of the mainstays of the inshore fishing trade of

Morecambe Bay, the Ribble Estuary and the Formby coast, being taken by various methods: spearing with a pronged fork; hooking on long, many-hooked lines which were trailed down the beach from stakes driven in above the high-tide mark; or even by feeling with the feet and catching by hand. Anyone who has ever stepped on a *fluke* while, for example, doing the sands walk across Morecambe Bay, will know how that operation could be achieved.

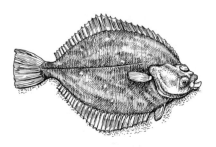

A fluke.

flying (fly) shuttle Until the **flying shuttle** was patented by John Kay in 1733, the width of cloth woven on a handloom was limited to the outstretched span of a man's arms, since the shuttle had to be returned manually. Any wider cloths (known as *broad-cloths*) had to be woven on one loom but with two operatives, one standing at each side to catch and return the shuttle. Kay's invention allowed the shuttle to be returned mechanically, using a *picker* (qv), and thus travel a longer distance but with only one man operating the machine, so allowing much cheaper and more efficient production of wide cloths.

fog (see *eddish*)

fold group of houses (usually a farm and its attendant cottages) built around, and facing onto, a common yard or small green. The *fold* was a pattern of settlement very characteristic of Pennine Lancashire and the adjacent parts of the plain, and numerous place-names, such as **Horrocks Fold** north of Bolton, remind us of how widespread it was. Many such groups of buildings have been lost, either through further development and infilling or, conversely, through the abandonment of all or most of the settlement, but some do survive to exemplify the appearance of the traditional *fold*.

football Although Lancashire's modern **football history**, a great and glorious record, dates from the 1870s and 1880s, **football** is a sport of great antiquity — people have kicked balls around for thousands of years, and many anecdotal recollections refer, for example, to children's games of **football** in which an inflated pig's bladder was used as a ball. Sometimes the game was on a large scale. At Kirkham, the Christmas Day **football match** was a great rowdy affair, resembling that which survives at Ashbourne, Derbyshire. The shutters in the town were closed after midday, and then the young men played football up and down the streets until nightfall, blaming the mythical *Roger-a-Moss* if any windows were broken or other damage caused. **Football** was played at Bury at Christmas and Shrovetide, and especially at Easter when the first two or three days of the week were given over to it. Large teams were chosen from among all the inhabitants of the town and the game was played through the streets, the 'goal' being the churchyard. At Rochdale the **street football** played between the various parts of the town often ended up in the riverbed.

footings workers' celebrations in a mill, especially when one of the women had announced that she was to be married. A mock wedding might be held, with the bride decorated in a sheet, and much mirth and telling of suggestive stories and jokes would ensue.

forest In medieval England the term **forest** did not mean wooded land, but land which was set aside for hunting or other special purposes (the word is from the same root as 'foreign'), and was therefore subject to a separate legal jurisdiction, the so-called **forest law**. The **Forest of Bowland**, the **Forest of Rossendale** and **Pendle Forest**, among others, thus originated as royal or noble hunting grounds, not areas with a dense tree cover.

Formby, George The Wigan-born film star and comedian (1905-1961) was, as Jeffrey Richards comments, a classic 'little man' in the Charlie Chaplin mould, one who, despite all sorts of adversities (including being Northern and working class), triumphs in the end. His films are perhaps now less familiar than his almost 200 songs, many of which, with their innuendo and dangerous naughtiness (for example, *My little stick of Blackpool rock*) were enormously popular in their day.

Forrester, Helen popular writer and novelist whose autobiographical accounts of her childhood and early adulthood in Liverpool during the 1930s have become worldwide best sellers. She was born in comfortable circumstances in Hoylake, Cheshire, but her family fell on hard times and were forced into conditions of dire poverty in the city, a tale which is powerfully and movingly recounted in *Twopence to Cross the Mersey*, *Liverpool Miss*, *By the Waters of Liverpool*, and *Lime Street at Two*. After the Second World War she married and moved to Canada, where she has lived ever since.

Foudroyant The *Foudroyant*, Lord Nelson's flagship, was restored in 1895, and anchored between the Central Pier and North Pier at Blackpool as a very popular tourist attraction. On the 16th June 1897, during a tremendous storm, the ship was wrecked when it broke from its moorings. It began to disintegrate in heavy seas and was eventually scrapped. Countless souvenirs were made from its copper, brass and timber, and large portions of its fabric were

The Foudroyant *beached at Blackpool in the summer of 1897.*

removed by sightseers as it lay on its side on the beach.

Friends of Real Lancashire organisation which campaigns for the restoration of the boundaries of historic Lancashire, the **County Palatine** (qv), as they existed before the 31st March 1974. It tirelessly publicises the need to emphasise 'proper' Lancashire in road signs, official publicity material, newspaper columns and other media, and it has recently begun to celebrate the 27th November as **Lancashire Day**. This was the date on which, in 1295, Edward I summoned Lancashire's first representatives ('Knights of the shire') to sit in parliament.

frog-i'-th'-'ole pudding now better known as 'toad in the hole', the dish comprised bits of meat, sausage or **black pudding** (qv) baked in batter; when cold, and heavy and solid, it was popular as a food to take to work in the fields or on journeys

front room The holiest of places in the Lancashire working-class home. The **front room** in my grandmother's house in Manchester in the 1960s was perhaps typical. It was bitterly cold all year round (never a fire); it had net curtains to screen it from the street (there was no front garden); there was a very large and uncomfortable sofa and armchair; a cabinet containing souvenir mugs from coronations and the silver jubilee of 1935; a small row of books, most of them Sunday school and elementary school prizes of the Edwardian era; and various photographs of members of the family. Forty years later I can still feel the cold, hear the silence, smell the slight mustiness and sense the sanctity of that room. (cf **back kitchen, living room**)

frumenty sweet porridge, ideally made of wheat grains which were simmered in water or preferably milk until they burst and softened to a jellied mass. Currants, raisins and spices might be included. *Frumenty* was a popular dish at Lancashire festivals such as Christmas and Easter Monday. A less agreeable version involved simply boiling oatmeal groats in water until they jellied, and then eating from a basin; a correspondent noted that she never tasted this because 'it looked like wallpaper paste'.

fulling process of cleaning woollen textiles, and removing their grease, dirt and other impurities, also known in dialect as **walking**. Frequently a cleansing agent such as **fuller's earth** (a naturally-occurring clay which had powerful grease-absorbing properties) or, more likely in Lancashire, *lant* (qv) was used. *Fulling mills*, where the process was undertaken on a large scale using water power, are recorded in the county as early as the 1240s, and their presence is an indication that, even in the thirteenth century, the textile

industry was developing beyond the purely domestic scale of cloth production. The cloth was placed in troughs of water or lye (an alkaline solution) under *fulling stocks*, which were huge wooden hammers. As these fell, they pounded the cloth and thumped out the dirt, at the same time thickening and felting the fabric itself to produce the desired texture for the material. An excellent example of *fulling stocks* survives in working order at Helmshore Industrial Museum in Rossendale.

fustian cotton-based fabrics, originally with a cotton and linen mixture. They were first woven in Lancashire in the late sixteenth century, by the mid-seventeenth century had become a mainstay of the county's textile trade, and were the foundation on which the great cotton industry was built in the eighteenth century.

fustian cutting Some *fustians* were woven with a looped pile. In order to produce the finished cloth, the pile had to be cut — the cloth was laid on a long table and, using a very fine-bladed and exceptionally sharp knife, the cutter ran the knife through the loops along the line of the pile. This was an extremely delicate and skilled process, demanding immense concentration and accuracy, and it produced cloths such as corduroy which had a raised nap.

G

galligoo local term for the great mounds of often toxic and always highly alkaline waste from the chemical industry which were deposited on open and vacant ground around Widnes, Farnworth and St Helens. In the 1960s much of the *galligoo* was removed for use as hardcore and infill in the construction industry — for example, the new road from the Widnes bridge to Speke was laid on a foundation of *galligoo* for much of its length.

galluses braces

Gannon, Luke The most famous of Blackpool's great showmen, responsible for many of the notorious exhibits and performances on the **Golden Mile** (qv) between the wars, including the celebrated displaying of the **rector of Stiffkey** (qv), the man with two heads, the pregnant man, the female Jesus and other highly undesirable shows of compulsive interest to the multitude.

Gaskell, Elizabeth The novelist Elizabeth Gaskell is perhaps most often associated with Knutsford in Cheshire, the small country market town which she portrayed as Cranford. She was, however, from Manchester, and as the wife of a Unitarian minister was deeply concerned with the pressing social issues of her day. She was one of the earliest writers of fiction who chose to depict working-class subjects, and in novels such as *North and South* and *Mary Barton: a tale of Manchester life* (1848) which were set in, and used a form of the dialect speech of, industrial Lancashire, she helped to heighten awareness among the middle class and non-Northern public of the human problems and tragedies which industrialisation and urbanisation had brought.

gate[1] In many Lancashire towns there are street names which include the word **gate**, from the Scandinavian word *gata* which means a track or road — for example, **Deansgate** in Manchester and Bolton, **Fishergate** in Preston and **Northgate** in Blackburn. Although it is often claimed in local newspapers and inadequately researched local histories that these indicate gates in the modern sense (that is, that the towns had walls and defended gateways), this is not the case. The word can also be used in a more general sense, as in *out o' th' gate*, meaning 'out of the way'. (cf *agate*)

gate² or **gait** pasturage for cattle. Many earlier estate and farm records, and documents referring to the use and management of common land, refer to the *cattle-gaits*, the grazing rights which specified the number of cattle which each tenant or owner was permitted to put on the land, and the periods of the year within which the grazing rights could be exercised. (cf *agate*)

gill in standard Imperial liquid measure, a quarter of a pint (0.15l), but in Lancashire a gill generally meant half a pint; my grandfather, who rarely drank, would say on special occasions if a drink was offered, *Ay, Ah'll 'ave a gill wi' yer*, and think himself very daring

ginnell narrow passageway between buildings (as in other dialect forms elsewhere in Northern England and Scotland, such as *vennell* and *jinnel*). A word with almost identical meaning in Lancashire and areas to the north is *weind* (qv). (cf *back-cut*, *entry*)

ginney In the coalfield areas of east Lancashire, and especially around Burnley, a *ginney* was a tram road which linked a colliery or outlying shaft-top with a canal wharf, road, railway sidings or yard. Some *ginneys* ran for several

miles across moorland and hillsides. They were usually operated with small tubs or waggons attached to a continuous chain.

gippo really excruciating pain, especially in the stomach or elsewhere in the insides

girdle variant of **griddle**, an iron plate used for baking or frying; also called a *girdlestone*

A girdle or girdlestone.

gist (see *agist*)

gobbin fool, a daft person, someone who does or says something silly or ridiculous

goit millrace or leat, a channel conveying water to or from a mill or other industrial premises

Golden Mile The most notorious and sensational part of the great Blackpool seafront, the **Golden Mile**, south of the town centre, originated in the decision of the borough council in 1899 to ban 'drapers, dealers in fancy goods of all sorts, quack doctors, phrenologists, palmists, cheap jacks, and all stands and stalls' from the

A ginney.

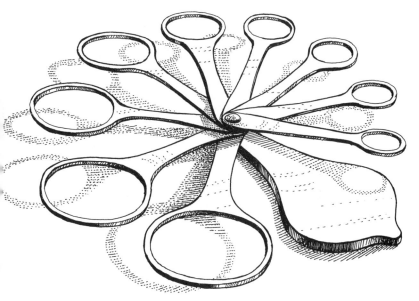

A gooseberry gauge (from Darwen).

beach and promenade area close to the centre. These people immediately moved southwards, taking over the gardens of houses on South Beach. The area was quickly turned over to raucous and often tawdry commercial uses, and so the Golden Mile was born. It has never looked back.

gooseberry contests In nineteenth-century industrial towns, the growing of prize vegetables and fruit was a popular pastime for those lucky enough to have a small plot of land or an allotment. In the Darwen area, the raising of **gooseberries** was the subject of fierce local competition, and there were several **gooseberry clubs**, the judges using graded ring measures

to establish the diameter of the fruit.

Goosnargh Cakes small, flat shortbread biscuits, into which a few coriander or caraway seeds are pressed before baking. Goosnargh is just north of Preston, and these cakes were traditionally baked on special feast days, including Shrove Tuesday when they were given to children who called at the doors of houses.

gormless (gawmless) slow, dull, vacant-minded; a word which is not confined to Lancashire. It derives from the word *gawm* or *gaum*, to understand or comprehend. This has fallen out of use, but the derivative remains in regular speech.

gradely very common word with a wide range of related meanings: proper, great, grand, very, good (*it's gradely, 'e were gradely ill*). Edwin Waugh uses it in this sense: *aw've no gradely comfort, my lass, Except wi' yon childer and thee*. It can also mean genuine, decent, proper, authentic. The dialect writer **Sam Fitton** (qv) wrote a humorous piece about the word, when an 'outsider' queried its meaning: *'He wanted to know what gradely meant, an' I towd him at that were nobbut one meaning for it an that were "gradely". It were a gradely word I said an if he couldno find it in th' dictionary it wernt a gradely dictionary.'*

grammar schools In the sixteenth and seventeenth centuries, numerous grammar schools were established in Lancashire towns and villages, often by local people who had left the area and made good elsewhere, and now wanted to immortalise their connection with a birthplace or ancestral property. There were, in total, almost eighty such schools. Some, such as **Manchester Grammar** and **Bolton Grammar**, were large and prestigious, and have remained as grammar schools to the present day. Others, such as those at Heskin, Rivington and Blackrod, were much smaller and more modest, and have long since been absorbed within the state education system.

Grant brothers The Grants, millowners and industrialists who

Common or field sorrel, once known as the paupers' food green sauce.

were largely responsible for the creation of the modern town of Ramsbottom, provided the model for the Cheeryble brothers in Charles Dickens' *Nicholas Nickleby*.

green sauce common or field sorrel, also known as sourdock (*Rumex acetosa*) or, less frequently, the curled dock (*Rumex crispus*). These weeds and field plants provided free and accessible food for the very poor in the rural parts of eighteenth and nineteenth-century Lancashire, giving a valuable potential source of greenstuffs in a diet which was otherwise almost entirely composed of carbohydrate. An additional advantage was that sorrel has very acid, sharp-tasting leaves, which lent a welcome sourness to the bland foods which most people ate all the time. *Green sauce dumplings* were made by chopping raw field sorrel, mixing it with suet and flour, and boiling as a dumpling in broth or water.

Greenwood, Walter In his 1935 novel *Love on the Dole*, set in Hanky Park, Salford, in the midst of the Great Depression, and in a number of other plays and stories, Walter Greenwood captured for many the hard times of the poor of urban Lancashire in a period of mass unemployment and distress.

griddle (see *backstone*)

grinning matches A favourite entertainment at wakes in the eighteenth and nineteenth centuries was a grinning match, in which the contestants had to pull

A contestant in a grinning match.

the most repellent and contorted face while peering through a horse collar which served as a 'frame' for the spectacle. The tradition has recently enjoyed something of a revival under the name of *gurning*.

guisings local festivals or frolics, or wakes, celebrated in many Lancashire towns and villages until the early nineteenth century. The term derives probably from *gystings* (that is, hirings), and may thus originate in the fairs at which servants and labourers hired themselves out. The alternative name, *wakes[1]* (qv), subsequently became general and was eventually transferred to holidays of a quite different sort.

gurning (see *grinning matches*)

gyste (see *agist*)

H

Hairy Ghost Weeton, in the Fylde, was reputedly haunted by 'the oldest of the ghosts' of the district, a hairy ghost which was alleged to resemble a satyr.

halfendole (see *aughendole*)

half-timers The *half-timer* worked part of the day in the mill and for the rest of the day went to school. In the mill such a child was often a *tenter²* (qv), one who minded the small and unskilled jobs on the loom, including sweeping beneath it. Most half-timers eventually graduated to full-time and more skilled work. The 1870 Education Act (which provided for elementary schooling from five to thirteen) exempted children over ten if they wanted to become half-timers. Only in 1911 was the minimum working age for children in the mills raised from eleven to twelve, and half-time working for those under fourteen was abolished under the Education Act of 1918, which came into effect in 1921.

ham '*Wi buri'd 'im wi 'am*' was the nineteenth and early twentieth century definition of *a good send-off* for many working-class families, not only in Lancashire but also elsewhere in Northern England. The significance is clear: meat was itself, until the later nineteenth century, a rarity for most poorer households, and to include ham in a funeral tea showed proper consideration not just for the deceased, but also for those still living who marked his or her passing. Furthermore, a meat tea (even though ham was much the cheapest form of 'proper' meat) represented a meal, whereas a cup of tea and a cake or biscuit was markedly inferior and snack-like. The difficulties of catering for large numbers of people in houses with inadequate cooking facilities and little space encouraged the development of the catering sidelines of organisations such as the Co-op Funeral Service, and provided local bakers and confectioners with very useful additional business. (cf *arval*, *wake*)

handball children's game which was once played widely in east Lancashire, whereby four or more stones were placed as the points of a diamond or other geometric shape. The thrower hurled the ball at the striker, who hit it away with his or her hand. The thrower then ran to catch it and in turn threw it at the striker, who was aiming to reach the next stone first.

handloom weaving Lancashire's great textile industry was not founded in mills or factories, but in the homes of the people. Spinning woollen thread and weaving woollen cloth were well established domestic trades by the seventeenth century. In the middle of the eighteenth century the cotton industry, hitherto relatively small, began to expand rapidly. Spinning was mechanised in the later eighteenth century, producing huge quantities of cotton yarn, but weaving was still undertaken on handlooms in cellars, attics or in specially-constructed loomshops at the rear of houses. This was the 'golden age' of the handloom weaver, and theirs could be a prosperous life in those years. But in the 1830s steam power began to be applied to weaving as well, and during the next thirty or forty years most of the industry was transferred from house to mill, from hand power to steam power. Many weavers were thrown out of work or earned ever lower incomes as the trade dwindled. For them the golden age was followed by the darkest of times.

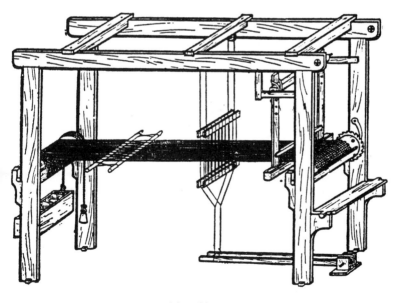

A hand loom.

ha'porth literally 'a halfpenny-worth', but in Lancashire used in phrases meaning 'a fool' — **daft ha'porth**, **right ha'porth**, or, more recently, **stupid ha'porth**; also, a small portion *'e put in 'is ha'porth*

Harland, John one of the county's greatest nineteenth-century local historians, and a well-known folk-lorist, born at Hull in 1806. He became a newspaper reporter and in 1830 he moved to Manchester, where — like some other local historians and folklorists — he became a reporter on the *Manchester Guardian*. He was soon deeply involved in local history, publishing many books and articles which, unusually for the time, showed an interest in social, economic and urban subjects. He published on the folk-speech of south Lancashire, ballads and songs of the county, and Lancashire legends and folklore (the last being published posthumously in 1873). Harland died in Manchester in 1868.

hash (see *'ash*)

haughendole (see *aughendole*)

have, to In his *Folk Speech of South Lancashire* (1901), Francis Taylor prints a table 'Conjugation of the Verb, To Have' which is a masterpiece. In his day the forms he records were still in everyday standard use, but a century later many have died out and others are declining. The following is just part of the table, for Taylor includes every form of the verb:

I have	*Aw'st*
You have	*Theaw'st*
He has	*He's*
She has	*Hoo's*
It has	*It's*
We have	*We'n*
You have	*Yo'n*
They have	*They'n*

haverbread, havercake The word *haver* is derived from the ON for oats, so the words *haverbread* and *havercake* are dialect variants of oatbread and oatcake. This form was particularly associated with the Pennine areas of the county, and with the equivalent parts of Yorkshire. Aikin, writing in the mid-1790s during the Napoleonic Wars, notes that when recruiting parties were seeking men for the army, they went round with an *havercake* stuck on the point of a sword, as a badge of local loyalty. The regiments thus raised were allegedly known as the **havercake regiments**. It should be noted that similar stories are found in the Calderdale area of Yorkshire. (See also *clapbread*, *jannock[1]*.)

hawes in the coastal areas of the Fylde and south of the Ribble, the sand dunes and the areas of blowing sand and grassland behind them; for example, **Layton Hawes**, which lay across the land where Blackpool Airport is today

heald part of the loom which is used to raise or lower the warp. The *healds* are a series of cords which are fixed to two or more wooden laths called *heald shafts* (they could either be threaded on the shafts or fixed firmly to them) and in the centre of every *heald*

Recruiting for a havercake regiment during the Napoleonic Wars.

was an eye through which the warp thread passed. The **healds** could thereby be raised and lowered as the shafts were moved. In this way a space, or **shed**, was created through which the shuttle passed.

heckle (hackle, hetchel)   coarse-toothed comb which was used for dressing flax and hemp in the linen and canvas industry

heivin'   (see **liftin'**)

hen pen   wooden hen-house or hut. Keeping hens was a favourite pastime (and potentially a useful supplement to family incomes) among working-class men in Lancashire industrial towns from the late nineteenth century, when reductions in working hours gave a modest amount of time for such pursuits. The wooden hut or shack on waste or vacant land around the edges of towns became a familiar feature of the landscape.

hen's back teeth   *What d' you know about hen's back teeth?* — in other words, 'you are completely ignorant and know nothing about this subject'. Hens do not have teeth.

Henry VII   In 1495 Henry VII and his wife, Elizabeth of York, visited Lancashire as guests of the king's stepfather, Thomas Stanley, first earl of Derby. Only five months before the visit, the king had ordered the execution of Thomas' brother, William, for treason. The king and queen stayed at Lathom House and, according to legend, the king climbed to the flat roof of the house to look at the view and inspect the property. While Henry

Henry VII.

was peering over the parapet, the earl's fool or jester is alleged to have whispered 'Tom, remember Will', meaning that the earl could take his revenge by pushing the king to his death. This would-be assassination was not to materialise, though, for Thomas was entirely loyal to the man from whose family connection much wealth and influence flowed.

hessians   leather water buckets; so called because of their vague resemblance to the military boots of the eighteenth-century Hessian regiments. In Liverpool in the 1770s, water supplies were so inadequate that a hessian-full cost a halfpenny (equivalent to perhaps £1 in modern values).

hey, lads, hey at times of pandemonium and confusion, when things had to be tackled fast and without delay, the cry *'hey, lads, hey'* was used. It was familiar all over Lancashire, and well within living memory in areas such as St Helens, Preston and Wigan. It meant 'come on, get going', or 'all hands to the pump', and might be used when, for example, there was a 'hue and cry'.

Hindle Wakes¹ Stanley Houghton's play, written in 1912, is set in the fictitious Lancashire mill town of Hindle, and is one of the popular works which highlighted the character of the independent-minded, high-spirited Lancashire mill girl (cf **Fields, Gracie**). The play was filmed in 1927, 1931 and 1952, but then languished in relative obscurity. However, it has recently enjoyed a revival and is now frequently performed by, among others, amateur dramatic groups in the county.

Hindle Wakes² remarkable dish, of cold chicken cooked with prunes and coated with a lemon flavoured sauce, which is usually claimed as being of traditional Lancashire origin. It is certainly medieval in style, but its true ancestry is somewhat obscure. The name is likely to derive from the 1912 play (qv) rather than vice versa, while the alternative explanation that the name derives from 'hen de la wakes' because it was a feast-day food is impossible on linguistic grounds.

hippin(g)s or *hipping stones*; stepping stones (the derivation probably being from 'hopping stones', for obvious reasons)

hippins baby's nappies (east Lancashire)

hobby horse The wooden horse-head, mounted either on a pole or placed over the head of a dancer, who is then covered with a cloth or sacking to conceal him from view, is a familiar figure in many of the more authentic and traditional **morris** (qv) and folk dances in different parts of England. In Eccles and Barton-on-Irwell, the hobby horse, with 'an enormous tongue of red flannel', was the central feature of the Easter dancing until the mid-nineteenth century, terrorising children and making leering and suggestive lunges at adults.

hog clamp or mound in which newly-harvested autumn potatoes were piled and then covered over with a thick layer of straw before being buried in earth; if properly made, it protected the potatoes from frost damage

Holden Rag At Holden Clough in Briercliffe, a *boggart* (qv) haunted the valley, causing diseases of crops and animals, mysterious noises and other anti-social goings-on. It could change its shape, sometimes appearing as a black fog, sometimes as a wisp of cloud or cloth. Eventually it was exorcised by a monk from Kirkstall Abbey and was confined under a cross on Delf Hill, there to remain as long as water flowed in the clough.

Holland, Bill Blackpool impresario and promoter, famous for his advertising slogan 'Come to the Winter Gardens and spit on Bill Holland's Hundred Guinea Carpet'

hollin holly; the word survives in numerous place-names, such as Hollinwood and Hollinclough

holly Holly has for centuries been considered to have a special significance at Christmas time, but it also had special powers in the rest of the year. It was traditional in Lancashire to hang a sprig in a new building to bring luck, or to place a branch in a house where somebody had died so that it would have a 'purifying' effect. Christmas **holly decorations** were left up until Shrove Tuesday and then burned in the fire, where their fierce, quick heat was ideal for frying pancakes.

hoo In south and east Lancashire this word meant 'she', and is normally used as such by the dialect writers in the nineteenth century, as well as in everyday dialect speech until the present day; but in south-west Lancashire, *hoo* was a more general term, meaning 'he', 'it' or 'they' as well as 'she'.

hoofed really 'down in the dumps', fed-up to the back teeth; the term was found in many parts of south Lancashire, from Liverpool to the Rochdale area

hoppit tray or basket, shaped to fit round the waist and hung from the neck. It was used to hold seed for broadcasting by hand at sowing time. The sower walked across the field, with each hand alternately dipping in and casting the seed in an arc to the front and side.

horse racing Horse racing became particularly fashionable among the upper classes after the Restoration in 1660, and there were racecourses outside many Lancashire towns by the early eighteenth century. The races were great social occasions, often attended by throngs of the county gentry and their families, and they could also be highly political — **Preston Races** were patronised by the Tories, the races a short distance away on Fulwood Moor were for the Whigs. The origins of the sport are much more ancient and less formal — the Lancashire place-name Hesketh (as in Hesketh Bank) is thought to derive from the Old Norse word for a racecourse. The Derby, named after its sponsor and founder, the twelfth earl of Derby, was started in 1780; and in 1829, William Lynn, landlord of the Waterloo

Holly

Hotel, opened a racecourse at Aintree to rival an earlier course at Maghull.

Hothersall Hall devil An ancient story states that the Devil undertook to grant three wishes to an inhabitant of Hothersall, in the Ribble Valley, in exchange for the man's soul. The man asked for a rope of sand, which the Devil could not provide, and in consequence Satan was imprisoned under a laurel tree at the end of Hothersall Hall, the penalty which had previously been agreed if he failed to keep his side of the bargain.

hotpot most famous of all Lancashire dishes, and one of the hardest to define. Almost everybody who cooks **hotpot** has a recipe which is claimed to be 'authentic', but in reality this was an all-purpose dish in which you included whatever was to hand. Its key ingredients were lamb, potatoes and onions, but **potato hotpot** was a commonplace in times when meat was scarce (sometimes known as *fatherless pie*). Some people put on a pastry crust, others are outraged at the suggestion and suggest that the 'true' version has sliced potatoes on top which are browned as a form of crust. It is a distant relative of Irish stew, and there are comparable one-pot oven-baked dishes in many other countries. It is unlikely that, say, 200 years ago many Lancashire people ate hotpot in its later form, since it requires an oven and only in the mid-nineteenth century, with the introduction of the range, did most households have such a facility. It is peasant cooking which is filling and cheap, and has survived to become a regional speciality — though some of the commercially-produced **hotpots** now served at *Lancashire neets* and other gatherings leave a great deal to be desired, with their sloppy mince and watery potato.

hotties discharge of very hot water from industrial processes into canals and rivers — for example, at St Helens, where boiling water used in the town's glassworks ran straight into the St Helens Canal, producing great clouds of steam

hullart evil spirit — in the Atherton and Tyldesley area, this was in the past often used as a threat to quieten children (*'Th' 'ullart 'll get thi'*); the phrase *black as a hullart* described a dirty person

Huskisson, William Although by no means the first victim of a railway accident, William Huskisson, MP for Liverpool and former President of the Board of Trade, was perhaps the most famous casualty of the nineteenth century. At the opening ceremonies for the Liverpool and Manchester Railway on the 15th September 1830 he was run over by *Rocket* at Parkside near St Helens, during a stop for taking on water, and died later in the day.

hush shops (see *jerry shops*)

hutch to shift closer, to move nearer to a person or place *We're o' reet … if I can get Craddy, here, to hutch a bit fur off* (Edwin Waugh)

I

ignaging A dance (which was accompanied by other forms of merrymaking) traditionally associated with Eastertide at Kirkham and other places in the Fylde until the mid-nineteenth century. It involved seven dancers-cum-actors, who included Tosspot, dressed in rags; the Grand Turk and his son; St George; a doctor; and a female character called Bessy. St George and the Turk fought, the Turk was killed, and the doctor brought him back to life with a potion after singing;

'I've a bottle in my pocket
    called alicumpane
Rise, brave Turk, and fight the
    battle again'

A **hobby horse** (qv) or horse-head on a stick was also carried, and Harland, the folklorist, believed that it was a version of an ancient sword dance — it certainly bore clear similarities to other very ancient folk rituals performed in other parts of the country. The origin of the extraordinary name is unclear; a corruption of *Ignis Agnae* ('fire of St Agnes') was one suggestion, but it is much more probable that the 'ig' element simply means 'egg', since this was an Easter festival.

Inglewhite Fair One of the great cattle fairs of the north of England was held at Inglewhite, north-west of Preston, where several roads meet at the large green, which is at the heart of the village and was the main fairground. The fair was the occasion for extensive drinking and entertainment, as well as serious sales; a nineteenth-century writer referred to it as 'the focus of the scum and the dregs of the neighbouring district'.

in her figure (see shawls)

J

jacquard component of a loom which allows, by use of punched card or needles, the movement of sections of the warp according to predetermined configurations so that patterned cloth can be woven. The development of the **jacquard** as a standard component of machine-weaving removed one of the main advantages of the hand-loom, namely that, until then, complex designs could only be woven if the movement of the warp was controlled by the weaver himself.

Jacobin The Jacobins were one of the leading factions during the French Revolution in the 1790s. Their name became synonymous with 'revolutionary', and in England many radicals espoused their cause. After 1815 the term was used in areas such as Lancashire, which had a tradition of popular discontent and civil unrest, to refer to anybody who might have 'revolutionary' notions. Ben Brierley, the great dialect writer, recalled how in 1830, when the people of Failsworth were celebrating William IV's coronation, he was refused any of the celebratory ox which had been roasted: *Nawe, thou mun ha' noane, thy gran-fayther's a Jacobin*, he was told by the old crone who was serving.

Jacobites The Jacobites, supporters of the Old Pretender or 'James III' marched through Lancashire in 1715 and 1745. Numerous tales, many highly implausible, are told about them. At Didsbury, for example, where the army crossed the Mersey in 1745, Dukes Hill was said to have been the place where the duke of Perth addressed the rebel army — but there was a family named Duke in the village in the 1590s, whose surname is a much more likely origin of the place-name. Almost every old house or pub on the main road from Warrington through Wigan and Preston to Lancaster has a story that fleeing Scots stayed there, hid in the barn, or married the innkeeper's daughter. A recent newspaper report about a converted barn near Garstang claimed that it 'sheltered some of Bonnie Prince Charlie's men back in the 1500s as they rested before battle'

— only 200 years out, and there never was a battle in 1745, but authenticity is not a strong point of such stories.

Jacob's Join social event where everybody brings food or drink to add to the communal feast. Such occasions are found everywhere, but the term *Jacob's Join*, for which no convincing explanation has yet been forthcoming, appears to be confined to north and mid-Lancashire. The word *joynin'*, to refer to a gathering when everybody provides something, was used by Samuel Bamford of his childhood in Middleton in the late eighteenth century, so is obviously traditional — but why Jacob should have put in an appearance is not at all clear.

jannock¹ cake or small loaf of oatmeal (thicker and more solid than a flat oatcake, although it was not raised). *Jannock* was allegedly introduced to Lancashire (some sources suggesting to Bolton before anywhere else) by **Flemish weavers** (qv) in the early fourteenth century, but there is no evidence at all to support this contention, which appears to have arisen with local mythology which appeared in print in the 1830s. The use of oatmeal as a staple foodstuff far predates the fourteenth century, and *jannock* is a basic method of using oatmeal. The first literary reference is in the early fifteenth-century Chester Mystery Plays, when the shepherds produce *'a jannock of Lancashyre'* to eat at a picnic. (cf *havercake*)

jannock² Because it was an essential and staple food, and perhaps because of its hefty physical qualities, *jannock* eventually became a term meaning honest, thorough, solid, reliable, straightforward; something underhand or improper might be referred to as *not jannock*

jessy (see *mollycoddle*)

Jeppe Knave Grave This cairn on the summit of the ridge leading south-west from the Nick of Pendle, above Wiswell, is allegedly the grave of a certain Jeppe, who was beheaded as a thief in 'Anglo-Saxon times'; a likely story!

jerry shops unsavoury and illicit drinking-houses of extremely low reputation and character, also known as **hush shops**; the drink served in them was often termed *jerry beer* and was notorious for its poor quality

jigger back lane or entry behind houses (Liverpool)

jinglin' neet (see *ringing the pan*)

Jinny Greenteeth fearsome being who lived in ponds and weedy water, and who would reach out and grab children and others who ventured near the edge or into the waters, pulling them under and drowning them. The threat of *Jinny Greenteeth* was used in Lancashire, into recent years, to discourage small children from going too near dangerous ponds and rivers. Marl pits, with their slippery sides and weed-filled muddy waters, were particularly dangerous, and Jinny certainly lived there. Indeed, it was from

A Jacob's Join.

Jinny Greenteeth on the lookout for another victim.

the long tangling weeds in such places such as those that the legend originated. An alternative name was **Jenny Long Arms**.

jockey In Liverpool before the Second World War, when bread was sold by weight, the baker would cut an extra slice if the loaf was underweight. This 'make-weight' was placed on top of the loaf before wrapping and so was known colloquially as a *jockey*. Children who had been sent to buy the bread would prefer to have the weight made up with biscuits, since these could be eaten on the way home and, all being well, mother would never know.

John of Gaunt The third son of Edward III, John of Gaunt (1340-1399) inherited the estates and title of the duchy of Lancaster from his father-in-law Henry, the first duke. In 1390 Gaunt's nephew, Richard II, made this title and honour hereditary, but when Gaunt died in 1399 that grant was revoked, and Richard took the duchy and its territories into the ownership of the Crown. This deprived Gaunt's son, Henry of Bolingbroke, of his inheritance. He rose against the king and seized the throne as Henry IV. After his accession he decided formally to separate the duchy of Lancaster and its estates from the Crown, but since the duke of Lancaster was king of England, henceforth the title would always be borne by the reigning monarch. Gaunt, although his personal interest in Lancashire was minimal, has

John of Gaunt.

always been considered something of a hero in the county, not least because of Shakespeare's *Richard II*, in which he is called 'time honoured Lancaster'. (See also **County Palatine**.)

jollop politely, the fat or juices from meat or other cooking, to be mopped up with bread or poured on potatoes; less politely, a quick-acting purgative which was a drastic remedy for being bound up (Samuel Laycock says of his friend Isaac Bradshaw that he has *pills for purgin' too, He says th'll oppen Chatwood's Safes, But that'll hardly do*.)

jolly robins foolish ideas, ridiculous notions; my great-grandfather

Cocklers using a jumbo and craam.

would ask my father, who years later would ask me, *'Who's been fillin' your head full o' jolly robins?'*

jorum measure, a dollop, a quantity; as in *a jorum of brewis* or *a jorum of porridge*

joynin' (see *Jacob's Join*)

jumbo in cockling (qv), a large heavy wooden board, about 4¹/ feet by 1¹/₂ feet (140cm x 45cm) with handles. The board was plac ed flat on the wet sand and rocke to and fro, the vibrations bringin the cockles to the surface so tha they could be scooped up with craam* (qv).

K

kail (cale) place or turn; children took a *cale* in games; you might ask someone to *keep mi' kail while Ah'm back*; or in a rush for seats you'd want to get *a good kail*. A related term is *keep kailie*, to keep a look-out.

Kathleen Mavoreen early twentieth-century euphemism for credit

kebbing fishing for codling, plaice or mackerel in the spring, using a line with several hooks weighted to rest near the bottom; a term used in the Morecambe Bay area and the Fylde coast

keck to turn over or tip, or to place insecurely so an object might be overturned — *'e keck't is cheer up on t' back legs*. In south-west Lancashire, other usages include *It's on a keck* (it's not straight) and *It jus' kecked over* (used especially when nobody claimed responsibility for a minor accident such as breaking a pot). Associated terms are *keck-handed* or *cack-handed* meaning 'left handed'. From this usage comes the assumption (which is quite wrong, as we left-handed people know only too well) that *keck-handed*

people are clumsy and make a mess of a job.

keep th' band i' th' nick to run smoothly, without interruptions; in early forms of spinning, the thread (*band*) had to run within the groove on the wheel of the spindle, and if it did not, the operation had to be stopped and repairs made

keigh-paw left-handed (cf *keck-handed*)

keks trousers; the word is found in east Lancashire and the West Riding of Yorkshire, emphasising the considerable linguistic similarities between the two sides of the Pennines

kempy rough, as in woollen cloth; the word is related to *kemps*, which were short and stubby hairs found among longer woollen fibres, and *kemp*, a defective fibre of wool which was thickened and 'lumpy', and so produced poor cloth — in particular, *kemp* would not readily absorb dyes

Kersal Cell The small monastic cell at Kersal near Salford was said to have been founded as a hermitage by Sir Hugh le Biron of

Clayton Hall, who pursued a hero-ically violent career slaughtering the infidel in the Holy Land, but then, filled with remorse, came home to Salford and found that his beloved wife had died during his absence. Distraught, he became a recluse and retired to a hermit's cell to ponder on his past misdeeds. In fact, the cell was founded for the Cluniac order in about 1150 by Ranulf, earl of Chester.

kid although officially meaning 'a child', a very frequent usage in Lancashire was that of brothers and sisters to each other (*our kid*)

Kilgrimoles There is consider-able circumstantial evidence that there was a Celtic monastic site known as **Kilgrimoles**, located in the vicinity of the modern town of St Annes. Although documentary proof is minimal, and the develop-ment of the town in the 1870s and 1880s may well have destroy-ed possible archaeological evid-ence, the name is recorded in medieval sources — *kil* is Irish for church (as in names such as Kilkenny), and *moles* is a form of the Norse word for sand dunes (as in North Meols).

kissing the shuttle The tradit-ional design of a shuttle in the cotton industry required the thread to be drawn through the eye of the shuttle by 'mouth suction', a pro-cess known as *kissing the shuttle*. It was long condemned as unhyg-ienic, and latterly identified as a cause of a range of mouth and lip diseases, including cancers, and deformities of the front teeth. The action also meant that weavers inhaled fluff and dust, so that lung and respiratory diseases commonly resulted. The problem was only remedied in the mid-twentieth century with the develop-ment of the self-threading shuttle.

kist chest or large box

kit can, as in the use of the term for a workman's tea-can; but the term is more familiar because it also meant the can or pail which was used for milking — children often remembered, and some still do, *carryin' t' kit*

kitlin kitten (ie *cat-ling*)

knackerty-knack (and many var-iations on the same theme) the sound of a handloom when weav-ing is in progress, a rattling clatter which for hundreds of thousands of Lancashire people before the mid-nineteenth century was one of the everyday noises of house and home. How many of them must have fallen asleep, exhaust-ed, as the clatter of the loom echoed in their heads? The sound, with its broken but regular and insistent rhythm, was reproduced as the rhythm of many Lancashire ballads, and is frequently referred to in poems and dialect:

> *'Knackety knicketty knicketty*
> *knack*
> *Thin water porridge and*
> *hardly that'*

knobstick blackleg or strike break-er; a workman who did not belong to the union, or who signed on for lower wages than the existing workers and so undercut their rates

knockdown brick game in which two bricks were placed on end, about twenty-five yards (23m) apart; two teams played, a member of each in turn trying to knock down the opponents' brick by rolling a *duckie stooan* or cobble

knocker-up figure now vanished from Lancashire's streets, but once ubiquitous in every milltown — the man who, at 5am or 6am,

A knocker-up at work.

would come along the streets, tapping at the upstairs window with his long stick to wake the workers. There was no alarm clock or radio then; instead, rain or shine, snow or storm, the *knocker-up* came by. Because of his central importance to working lives — to be late at work meant the sack, or docked pay — the *knocker-up* also assumed a key place in the folklore and popular culture of the county, celebrated in dozens of postcards, verses, cartoons and fond recollections.

knockin'-up stick The *knocker-up*'s stick was a long flexible rod, sufficient to reach the upstairs windows of a standard terraced house. At the end it usually had a few buttons, a bundle of twigs, or a stout wire, which would be rattled against the window pane.

knout cheeky, insolent or impudent person *tha young knout*

knur and spell game formerly very popular in east and south Lancashire, whereby a *knur*, a round made of pot or wood, was thrown into the air by a spring (in more recent times) and then struck with a *spell*, a three or four foot (1-1.2m) long wooden club or bat with a flat paddle at the end. The winner was the man who hit the *knur* furthest, the distance being measured in scores of twenty yards (18m). Herbert Collins quotes the example of Old Bark, the champion from Heyhead on the Yorkshire border above Todmorden, who was recorded as twice hitting twelve score and eight yards

(almost 750 feet/230m) in one match. (See also *billet, buck-out-of-the-wood, tipcat, trippet*.)

kurn-shuttin' celebration at the end of harvest (*corn-shutting*) when bread, cream, fruit pies, cold meat and other delicacies were provided for the harvesters

Knur and spell: a pummel, and a spell with a knur ready to fire.

L

lad invariable and everyday word for 'boy' in Northern England. The connotation is now changing as the word has become adopted nationally in words and phrases such as 'one of the lads' or 'laddishness' (although **laddish**, for 'boyish', was a standard Lancashire word).

Lady Sybil According to legend, Lady Sybil was the owner of Bernshaw Tower at Cornholme above Todmorden. She sold her soul to the Devil to obtain supernatural powers and become a shape-changer, and as a white doe she appeared to Lord William of Hapton Tower, who had long loved her. Following instructions given to him by a witch, he captured the doe and took it back to Hapton, where it changed back into Sybil and the pair were duly married. To cut a long story short, she resumed her witchcraft and changed into a cat, which had its paw cut off by William's manservant, before resuming human form and thereafter wasting away. Before her languishing death she was reconciled to God and died in peace, but tradition related that she was buried in a cold grave high above the gorge at Cornholme, and 'on the even of All Hallows the hound and milk-white doe meet on the crag, a spectre huntsman in full chase'. Such stuff sent a thrill of excitement down early Victorian spines.

lake (laik, lyke) to play; until the early twentieth century, this was a common word for playing by children (*a lot of us lads were laikin' in t' street*) but the word is now becoming obsolete (AS *laecan*)

Lancashire acre The statute acre of 4,840 square yards (4,046m²) was defined in the reign of Edward I, but in many parts of England, local measures, often very different from the official ones, remained in everyday use for another 600 years, only disappearing in the late nineteenth century. The Lancashire acre was a well-known example of such a measure, often calculated at 10,240 square yards (8,560m²)and thus more than twice the size of the statute acre. But within the county there were in fact many local variations even

Lancashire gloves — an ironic term.

on this measure, and when using older documents which give the acreages of land, local historians must be vigilant in trying to determine which measure has been employed.

Lancashire Authors' Association The idea of founding the LAA was put forward by the writer **Allan Clarke** (qv) ('Teddy Ashton') during a meeting of dialect writers and other interested parties at Rochdale in April 1909, commemorating the 200th anniversary of the birth of **John Collier** (qv). In November 1909 the LAA was established 'for writers or lovers of Lancashire literature and history', and its first president (1909-1933) was Dr Henry Brierley. The society has flourished ever since, encouraging the study and writing of literature (whether prose, poetry or drama) in dialect or devoted to Lancashire subjects, and it has been a major force in promoting Lancashire's rich literary heritage, past and present. Its publications include a great deal of contemporary dialect writing in poetry and prose, as well as historical material.

Lancashire gloves bare hands — an ironic term used by nineteenth-century paupers

Lancashire Plot This name was given to an alleged conspiracy, 'exposed' in 1694, in which various Catholic gentlemen of the county were said to have plotted to overthrow William III and restore James II to the throne. Eight conspirators were arrested, imprisoned in the Tower of London, and then taken to Manchester for a show trial, which the government confidently expected would result in their execution for treason. The local jury, however, acquitted the eight, after hearing in court how government agents had fabricated the conspiracy and after observing that key witnesses were patently fraudulent or perjurers. It is also evident that Lancashire jurors were very reluctant to convict Lancashire men simply because the authorities in London were pressing them to do so. The openly partisan judge, in telling the men that they were free, evidently thought them guilty, for he told them not to do it again: 'go and sin no more, lest a worse thing befall you'.

Lancashire witches 'beautiful women', an ironic play of words upon the story of the Pendle and other witch trials of the seventeenth century (see **witches**). In the nineteenth century it was customary among those who proposed toasts to 'the ladies, God bless 'em' to refer to the 'fair witches', who had captivated, bewitched and ensnared their menfolk by their beauty and charm

Lanky very old and affectionate abbreviation of 'Lancashire', used in all sorts of circumstances but always with approval and as a measure of quality and solid reliability. Something might be described as *real Lanky*, *proper Lanky* or, conversely, *not Lanky*. The Lancashire & Yorkshire Railway, which served much of the county and was a homegrown product not run from a distant London

headquarters, was generally known as *the Lanky*, and more recently the language or dialect of the county is often referred to as *Lanky*.

lant urine. This was an essential ingredient in the cleansing of woollen cloth, as a soaking in urine helped to strip the natural grease from the fibres. In areas such as Rochdale and Rossendale, where the woollen industry remained important until the end of the eighteenth century, it was usual for cottagers to collect human urine in large *lant jars* which were kept outside the door and collected at intervals. It was alleged that Methodist urine was better than Anglican, because Methodists did not drink and so their urine was not polluted by alcohol; *lant jars* were sometimes placed round the backs of chapels for those who wanted to relieve themselves after services. **Chamber lye**, an alternative name, referred specifically to urine which had been fermented and was used as a cleaning agent (including washing household linen) because it had powerful detergent qualities. Fortunately we now have washing powder. (See also *fulling*.)

lap thick sheet of combed, cleaned and separated fibres which emerges from the **carding engine** (qv), and is ready to be spun out into yarn

lappets striped cotton cloths which were very popular for cheap everyday clothing in the nineteenth century. Lancashire developed a large export market sending these cloths to the Far East and Middle East, and today *lappets* are still made at several mills in the county, including Vale Mill (opened in 1835) at Calder Vale near Garstang, which produces shawls for the Middle Eastern market and is owned by the Al-Ajlan family.

laps makeshift aprons cut from ends of cloth, worn by weavers to protect their clothing from oil and grease

lass standard term used throughout northern England and Scotland for a young unmarried girl or a female child, but also as an endearment for older women

lathe (laithe) barn, especially in north Lancashire (ON *hlatha*)

Lathom House The greatest loss to Lancashire's architectural and historical heritage was perhaps the destruction of the great late medieval palace of Lathom House near Ormskirk, the seat of the earls of Derby. The house was built in the 1490s by the first earl, and was besieged 150 years later by the parliamentary forces during the Civil War. It was heroically defended by the countess, Charlotte de la Tremouille, and held out until the very end of the war in the winter of 1645. Afterwards the house was partly destroyed, and in the early eighteenth century the remainder was pulled down and replaced by a modern building (itself now largely demolished). No reliable picture of the medieval house survives, but it

was known to have been a large and very impressive fortified complex, an ostentatious and spectacular cross between a mansion and a castle.

laughing like a drain to laugh heartily, or uncontrollably; from the similarity between the gurgling made in such laughter and the sound of water going down the drain

Laycock, Samuel Laycock was one of the most famous and highly-regarded of the Lancashire dialect poets, though he was really a Yorkshireman. He was born at Marsden near Huddersfield in 1826, and in 1837 moved with his family to Stalybridge in Cheshire. Initially he worked in the mills, but this affected his health, and after a time as caretaker and librarian at the Stalybridge Mechanics' Institute, he moved in 1867 to Fleetwood and shortly afterwards to Blackpool, where he worked as a stationer, confectioner and baker. He died in 1893 and is buried at Layton. Laycock began to write dialect verse in his early twenties and it is for this that he is remembered, although he also produced a great deal of sentimental poetry in typical Victorian style. His dialect poems concern everyday situations and the hard lot of ordinary people, as well as family, friends and local scenery. Among his best-known works are *Bowton's Yard*, *Thee and me*, *Mi gronfeyther*, and the series of twelve 'Lyrics of the Cotton Famine' of which one, the tender

Samuel Laycock.

and gentle *Welcome, bonny brid*, is perhaps the most popular of all Lancashire dialect poems.

layer-out person who did the *laying-out* (qv) of corpses. Most villages and urban neighbourhoods had recognised *layers-out*, just as, at the beginning of life's cycle, they had midwives. My great-grandmother, four feet ten inches tall, was the *layer-out* for her district in Openshaw, Manchester, in the 1920s — because she was small, my grandfather helped her with the lifting. It was skilled and respected work which, in areas of high mortality, was often needed. To be trusted by the community to act in this way was a very great honour.

laying-out part of the series of burial rituals which have now largely been taken over by the undertaker, funeral parlour or other euphemistically-titled outside agency. The *laying-out* of the corpse was the essential preliminary to the funeral itself, and the procedures were strictly prescribed. The body was lifted onto a table or bench, washed and cleaned, dressed in suitable fine clothes, and arranged decorously and beautifully (*"e made a lovely sight'*). Placed either on the table or the bed, the body was then displayed for the visitors to see. Many an older Lancashire person can remember to this day the terror and horrified fascination of having to look, as a child, at the body of a dead relative, friend or neighbour. But rituals such as this, in times of poverty and frequent death, represented a moving and effective way of giving a dignified and respectful departure from this world.

lea (see *cut²*)

lead large vat for holding liquids; in the textile industries, a *lead* was used for dyeing, but the word was also used in brewing, in which the *lead* was the fermenting vessel

leaps in the North Meols and Southport area, willow baskets in which fishermen and shellfishers transported their catch for sale in the town (see also **shrimping**)

leather to thrash, beat or belt *Give over or Ah'll leather thi'*

Lees, Joseph dialect writer, of Glodwick in Oldham (1748-1824). He was the author, with his drinking companion Joseph (Joss) Coupe, of the comic ballad *Jone o'*

The origins of liftin' *are shrouded in mystery.*

Grinfilt ('John of Greenfield'), composed in about 1805. This tells how John decides to become a soldier because times were so hard — it was written in the middle of the Napoleonic Wars — but, being an ignoramus from a backwater, he has no idea where France is. He therefore goes all the way to Oldham (four miles!) to find the French, and when he reaches there he thinks he is indeed in a foreign country. Poking fun at the ignorance of country people, the song became a bestseller in broadsheet form, and many versions were made in imitation.

length   cloth was woven in *lengths*, but the term implied no precise measurement and so was used for any piece of cloth of any sort and of whatever size

lestering   spearing fish in rivers and brooks. A nineteenth-century description of the River Roch tells how 'at night-time men would venture into the river with a lighted lantern held in the left hand and the trout being attracted by the light they were then speared and captured'.

liftin'   bizarre custom, also known as *heivin'*, which was common in the Bolton and Manchester areas, around Wigan and in the Fylde in the eighteenth and early nineteenth centuries. On Easter Monday, men lifted women: several men would take hold of a woman, at least one per arm and one per leg, and raise her horizontally into the air, three times. On Easter Tuesday, groups of women would

Lestering.

lift men. The objective of the exercise must remain the subject of speculation, but the 'proper' version was that it commemorated the lifting of Christ from the cross. This seems rather unlikely. (See also ***buck-thanging***.)

Lights, the   Known, more properly perhaps, as the Blackpool Illuminations, these are one of Lancashire's greatest popular attractions. Others may sneer, call them tawdry, claim that towns elsewhere do better, but we all know that such notions are nonsense and Blackpool's lights reign supreme. They were first installed, on a much smaller scale of course, for the 1912 and 1913 seasons, and from 1925, except for the years of the Second World War, they became an annual event which was increasingly the highlight of the resort's season. The vast crowds, the immense queues of traffic, and the almost inevitable question, *'Goin' t' Lights this year?'*, testify to their enduring popularity.

like The characteristic Lancashire use of *like* at the end of a sentence, for dramatic effect or to reinforce the message, is described in Nodal and Milner's 1875 glossary: 'used in a curious manner for the purpose of intensifying an expression — as, *"I'm all of a dither, like"*, meaning, "I am trembling violently".'

like likely *e's not like t' get theer*

likely handsome, sharp, on the ball; now often associated with Tyneside (*The Likely Lads*) but formerly used throughout Northern England

limb o' th' devil wicked or particularly mischievous person; the phrase was often abbreviated, so a naughty child might be referred to as a *young limb*

limegal small pony (*gal* = galloway, a name given to the breed of hardy animals originally raised in the Galloway region of Scotland) employed for transporting slaked lime from the kilns in areas such as Clitheroe and Carnforth down into south Lancashire for the building trade and for dressing the land to reduce the acidity of soils. The use of ponies for this purpose was greatly reduced by the growth of the canal and rail networks, but some *limegals* were still trotting down from Clitheroe into Rossendale as late as 1902.

lint general English word for fluff, but in Lancashire particularly associated with the huge quantities of loose cotton fibres which accumulated in any spinning or weaving mill, floating around the looms or frames before settling in dusty piles on the floor and any other flat surface. The *lint* had to be swept up constantly because, as practical experience soon demonstrated in the early mills, it represented an acute fire hazard, particularly if mixed with the oil which seeped from the machinery. Small children were employed in the early days to undertake this task, since they could reach under the looms and other working machinery to sweep otherwise inaccessible recesses, and innumerable industrial injuries resulted from this practice.

lip-reading was also known as *weighvers' talk* or *mee-mawing*. The deafening noise in a loomshop or weaving shed meant that normal forms of communication among weavers were impossible. They therefore developed lip-reading as a way of conversing and passing messages — a method which, by happy coincidence, managed to avoid the rules against conversation which were enforced in most nineteenth-century mills. Different mills developed their own specia 'languages': one description of a Rossendale mill refers to the 'long, bawdy and derisive conversations across the floor of the mill', in which the manager and the **tacklers** (qv) were the objects of scurrilous and slanderous wit. In recent decades, lip-reading has largely died out as mills themselves have disappeared and the level of noise in those which remain working has been considerably reduced.

lips an' lugs poorest form of offal or scrap meat: the trimmings of a sheep's head, two pennyworth of which might be bought to make a stew with potatoes, or a broth which could be thickened with a bit of stale bread

lish lively, active (with an unsubtle alternative meaning of 'over-sexed', as in the well-known north Lancashire and Westmorland folk song *'It was the lish young buy-a-broom that led me astray'*)

lithe to thicken broth or stew with flour or meal; in fact, to produce the opposite effect to the usual English word *lithe*, meaning lively and active. *Lithin'* was a dialect name for pancake batter.

lither lazy, idle

littledoms A delightful obsolete term meaning small portions or penny packets; an eighteenth century diarist, writing about Lancaster market, said that 'they dealt the oatmeal in *littledoms* to everybody there'. An equally attractive, though regrettably obsolete, term was *fewtrils*, or little things.

little house privy, sometimes called the *netty*, but in Lancashire the most commonly used alternative terms were *petty* or *bog*

Little Ireland This name was given to the worst of all Manchester's many slums, the area just south of the city centre where, in the mid-nineteenth century, thousands of poverty-stricken Irish immigrants were crowded into insanitary hovels perched on the edge of the filthy and polluted Medlock. This appalling place was observed by the German merchant **Friedrich Engels** (qv) in the early 1840s and his experience helped him, with his friend and colleague Karl Marx, to formulate the theories of Communism. The name *Little Ireland* was also used for Irish ghettos in other towns, such as Southport (where it was a collection of cottages and shacks close to the present Hesketh Park).

Liver Bird celebrated mythical bird which is the symbol of Liverpool and appears on taxis, tourist literature and many another likely or unlikely place. The most prominent examples are of course the great birds which perch on top of the towers of the Liver Building (completed 1911) at Pierhead. The original badge of the city was an eagle with a sprig of foliage in its beak. In 1797 the borough was granted a new coat of arms which included a cormorant carrying a piece of seaweed, symbolising the fact that Liverpool was by then a great international port. It is said that the seaweed was laver, and that its use was a heraldic pun on the first part of the city's name. Whether or not that is so, ever since that time the cormorant-like bird has been known as the Liver Bird.

Liverpool gentlemen 'Manchester men and Liverpool gentlemen' was a favourite Liverpudlian epithet of the nineteenth century. Manchester, and its enormously wealthy cotton merchants and businessmen, prided themselves on their down-to-earth, honest, 'grown from the soil and not ashamed of it' approach to business, but Liverpool, an ancient corporate borough, regarded the Mancunians as coarse upstarts. Manchester, in turn, considered the wealthy shipping owners of Liverpool to have unwarranted airs and graces and, just as important, felt that the seaport acquired its great prosperity by milking and exploiting the entrepreneurial activities of Manchester's cotton trade. The two great cities have never lost their fierce rivalry.

living room Though certainly not confined to Lancashire, this term was and is particularly common in the county. It recalls the time when almost all houses had only one room for cooking, eating and daytime living or, rather later, the period when, in a two-up two-down, the other downstairs room was the never-used, icy cold, sacred shrine of the parlour or *front room* (qv). The words *living room* implied a place that was noisy, hot, cosy, crowded and busy, while *front room* suggested the exact opposite. (cf *back kitchen*)

livin' up t' stick living together without the benefit of marriage: one of many euphemisms for this state of affairs, which was far more frequent in the past than present day moralists like to believe. Other terms include *tally* and *livin' o'er t' brush*.

loading to carry; a term used when, for example, taking wood to the timber yard, or hay or corn from the fields to the barn. Other spellings in older documents include *lading* and *leading*, and it can mislead the unwary who assume that it simply means 'piling the stuff into the cart' in the modern sense.

lobscouse According to one nineteenth-century definition, this was 'a dish consisting of hashed meat, cooked with potatoes and onions', while another describes it as 'a sort of Irish stew'. Normally known simply as *scouse*, it was the southwest Lancashire and Liverpool version of *'ash* (qv). Some writers have claimed to give the 'authentic' recipe for *lobscouse*, but in reality it was, like its near-identical twin, an all-purpose, anything-goes dish, in which whatever was to hand and in any way suitable was boiled up to make a (with luck) fragrant, rich and tasty meal. Or, in times of poverty, it was a thin, watery broth with anonymous bits of this and that floating in it, not satisfying but better than nothing. What sets *scouse* apart, though, is its inextricable ties with Liverpool. The word is probably Scandinavian in origin

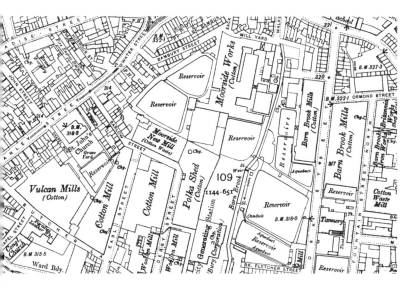

Lodges, shown as 'reservoirs' on this 1910 OS map of Bury.

but the Liverpool connection developed because, when made with hard sea-biscuits rather than potatoes, it was an ideal shipboard meal. The long cooking softened the rock-like, weevil-infested biscuits and made them comparatively palatable. *Blind scouse* was scouse which was made without any meat, a food of the poor or a dish eaten when the money had run out at the end of the week.

loce (loose) loose, a word used in the modern sense, as of clothes or footwear, but also employed with the wider connotation of 'to let go' or 'release': William Baron wrote in the 1890s of *'when t' factory loces uv a neet'*. When they had finished their term of seven years, apprentices were *loosed from their bindings*.

lodge reservoir of a mill or other factory, or a colliery. The term could also be used for other ponds and small lakes, but in the nineteenth century it became associated particularly with industrial sites.

Lofthouse, Jessica popular writer on Lancashire and Cumbrian subjects, who grew up in Clitheroe and whose many books published between 1945 and 1975 celebrated the landscape and 'folk history' of the county and its neighbours. Historical accuracy was not always her strong point, but she had a fine sense of the romance of history and a talent for topographical description. Her works were often structured as travels or itineraries around the chosen area.

longwall   (see *stop and room*)

long curtains to have full-length curtains, or curtains which covered all of a window even if they did not reach the ground, was a mark of distinction in many urban working class areas: most people could not afford them. Thus, of a woman who spoke 'posh', it might be said that *Hoo* [she] *talks long curtains*.

long stick measure for cloth, of 36^1/$_2$ inches (93cm). The extra half-inch allowed for the folding of the cloth.

loose end nothing to do *come by if you're at a loose end* or, more threateningly to a child, *if you're at a loose end why don't you* [tidy your bedroom, do your homework, clean up that mess...]

Lowry, L S The name of Laurence Steven Lowry has become internationally known because of his particularly idiosyncratic style of painting, portraying the industrial and urban landscapes of the North-West in the early and mid-twentieth century. The dark and gloomy scenes, matchstick people, industrial chimneys belching smoke, the grimy Victorian buildings of mill and factory towns, the docks and the stray dogs are instantly recognisable. So close has the connection become that such scenes are now sometimes described as **Lowryesque**.

loyal toast Elizabeth II, like every English monarch since the accession of Henry IV in 1399, is also duke of Lancaster. Lancashire's loyal toast therefore celebrates this special connection with the county: 'The queen, duke of Lancaster'. (See **duchy of Lancaster**.)

lug, lughole ear, earhole

lurry until the 1920s the standard Lancashire form of the word 'lorry', in written form as well as everyday speech. Today the written spelling is obsolete, but the older pronunciation is still widespread. Historically, a lorry or *lurry* was a long farm-cart, with four wheels but without sides. Its name was then transferred to the 'motor lorry' and hence to the modern vehicle. *Lurry* could also be used as a verb, meaning 'to drag, to pull along'.

Lyon, George The notorious highwayman of Upholland, George Lyon was to some a 'Robin Hood' figure, romantic and dashing while to others he was a vicious and unrepentant criminal. He was born in 1764 and his known criminal activities began as early as 1786, when he was convicted of highway robbery. In 1814 he led a gang of thieves who allegedly terrorised the neighbourhood for some months, but he was eventually captured and tried on eleven counts of robbery and burglary. With two accomplices he was executed at Lancaster on the 22nd April 1815, and his body was buried in Upholland churchyard. The grave rapidly became an object of reverence and pilgrimage, to the very obvious and not unreasonable dismay of the local clergy.

M

Mabs Cross Mabs Cross in Wigan is associated with an early legend which states, that in the time of the Crusades, Sir William Bradshaigh was away from home for ten years. Making the assumption that he was dead, his wife Mab (Mabel), daughter of Hugh Norres of Haigh, remarried. Sir William subsequently returned home and slew the man who had supplanted him. Mabel, as a penance, agreed to walk barefoot once every week from Haigh to the cross on the edge of Wigan, while Sir William was outlawed for a year and a day. Although she continued to do her penance weekly for the rest of her life, Mabel and Sir William were reunited and lived happily ever after. The story fascinated Sir Walter Scott, who used it in *The*

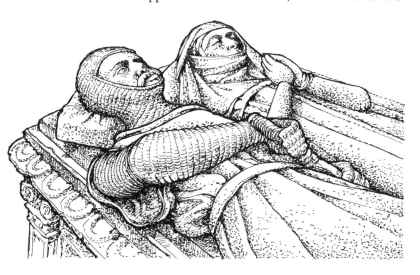

The tomb of Sir William and Lady Mabel Bradshaigh in Wigan Parish Church.

Betrothed, but comparable legends appear in many European countries and elsewhere in England, and there is no truth behind it. Sir William and Lady Mabel, although historical figures, actually lived in the early fourteenth century, a considerable time after the Crusades.

mad fierce, angry (*mind, now, plate's mad 'ot*)

Mag Shelton Mag Shelton was a witch from Singleton in the Fylde whose staple food was haggis, made of boiled groats mixed with herbs (nothing remarkable in that — many Lancashire people lived on such fare), and one of whose somewhat innocuous 'deeds of darkness' included milking her neighbour's cow into a pitcher in the shape of a goose. The neighbour, suspecting that something suspicious was afoot, struck the goose and it broke into pieces, spilling the milk. This all seems fairly prosaic, but Mag's fame was widespread. She is said to have been buried beneath a boulder in Woodplumpton churchyard.

maiden clothes horse

Mally until the mid-nineteenth century, a very common diminutive of the girl's name Mary

Malvolio For many years advocates of the 'Shakespeare spent time in Lancashire' theory have suggested that Malvolio, the hapless steward in *Twelfth Night* who is one of the greatest of all comic victims, was modelled on Sir William Farington of Worden Hall in Leyland, steward to the earl of Derby in the early 1590s. The theory is a good deal more plausible than some which have been put forward about the plays, for **Shakespeare** (qv) certainly had close associations with other members of the Stanley family, and there is circumstantial evidence to suggest that Farington may indeed have been the inspiration.

Manchester Guardian Originally a weekly paper, but from 1836 published twice weekly and after 1855 a daily, the *Manchester Guardian* became the voice of liberal England and one of the greatest of all provincial newspapers. In the twentieth century this role was extended as it gradually developed a national circulation under the editorship (from 1872 to 1925) of C P Scott, until eventually, and sadly, the word 'Manchester' was dropped from its title. The *Guardian* retains, however, a strong involvement in the North of England, and its coverage of issues and stories from the north is better than that of any other national paper. It has a proud record of supporting worthy causes, and many important literary, political and socially enlightened figures have worked for it or contributed to it.

Manchester Martyrs In 1867 there was an abortive raid by the Irish nationalist Fenians on the military armoury at Chester Castle. Two of the organisers were arrested in Manchester, but as they were being moved to Hyde

Road Gaol, a group of between thirty and forty armed men attacked the convoy and freed them. During the gun battle a policemen was killed, and as a result three Irishmen were convicted and publicly hanged at Salford Gaol in December. The execution of the Manchester Martyrs (among the last public hangings in England) outraged the Lancashire Irish and inflamed nationalist sentiments, although to most English people the men were murderers.

mangle Until the advent of the washing machine and tumble drier, the *mangle* was an essential item in many Lancashire households. It would usually be kept in a shed in the backyard, its heavy cast-iron frame rusting slightly and its great rollers waiting to be fed long lengths of soapy wet clothes, sheets and towels. My grandma would carry out the heavy, dripping washing from the sink in a tub, put the items through the **mangle** by turning the large iron wheel, and out would pour a stream of greyish-blue fresh-smelling water, running down the flags of the yard into the grid. Later, the rinsed washing would be put through again, and the yard swilled down with any leftover water to remove at least some of the accumulation of soot and grime.

marl a light and, ideally, slightly limy soil, which was dug very extensively in Lancashire until the end of the nineteenth century for use as a top-dressing on heavy clay or acid peat land. It was worked from deep pits in the fields — a large proportion of the county's surviving field ponds are the result of **marl-working**. The **marl** was dug in spring and especially in mid- to late autumn, after the harvest and when the other work on the farm was limited. In many places the end of *marl-getting* was the occasion for a celebration, often known as *shutting the marling*, when a 'lord' and 'lady' would be chosen from among the **marlers** and, dressed up in costume, would be drawn on a cart out of the pit by horses decorated with ribbons. They then presided over a feast.

marlock mischief, tricks, frolicking
'When t' ones bin strivin' o' he con
To awter wicked men,
Then t' other may's some
marlocks, an
Convarts 'em o'er again'
                (Edwin Waugh)

marred soft, spoiled, pampered

marrow, marrah a friend — usually with the implication of 'best friend' or 'mate'. The word was found throughout Northern England and is still in everyday use in the North-East. A related meaning was 'pair, equal, match' (*aw never seed 'er marrah*).

marshgates allocations of grazing land within coastal and estuarine marshes (from *gate*, to go), as on the Freckleton Marshes on the north side of the Ribble

mash in the weaving trade, a term for bad work or work which has gone wrong

mass trespasses In the 1920s and early 1930s there was growing pressure for the public to be given access to open moorlands and hillsides in the south Pennines, close to the Lancashire and Yorkshire conurbations. Leisure time was increasing, tram, rail and motorbus services gave access to the edges of the open country, and there was a powerful feeling that these areas, held sacrosanct as grouse moors for shooting, should not be the private preserve of a privileged few. To highlight the cause, **mass trespasses** were held. Groups of ramblers and supporters walked onto the grouse moors in such numbers that the keepers and police could do nothing. The movement led, after 1945, to the creation of rights of access to at least some of the uplands along the county's eastern boundary, but half a century later there are still extensive areas of beautiful countryside which remain legally inaccessible to the general public.

maunder to be listless, wander aimlessly, be distracted or not pay attention

mawkin dirty, sluttish, slovenly, filthy, shabby,

mawt target or objective in a game

May Day This festival was celebrated in many Lancashire communities until the mid-nineteenth century. At Poulton-le-Fylde, for example, the streets were strewn with flowers and there was dancing and drinking. In the Briercliffe area, May Day was known as *Laying May* and the younger members of the population indulged in unruliness, carrying off all sorts of movable items ('brushes, mops, buckets, dollytubs and anything else we could find') from outside houses and taking them to the top of Cockden Hill, where the unfortunate owners had to sort out their possessions the next day. At Burnley and many other places, **May Day** was marked by decorating houses with garlands and branches. In nineteenth-century Liverpool the carters and horse-van drivers bedecked their carts with ribbons and brightly-coloured cloths, and covered the harness with elaborate ornaments. By the 1880s this had become so popular that processions of floats were arranged, and the mayor and corporation attended. In Manchester the coaching companies and carriers decorated wagons and horses, while at Clifton and Kearsley the activities of *Ribbin Horse Day* included dressing-up of the carts and horses of the local coal companies and driving them in procession through the area, a custom maintained until 1917.

May washing to wash in fresh dew on May Day morning was held to be a recipe for eternal beauty

maypoles Most places in Lancashire had **maypoles** until the late eighteenth century, but a combination of large-scale economic and social change, and concerted efforts by the Church authorities to stamp out the 'unseemly' goings-on which were associated with **maypoles**, meant that by the 1860s few survived. John Lucas's 1732 history of the parish of Warton (near Carnforth) tells how the village lads and lasses would go to a *rushbearing* (qv) and then dance in the open air round the **maypole**, which was adorned with evergreens and flowers, for the rest of the day and much of the night. At Abram the **maypole** was associated with **morris dancing** (qv), and custom dictated that if the dancing was not performed for twenty years, the right to the land on which the pole was situated would lapse.

May, singing in the It was traditional in south Lancashire and north Cheshire for bands of men to go from farm to farm and village to village during April, 'singing in the May'. They led a nomadic life, sleeping in outhouses but receiving food at the farms and houses where they entertained. The custom is recorded in Langton's history of Flixton (1898) as having been commonplace within relatively recent times.

meal Oatmeal was the staple food of the Lancashire poor for centuries, the difference between life and death on countless occasions. It was usually known simply as *meal*, since oats were by far the commonest grain, although the poor also ate ryeflour and made ryebread or dumplings, and in times of utmost deprivation would also eat barley. Wheatflour was

so expensive that, until the nineteenth century, few poor Lancashire people had ever tasted wheaten bread and many had never even seen it. *Arks* (qv), the great chests in which oatmeal was stored, were treasured heirlooms for those able to afford them; and porridge, *oatcakes* (qv) and *jannock* (qv) were the almost invariable daily fare in many Lancashire households.

meanygate In the mosslands of south and west Lancashire, the long straight tracks which led onto the moss (and which today cross the farmland created when the mosses were drained after 1700)

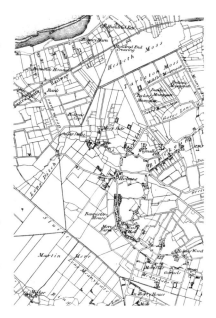

Meanygates are shown crossing the mosses near Tarleton on this OS map of 1845

The mechanics institute, Burnley, in 1855.

were known as ***meanygates***. The word means 'communal track', and these routes were used by local people for leading their animals and to give access to the peat-workings which supplied their fuel. Today the word is still used as a noun, but also survives in road and lane names such as **Longmeanygate** in Leyland and **Boundary Meanygate** in Becconsall.

Mechanics Institutes The first 'Mechanics' was established in Manchester in 1824 and the idea quickly spread throughout Lancashire and Yorkshire — twenty-five were founded in the next two years. They were intended as places where working men could improve themselves, with reading rooms and libraries, lectures and discussions, and other wholesome pursuits. Although often seen as working class in origin, they were in reality sponsored by the middle classes. That is not to deny their usefulness and importance in providing opportunities which were hitherto unavailable, but it is clear that they benefited only a small minority of skilled labourers — much better than nothing, even so.

mend to get better or improve; someone recovering from an illness might be described as *in a mendin' way* or *on the mend*

mental deficiencies There was a wide range of euphemisms, more or less tolerant, for people who were 'simple'. Many were used of those who were slightly backward, but others were applied to people lacking in commonsense or who did stupid things — not with psychiatric or mental health problems, just *plain daft*. Examples include *nowt between the ears*, *away with the fairies*, and *daft as a brush*, while *not right in th' head* was a common term for those with more serious difficulties. *Ninepence to t' shillin'* and *nineteen n' six in t' pound* were monetary ways of saying the same thing. In Rainhill somebody might, usually with sympathetic understanding, be described as *from the Building*, the local name for the great Rainhill Mental Hospital.

mercerising process by which ordinary cotton thread acquires the texture and high lustre of silk, taking bright dyes and becoming a 'luxury' product. The process, which greatly extended the potential of the cotton industry to provide more expensive and fashionable fabrics for the growing middle-class market, was invented by John Mercer (1791-1866) of Great Harwood.

mere lake. The word is now more usually associated with the Lake District (as in Windermere) but the comparatively few natural lakes in lowland Lancashire were also called *meres*. **Martin Mere** and **Marton Mere**, near Rufford and Blackpool respectively, were

the largest; in both instances the first word means 'place on the lake', so the names are tautologous.

merril board game which was popular in Lancashire for centuries, played using counters and a chequered pattern of squares. The aim was to get as many counters in a line as possible, and the game was a variant of Nine Men's Morris, which was played throughout medieval Europe and is from the same family as chess and draughts.

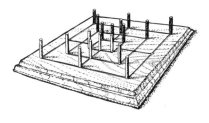

Merril.

mester (maister, mesthur and master) man with authority; used, for example, by women of their husbands or workers of their immediate boss

***Mexico* disaster** In December 1886 the German barque *Mexico* got into difficulties off the Ribble mouth in atrocious weather and sea conditions. The local lifeboats were launched but, in the worst disaster in the history of the British lifeboat service, all thirteen men on the St Annes lifeboat, the *Laura Janet*, and fourteen of the sixteen crew of the Southport boat, the *Eliza Fernley*, were lost. Memorials at both towns commemorate their sacrifice.

mich, mitch to play truant or get away from where one is supposed to be

midden, middensted The *midden* was the muck-heap, a ubiquitous feature in rural areas where the contents, after a suitable period of rotting down, would be spread on the fields or the smallholding, having been used by hens for pecking over and perching on. In towns, however, the *midden* represented more of a problem, since the lack of sanitation and the absence of scavenging services until the late nineteenth century meant that *midden heaps* grew, large, high and offensive, in streets and backyards. In Preston in the 1670s and 1680s, for example, numerous *middens* partially blocked the three main streets of the town, and despite orders for the removal of the heaps, repellent to eyes and noses and highly unpleasant to the feet, the householders let them remain there for many years at a time. *Middens* were popular places to hurl people who had offended society's rules, or for small boys and teenagers to dump their fellows as a joke.

Milnrow bonnet style of woman's head-dress common in south Lancashire in the nineteenth century (known in dialect as *Mildro' bonnet*); a white mob-cap over which was tied a large coloured handkerchief in the manner of a headscarf of the mid-twentieth century. Edwin Waugh records going into Milnrow in the late 1860s and meeting a woman 'with a chocolate-coloured silk kerchief tied over her snowy cap, in that graceful way which is known all over the country-side as a "Mildro Bonnet"'.

mimpin' simpering, prim, proper, straight-laced *hoo looks verra mimpin'*

mind your own business The phrases which parents used to tell children to mind their own business were numerous and often eccentric (*'What are you making'? 'Shimshams for meddlers'*). A particularly colourful one was used in the 1930s in St Helens if a child asked who a mother and the neighbour were talking about: *'Icky the firebobby and Bones the ragman'*.

Mischief Night This was the older version of the 'trick or treat' antics of Hallowe'en or All Souls' Eve. The assumption is often made that this is an American invention, but it was ubiquitous in Lancashire and elsewhere in the North until the late nineteenth century, when it began to die out. Its recent revival is certainly transatlantic in origin but, as with many American customs, it preserves an authentic English tradition. Doorhandles would be tied together or smeared with unmentionable substances, chimneys blocked up with rubbish so that houses filled with smoke or the soot fell, and other forms of mayhem and minor damage inflicted on hapless householders.

mither There are two main meanings of this common word. The older is 'confuse, perplex, bewilder, frustrate', especially with the earlier spelling used by dialect writers: *moither* or *moider* , as in *a 'ad that much on, a' were fair moithered by 't th'end*. A more recent, but now more common, meaning is 'worry, fret, pester'. A mother might say to a child pulling, literally or metaphorically, at her skirts, *'Give over mitherin' mi''*.

mixen heap of dirt or filth and, as an extension of that meaning, to sweep up or clean up

mock corporations In Catholic Lancashire there was strong support for the Jacobite cause during the reigns of William and Mary, and Queen Anne. Such activities were illegal, and various Jacobite societies were therefore established under the guise of drinking and social clubs: drinking toasts to the Stewarts loomed large in the business of their meetings. They often, as an additional though rather transparent cover, labelled themselves 'corporation'. For example, the **mock corporation** of Rochdale was founded in 1712 and its members, prominent in local society, enjoyed punch, politics and puerile humour. The **corporation** at Walton-le-Dale, founded in 1701, continued as a respectable but politically subversive society until the 1760s, when it was taken over by rowdier elements. At Sefton, in contrast, the **mock corporation** does not seem to have been founded until the 1770s, and was always a highly exclusive club for local society.

modiwarp (see *mowdywarp*)

mollycoddle now used mainly as a verb, meaning 'to over-protect, to indulge to excess', as in the bringing-up of a child. In the past the word was used in Lancashire as a noun to describe a man who did the work of women — for example, hung out the washing, sluiced down the step or cooked meals. It was just about permissible to do these things if nobody saw, but to do them publicly brought instant and almost ineradicable shame and humiliation on both man and wife. Other terms used in this sense were, and are, *jessie* and *peggy*.

monkey walks perambulations by courting couples. On Saturday evenings or sometimes Sunday afternoons in spring and summer, the monkey walks in many Lancashire towns were when young people walked hand-in-hand or arm-in-arm up and down the streets, or around a local park (also known as the *monkey run*).

mopstone (see *donkey stone*)

Moravians In 1773, Protestant refugees from Moravia (now part of the Czech Republic, then part of the Austrian empire) fled from religious persecution and came to England, where they founded several new communities, among them one at Fairfield between Manchester and Ashton-under-Lyne. The new settlements were planned and carefully laid out, with fine formal architecture, and

A monkey walk.

The Fairfield Moravian settlement, in an engraving of 1795.

were designed to be self-sufficient. The Fairfield Moravian settlement still survives, tucked away just north of Ashton Old Road, as an unexpected oasis of elegance and calm amid the somewhat down-at-heel suburban surroundings.

Mormons The Preston branch of the Church of Jesus Christ and the Latterday Saints was founded in 1836 and is the oldest continuously existing Mormon church in the world outside Utah. Substantial numbers of people from the Preston and Leyland area, including a large contingent from the village of Longton, migrated to Utah in the late 1830s, as a result of zealous work by the first band of Mormon missionaries ever to leave Salt Lake City and travel abroad. The special place which Preston has in the history of the Church is reflected in the building on the northern edge of Chorley of Britain's second Mormon temple, opened in 1998 and a dramatic landmark from the nearby M61.

morris dancing general term which covers various types of folk dancing and traditional dancing. It was formerly very widespread in Lancashire, with innumerable local variations, and numerous dances which were unique to their particular town or district. **Morris dancing** was traditionally associated with particular feast days and celebrations, and involved men dressing in elaborate and brightly-coloured costumes. It began to die out in the mid-nineteenth century as these customs and local feasts themselves dwindled away, and by the early twentieth century, few examples remained. At that point there was a national revival of interest in folk customs, including music and dancing, and the tradition was reinvigorated, so that today no Lancashire festivity seems complete without **morris men** and (though the dancers of 300 years ago may be turning in their graves) **morris women**. Much is therefore not truly old, but traditional styles are maintained, and some Lancashire teams are indeed heirs to an ancient legacy.

moss Although the term is frequently found as a name for upland bogs in the Pennines, it is particularly associated with the lowland peatbogs of the North-West. Large areas of the Lancashire plain were

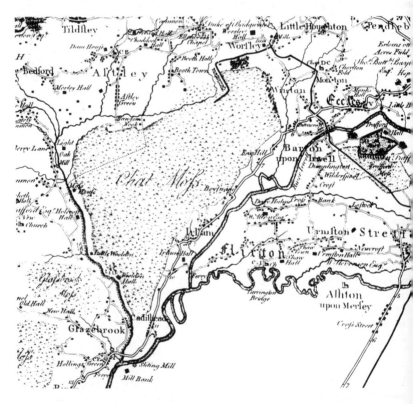

Chat Moss, from William Yates's map of 1786.

formerly **mosslands**, where thick deposits of waterlogged peat were covered with coarse grasses and a scrub of birch, willow and alder, interspersed with shallow pools and small lakes. These ecologically rich and haunting landscapes had largely been drained by the end of the nineteenth century to provide agricultural land, so that today only a few areas — notably **Chat Moss** and **Astley Moss** — survive in anything like their original state.

moss rooms   Until the late eighteenth century, turf or peat was dug on the **mosses** (qv) and moorlands of west and north Lancashire, where it was the most important fuel. Only in the coalfield areas was there a viable alternative. The rights to cut peat (technically known as turbary rights, from the medieval Latin *turbarium*, a peat-working) were jealously guarded, and each family or household would have its own plot of **moss** or moor where it alone had the right to dig the fuel. These plots were either unmarked, or were identified by posts and sticks driven into the soft ground, and were known as *rooms*.

motty   literally, a small sum of money — for example, the contributions made at 1d (¹/₂p) per week to a communal fund or kitty such as a burial club or holiday fund; but the alternative meaning was, to use words familiar to all those born before about 1960 but which are themselves fast becoming obsolete, a **penn'orth** or

A mowdywarp.

ha'-porth. Thus, someone who added his **ha'porth** to an argument might be said to *put 'is motty in*.

mowdywarp   the mole

muck-pit   In the nineteenth century this was the name given to the *middens* (qv) or open-air cesspools which provided, without any shelter or screen, the communal outdoor toilets in many Lancashire industrial areas. They were eventually superseded by the introduction of the (by comparison) relatively sophisticated privy or *petty²* (qv). The *muck-pit* was a noxious hole, across which a narrow rail or plank was supported on two uprights. That was all. For someone to put on airs might incur the comment that he or she was *nice-minded about the muck-pit*.

mug   Today a mug is pottery drinking beaker (now ubiquitous following the decline of the cup and saucer), but historically any earthenware vessel with a cylindrical shape was given this name. Thus there were *ale mugs*, usually of about one pint (0.6 litre) capacity, and *salt mugs* in which quantities of meat or vegetables were preserved under salt. *Butter mugs* were very large pots, which would hold about 21lb (9.5kg) of salty butter, with wooden caps which fitted in, and were then sealed over with wax or tied with cloth and string. Most *mugs* used in south Lancashire were made at Prescot, where from the sixteenth to the nineteenth centuries there were large potteries producing cheap earthenware.

mule cotton-spinning machine. Various inventors in the early eighteenth century experimented with the development of an efficient powered spinning engine, but the first viable model was produced by Samuel Crompton in 1779. His machine combined the key elements of Arkwright's water frame (especially the roller drawing of the yarn) with the carriage-drawing of Hargreaves' **spinning jenny** (qv). As a result it was called a **mule** because, like that animal, it was a cross between two different parents. The **mule's** carriage drew out and twisted the yarn as it moved outwards, and then as it returned it wound the yarn onto spindles.

mun must; in the negative, *munno* or *munna*, must not (Icelandic, *muna*)

mussled to be afflicted with the acute stomach-aches and cramps which result from eating unfit shellfish

N

nab prominent peak or summit of a hill, often with a sharp slope at the end of a long ridge; for example, **Whalley Nab**, high above the town and the River Calder

narrow callies (see *cally*)

nazzy peevish, short-tempered, cross

neave, neive fist, a man's clenched hand

neb peak of a cap; the bill of, for example, a duck, swan or goose; in slightly joking fashion, a nose

neckleton in Rossendale, a local equivalent to an *aughendole* (qv), a measure of meal

nesh soft, feeble, weak, delicate. Although in origin a word which could be used in any such sense, it latterly acquired a disparaging or contemptuous air, so that somebody who could not take a bit of roughness or physical difficulty might be told *'Eeh, lad, th'art nesh'*.

nettle beer popular traditional drink, made from new spring nettles which were lightly fermented and produced a very mildly alcoholic sparkling beverage (comparable with the elderflower champagne beloved of many home winemakers). **Nettle beer** was widely recommended as a tonic, and it was held to *cleanse the blood*, removing all the impurities of the winter — though it probably did more to refresh the tired mind. It was still being sold to visitors on the village street in Heysham in the early 1950s.

nettle porridge Boiled stinging nettles, gathered from the roadsides and waste ground, were a common starvation diet in Lancashire, especially in the years around 1800 but even as late as the 1840s. When chopped and boiled, nettles quickly form a mushy paste (like overboiled spinach) and they lose their sting. At this time oatmeal, the staple food of the Lancashire poor, was too expensive for many unemployed handloom weavers, so nettles and other roadside weeds were their only alternative. If possible, they would add a few handfuls of meal to thicken and bulk out the khaki-coloured pap.

netty outdoor toilet (cf *bog*, *little house*, *petty*)

*The stinging nettle, used to make
nettle beer and nettle porridge.*

nicknames Before the general use of **surnames** (qv) and when the range of first names in use was much more limited than it is today, nicknames were a very common means of identification in Lancashire. *Puddin' Jane*, *Dick-in-a-minnit*, *Reawnt Legs*, *Bull Robin*, *Bonny Meawth and Fiddler Bill* are examples quoted by Edwin Waugh from the Rochdale area in the 1860s.

Nick o' Thung's Charity strange custom which began in the 1850s, when, on the first Sunday in May, hundreds of men from the industrial areas of the Calder Valley, between Burnley and Colne, would climb Pendle and join in a collective feast, of pork, beef, mutton and rabbit, nettle pudding

and copious quantities of beer. It was ostensibly a mass ramble and picnic, but in fact was a not-very-good cover for various illegal activities such as **cock-fighting** (qv) and dog-fighting.

nobbut naught but, or not but. Nodal and Milner (1875) say that it is 'a peculiar negative or emphatic form of the conjunction *but*', and quote Ben Brierley *'If th' rain'll nobbut keep off a bit'*.

nobbys fishing boats, with a full deck, shallow draught and small 'cockpit', as used by the fishermen of the Southport and Formby coast for inshore work. In 1892 there were over eighty boats of this type at Southport alone. The forty foot (12m) boats could also be used for rather deeper waters, but the thirty-two foot (10m) boats had a draught of only four feet (1.2m), and so could work very close inshore.

North West Sound Archive Based at Clitheroe Castle, the NWSA is the most important repository for sound recordings of Lancashire dialect, and has for many years conducted a programme of recording and transcribing interviews which not only preserve dialect speech and accents, but also give vivid and often moving first-hand accounts of events, activities, daily life and labour in the region. They have published a very useful series of dialect dictionaries, and also produce CDs and tapes for sale.

notchel crying practice whereby a husband publicly announced to the local community (often on

Nobbys.

market day or some other public occasion) that he would no longer be answerable for or honour his wife's debts. Less frequently, the wife made a public declaration about her husband's finances. Harland gives a detailed account of an example at Accrington in 1859, but the custom was an ancient one. The records of the bishop's court in Chester for 1633 include a case where a Prescot man publicly denounced his wife at the market cross there, ' warning all people nethere to lend her any thing or to buye any thing of her'. Harland also notes a case when a woman denounced her

143

A nude race in progress.

husband after he had made such a pronouncement, telling the world that he had for a long time been living on her (immoral?) earnings.

nowt　nothing; a Lancashire pronunciation of the word 'naught' which survived here, and in other parts of the North, when it had become obsolete in the South and Midlands

nowt so queer as folk　wise and true saying still in general use; a widespread variation was *'They're all queer here 'cept thee and me, an' Ah'm not too sure about thee'*.

nowty　usually explained by older dialect dictionaries as 'naughty', of which word it is a variant, but in reality its meaning is not the same: *nowty* usually implies 'bad-tempered, disagreeable, irritable, grumpy', rather than straightforward naughtiness

nude racing　Several nineteenth-century sources refer to the popularity of foot-racing in the more remote and by implication less civilised parts of Lancashire. These races were often unusual insofar as the participants ran either with only a small loincloth or (more excitingly for the spectators) stark naked. Harland quotes examples from the 1820s at Whitworth, where six men ran seven times round a one-mile circuit on Rooley Moor, but he also notes (in the late 1870s) that 'races by nude men are not yet extinct in many parts of Lancashire, notwithstanding the vigilance of the county police'.

Nut Nan　terrifying old woman who prowled in dark woods ready to seize little boys who went thieving; she carried red-hot irons *to brun nut-steylers their e'en eawt* (to burn nut-stealers' eyes out)

O

oatcake (see *backstone*, *brade flake*, *clapbread*, *havercake*, *jannock*, *meal*, *pigwhistle*)

oer faweed outwitted

o'er t' brush (see *living up t' stick*)

off from; a usage still extremely common all over Lancashire, as in *'Eh, in't that so-and-so off Coronation Street?'*

oilers people employed in a spinning or weaving mill to oil the moving machinery; lack of oil meant that friction made the parts red-hot and fire could easily result. Oilers often used feathers dipped in a can to apply the oil, a more delicate and precise method than pouring it straight from the can itself. As Fowler and Wyke note in their biography of Sam Fitton, the spindles, once freshly-oiled, could revolve at 8,000rpm, so that a fine spray of oil was dispersed into the atmosphere of a spinning room, while drops of oil splashed onto the waist and groin of the spinner; *spinner's cancer* was a frequent long-term consequence.

Old Dun Cow An old dun cow of monstrous size was, so old legends said, once resident in the Chipping area, where it roamed across the moors and hillsides and drank at Nicks Water Pot, a spring on the top of Parlick. The vast and generous animal happily dispensed milk to allcomers, so that none went away with pail or jug empty. Eventually, another elaboration of the story recounts, a **Pendle witch** (qv) milked the cow into a *riddle* (sieve) which was thus never full and the cow, exhausted, finally died. Her rib was preserved at Old Rib Farm near Whittingham, north of Preston. It is easy to speculate, and impossible to reach any conclusion, about the origins of a story such as this. The fertility and richness of the local pastures might explain the 'flowing with milk' element, while the discovery of a large fossil bone could perhaps have prompted the idea of the gigantic cow. We will never know.

oller (see *alder*)

o'on oven; an *oon-cake* was one baked in the oven, with or without a dish, in contrast to one baked on a griddle over the fire

Owd Ball, formerly a south Lancashire custom.

147

Ormskirk gingerbread famous local delicacy as early as the eighteenth century; travellers on the coach from Liverpool to Preston would be met by gingerbread-sellers when it stopped in the town, and itinerant women sold the gingerbread all over south Lancashire

otter-hunting once a popular sport in the county. Nicholas Assheton, one of the earliest Lancashire diarists, records **otter-hunting** among his activities in 1617, while *The Radcliffe Otter Hunt* was a popular eighteenth-century ballad, telling (the narrator being the otter himself) of a hunt along the Irwell from Radcliffe down to Agecroft.

overlooker man in charge of a *mule room* (qv) in a spinning mill, or in charge of a group of weavers (see also **tackler**)

Owd Ball Originally a nickname for a large and lumbering cart-horse, *Owd Ball* was also an Easter custom found in various parts of south Lancashire. A great wooden horse head was made, with the bottoms of broken bottles for eyes, moveable jaws, and nails for teeth. The head was fixed on a pole and, as with a **hobby horse** (qv), the boy playing the beast was covered with a cloth or sacking. Looking through the horse's mouth, he ran into the crowd, snapping the jaws at potential victims (especially girls and women) and 'creating a scene of the most boisterous and ridiculous mirth'.

owt aught (anything) *'Do you know owt about our Nellie?'*

oynin' Edmund Battersby defines this word in his article on Accrington dialect as 'not doing right by. You kept a dog badly, you *oyned* it. Bad parents *oyned* their children.'

P

pace eggs ancestors of our Easter eggs. They were ordinary hen's eggs which were usually hard-boiled, and painted in bright colours and complex patterns. The boiling could include dyeing the shell with, for example, onion skins to produce a soft yellow-brown colour. (From the medieval Latin *pascha*, meaning Easter; cf modern French *pâque*.)

pace-egging This custom was observed all over Lancashire until the late Victorian period. It was usually performed on Good Friday, when troops of children and young people, dressed in costume and carrying a variety of baskets and other containers, would go from house to house, and at each door would sing or chant verses, in return for which they were given money, sweets or painted eggs. As numerous contemporary commentators observed, the former was much the most acceptable. Each town or village had its local variations on the theme. At Aughton near Ormskirk, for example, the *pace-eggers* wore coloured ribbons and one, *Tosspot*, held the basket for contributions, while the troop performed a 'sort of rude play with wooden swords' based, apparently, on the legend of St George and the Dragon, but including more topical references to Lord Nelson and the British navy. At Hindley there were white *pace-eggers*, who came in the daytime and decorated themselves with ribbons; in their drama the hero was *Bold Slasher*, who was resurrected (presumably a recollection of a medieval mystery play). In the night-time came the black *pace-eggers*, who had black faces and were 'dressed as hideously as they could devise'.

pad path or trackway. Old route-ways were often called *pads* in Lancashire — for example, **Danes Pad** and **Kates Pad**, which were prehistoric or Roman roads in the mosslands of the Fylde. The place-name **Padgate** near Warrington is a tautology on the same theme — *pad* with *gate*, from the Scandinavian word for a track or road.

paddock toad or (less commonly) a frog

parents In parts of south Lancashire, including the St Helens area, the following terminology was used to describe parents and grandparents:

father	=	*dad*
mother	=	*mam*
grandfather	=	*father*
grandmother	=	*mother*

so that if *yer mam wuz with yer fayther*, your mother was at your grandfather's house.

parkin (see *tharcake*)

Paslew, John John Paslew was the last abbot of Whalley, and was hanged in March 1537 for his complicity in the Pilgrimage of Grace, a popular uprising which in 1536 had sought to restore the dissolved monasteries and reverse the religious upheavals of the Reformation. His execution took place on Lancaster Moor, after trial for high treason, but a series of legends swiftly gathered around his death. One suggested that he had been hanged from the gatehouse of Whalley Abbey itself, while another claimed that his execution took place on a mound in a field close to Whalley Bridge.

passion dock common bistort (*polygonum bistorta*), a wild plant of which the spring shoots and young leaves were once eaten all over Lancashire, Yorkshire and the Lake Counties, either as a green vegetable, as an ingredient of soup and broth, or chopped and mixed with suet, flour and onion to make a pudding which was boiled in a cloth. Now its use is very localised, although the

Passion dock, used to make dock pudding.

revival of interest in regional cookery and 'food for free' has meant that a number of recipes have appeared in print in the past thirty years.

patty-pans earthenware dishes in which small cakes, tarts and pies could be baked; they were immortalised in English literature by Beatrix Potter's story *The Tale of the Pie and the Patty-Pan*, published in 1905

paupers' food Many of the entries in this dictionary concern the food which was eaten by the Lancashire poor in the past (in some cases, the all too recent past). For thousands of people in the eighteenth and nineteenth centuries, starvation was only a frugal and inadequate meal away, and they had to eke out meagre fare or scratch around to find something to eat. Typically, the very poor lived on oats, eaten in the form of *meal*, which could be made into some sort of porridge or, if they were slightly better-off and could afford a *girdle*, baked as *oatcakes*. In the hardest times the poor could not afford milk, **treacle** or other ways of enriching the porridge, and the names given to their thin and inadequate gruel tell their own story: *nettle porridge*, *Waterloo porridge*, *pobs*, *pigwhistle* and *salt cap*. Others ate the indigestible barley bread known as *ran dan* or *Brown George*. If times were a little more comfortable they might be able to afford some small variety in the diet, and could eat *dib i' th' oil*, *brewis* or *rap*, or perhaps even *'ash*, *lobscouse* or *lips an' lugs*, but until our own times many Lancashire people were brought up on not much more than *wet nelly* and *tater ash*.

payshulls pea pods (*pease-hulls*)

Pea Dick common nickname for a man who came round the streets, usually in the late afternoon or evening, carrying cooked peas which he ladled out from cans of hot water. In the nineteenth century the cans were often carried on a yoke, but later this was usually replaced by a wooden black-pea cart. Superior traders would carry plates, spoons, and salt and vinegar in the pockets of their large aprons.

pea saloons Also known as *pea booths*, or, less properly, *pea-oils* (pea-holes), these were tents or wood and canvas huts, which were erected at fairs and wakes, in which hot peas were served. Similar stalls were found on most Lancashire markets in the nineteenth century and well into the twentieth, serving 'a saucerful with plenty of green water and a lead spoon to eat them with'. Salt and vinegar were provided, and some sold pies and other food as well, but it was the peas — green, grey or the hard *pigeons* — which were the main offering.

Pea Soup Year According to legend, in the autumn of 1799, after a disastrous summer harvest, a ship laden with dried peas was wrecked on the shore at Blackpool. The peas allegedly saved the local population from starvation, a prosaic version of the events in *Whisky Galore*. The story is first recorded in print in 1839, and may be a heavily-embroidered version of an actual event, but there is little authentic contemporary evidence. Another, even less plausible, version claims that the ship arrived at a conveniently unnamed port during the **Cotton Famine** (qv).

pea whack   (see *whack*)
pee-a-bed   (see *pissabed*)
peel   baker's shovel, large and flat, with a long handle, so that bread, cakes or pies can be slid into the inner recesses of the hot oven
Peel, Sir Robert (1788-1850)   Conservative prime minister from 1834-5 and 1841-6, and a local hero in Lancashire. He was the first prime minister born in the county, and his birthplace at Chamber Hall near Bury was long venerated. Peel is today commemorated in many road names, and in the Peel Monument, built in 1852 on Holcombe Moor above Ramsbottom. Among his achievements were the introduction of regular income tax (1842), the creation of the Metropolitan Police when he was home secretary in 1829, and the repeal of the Corn Laws in 1846 — which split his government and led to his fall from power.
peggy¹   see *billet*
peggy²   (see *mollycoddle*)
Pendle (Hill)   Pendle dominates much of east Lancashire and the Ribble Valley, its great whaleback appearing in countless views. Many legends and myths are associated with the hill, notably of course the famous **witches** (qv), but it was also the subject of an old rhyme which grossly overstated its height:
'Ingleborough, Pendle Hill
and Penyghent
Are the highest hills between
Scotland and Trent'
This is true for none of the three,

for Cross Fell (2,960 feet/902m) in the north Pennines is 300 feet (90m) higher than Ingleborough, while Pendle is much lower than either of the two Yorkshire hills. The rhyme also, of course, ignores dozens of Lake District summits and the Cheviots. The massive bulk of Pendle, and the fact that it rises so prominently from relatively low-lying country, explain the exaggerated idea of its altitude; only with precise surveying by the Ordnance Survey in the 1840s was its true (and comparatively modest) height of 1,831 feet (557m) finally established. Another Pendle rhyme strikes a chord with those who see the low cloud which frequently swathes its upper slopes:
'When Pendle wears its woolly
cap
The farmers all may take a nap'
Pendle Witches   (see *witches*)
Penny Stone   rock about half a mile (800m) offshore from Norbreck, at the north end of Blackpool, and visible at the lowest tides. Many stories were associated with it, among them that it was all that remained of a village which had been washed away by the sea, or that it was the last trace of an inn which had sold ale at a penny a pot. While these stories had no foundation in detail, it is clear that they were a folk memory of an actual event: the soft cliffs of Bispham had indeed eroded rapidly and the stone was a fragment of the old coastline, lost to the sea centuries earlier.

perish to freeze, or (less commonly now than in the past) to starve with cold and hunger *'Shut t' door, it's perishin' in 'ere'*

Peterloo One of the most important events in English history, the **Peterloo Massacre** was swiftly engraved on the folk consciousness of the nineteenth century. On the 16th August 1819, an unprecedentedly large mass meeting was held in St Peters Fields, on the southern edge of Manchester town, to press for suffrage reform and the extension of civil liberties. Estimates of the numbers present ranged from 30,000 to 150,000. They had come to hear an address by the Radical leader Henry 'Orator' Hunt. The authorities panicked and sent in the militia, who charged the unarmed and peaceful crowd, wielding sabres and cutlasses. At least eleven people died, and the massacre was immediately christened **Peterloo** in bitter parody of Waterloo four years earlier. The Midland Hotel now lies on the site of those tragic events. (cf **Bamford, Samuel; Westhoughton riot**)

petty outdoor toilet (cf **bog**, **little house**, **netty**)

picking sending the shuttle through the **shed**, the space between the warp threads, on a loom; the

A contemporary illustration of the Peterloo Massacre.

153

THE

Preston Pickle Factory,   KILSHAW STREET,

NORTH ROAD, PRESTON.

PROPRIETOR : MR. JOHN CRANK, (LATE A. THORNLEY).

IF there be a name calculated to make one's mouth water, in these days of imitation and substitution—baneful results of modern competition—it is that of "home-made pickles." It awakens memories of home and the days of our youth, when a few thick slices of cold meat, or a chunk of bread and cheese, when accompanied by a plate of bright crisp pickles—which gave such a relish to the meal—tasted like a banquet.

In our search, the other day, for some of these most appetising accessories to a "gradely" homely meal, we came across the Preston Sauce and Pickle Manufactory of A. Thornley, situate in Kilshaw Street, North Road. Having quite an old-established reputation—extending over a quarter of a century—operations were very active indeed, the staff of clean, bright looking girls, under the active superintendence of Mr. John Crank, the present proprietor, being quite busy putting up various tempting kinds of pickles and sauces. On testing the pickles, we found they possessed the true "home" flavour, together with that delicious crispness which is only to be found in pickles which are carefully prepared, in the finest and purest vinegar, by a practised hand. The flavour of the sauces produced so largely here was most excellent, and must commend them to all persons of taste.

Both pickles and sauces are put up in suitable handy-sized bottles for home use, also for the grocery and provision trades, restaurants, coffee taverns, dining rooms, etc.

This enterprising firm are commemorating the advent of the Coronation of King Edward VII. and the Guild of 1902 by the introduction of a piquant novelty of the most delicious description, for which the present writer can vouch. They are happily named the "**Royal Beano Pickles**," and fit for the table of a king, and, as they are produced at a moderate price, they are bound to secure a wide popularity. This new departure means further space, and the necessary extensions are now actively in hand

A 1904 advertisement for pickles.

horizontal action of weaving, which on a handloom was originally done by passing the shuttle from hand to hand, and then later by the development of the *picking stick*, which mechanically sent the shuttle across and allowed the weaver to work on a wider cloth (see also **flying shuttle**)

pickles The diet of the Lancashire poor was very dull and monotonous diet, so **pickles**, with their sharp and biting flavours, were a very popular *taste* (qv), and so they have remained — what would a *Lancashire neet* be without the red cabbage to go with the *hotpot* (qv)? As Edwin Waugh wrote in his short story *A Ramble from Bury to Rochdale*: 'Dun yo like pickle, measther?' 'I do', said I, 'just for a taste* [qv]'.

piece length of cloth. In different fabrics a specific measurement was often implied, especially by the nineteenth century — thus twenty-eight yards (25.5m) was a *cotton piece*. However, the term was also used in a more general sense to mean any length of cloth which was being woven, as in Richard Rome Bealey's poem about approaching death, *My piece is o bu' woven eawt.* (see *woven m piece*)

piecer worker who fastened together the broken ends of yarn on a spinning *mule* (qv). It was a task which required nimbleness, agility and dexterity, and wa often given to the young — the *little piecer* was a well-known figure in the cotton mill, although not all *little piecers* were in fac young people. It was potentially a dangerous job, for feet could slip on the oily floor and the *piecer* might fall into or under the inexorably moving machinery. *Little piecers* would usually graduate to become *big piecers*, and some might then move up to become a spinner, after years of training, watching and gaining experience. Spinning mills had wooden floors, and as most *piecers* worked barefoot in order to gain a better grip on the surface, they frequently caught their skin on the *spells*, or splinters, of the boards, and a mixture of oil, dirt and blood was ingrained into the soles of their feet.

piffy Who (or what) was piffy? Nobody appears to know but, for generations of Lancashire people, he (or she, or even it) has been a familiar friend, because when they are waiting for something to happen, and yet nothing seems to be moving, they are *standin' around like piffy* (see also *pilgarlic*)

pigeons (see *pea saloons*)

pig in an entry it might be said of a bandy-legged person that he *couldna' stop a pig in an entry*

pigwhistle oatcake broken up and crumbled into weak beer, and eaten as a kind of gruel (cf *brewis*, *salt cap*)

pilgarlic Just as in much of Lancashire you could be *standing around like piffy* (*till the cows come home*, indeed), so in southwest Lancashire you might be *standing here* or *there like a pilgarlic*, though here the derivation

is rather more obvious (sixteenth-century English slang, *pillicock*, the male organ)

pillar and stall (see *stoop and room*)

pissabed dandelion, so called because its juice is a powerful diuretic; compare the identical French term *pis-en-lit*. Slightly more refined people might have said *pee-a-bed*.

pissabed: the common dandelion.

pit brow lass In the Wigan and Leigh area, girls and women (who had been forbidden to work underground in coalmines from the 1840s) were employed on the

Pit brow lasses.

surface at picking, sorting and grading the coal as it was brought from the shaft-top. It was very hard manual labour, of the sort which many middle-class Victorians thought was not 'respectable' for females, and by the late nineteenth century the *pit brow lasses* had become one of the sights of the area for photographers and for the type of visitor who found a certain voyeuristic attraction in such a pleasurably shocking spectacle.

plague stones In many places in Lancashire, as in other parts of the country, large boulders and stones which have a slightly hollowed top or (as in the **Plague Stone** at Stretford) deep cavities, are pointed out even today as **plague stones**, where people are said to have left money and food for plague victims at unspecified times in the past. While there is a little evidence, from places such as Eyam in Derbyshire, to suggest that this practice may have been followed, it must be said that there is no reliable information to support the story in most instances. Some stones to which this legend is attached were probably the bases of wayside crosses destroyed at the Reformation.

platt¹ footbridge, or plank bridge, across a ditch or small stream; for example, Nutters Platt near Penwortham

platt² area of land; in south Lancashire, a garden lawn was often known as a *grass platt*

playin' ironic term for being out of work

Pleasure Beach The mecca of Blackpool's south shore began to develop in the 1890s when a small fairground was laid out among the sand hills. In 1904 the first ride was introduced (Maxim's Flying Machine), and since then it has continued to grow and change, reflecting every fashion, always seeking to thrill and terrify in ever-more sensational ways, never still and invariably trying to beat records. For a century it has been one of the greatest of the county's attractions, and for millions of Lancashire people the carefree fun of the Pleasure Beach has summed up what is meant by the word 'holiday'.

plod form of the word plaid, striped or checked cloth; *plod-weaver* is an occupation often mentioned in local documentary sources before the late eighteenth century, although plaid production was not important in Lancashire later in the industrial period

Plough Sunday On the second or third Sunday in January, a decorated plough, decked with garlands, would be taken to church and blessed, as a preliminary to the ploughing season which would soon begin. It was, therefore, equivalent to the harvest celebrations at the other end of the farming year. On the following Monday, *Plough Monday*, ploughmen might be given a day's holiday. The festival was very popular, and Bennett records that it was celebrated even in urban industrialised Burnley as late as the 1860s.

plug-drawing During the endemic industrial unrest of the 1830s and 1840s, *plug-drawing* was a common means of attacking the machinery which (it was felt) was putting men out of work, and so seriously inconveniencing the employers and industrialists. Rioters or demonstrators would occupy mills and other factories, draw the plugs from the steam engine boilers, letting the water off and so bringing work to a standstill.

pobs, pobbies bread and milk. A legendary supper food for children (only really palatable if it included plenty of sugar and perhaps nutmeg), but also a pauper's food and popular for feeding elderly people in the days before false teeth. The term could also refer to any other dish of bread or oatcake, soaked in a liquid such as broth or weak ale. (See also *brewis*, *pigwhistle*)

poke a bag, shaped like an ice-cream cone, which tapered towards the bottom (in contrast to a **sack**, which was rectangular)

pop his clogs to die; the clogs of a living person would never be pawned (*popped*), so it was only after someone's death that his clogs could be *'tekken' t' uncle* (qv)

pop shop pawnbroker

pool stream or tidal creek; not, as is often thought, a small lake. The word is particularly associated with the Fylde and the name **Blackpool**, for example, refers to a stream which once flowed from the low ridge behind the modern town down to the sea somewhere in the vicinity of the centre. Other examples include **Skippool** ('ship-creek') at Poulton-le-Fylde, and **Freckleton Pool**, the narrow estuary of the Dowbrook.

poorly (see *badly*)

Portus Setantiorum The destination of the Roman road which led from the fort and small town at Kirkham westwards into the Fylde has long been the subject of debate among historians and archaeologists. The Setantii were a small sub-tribe living in the North of England in the early Roman period, and one widely-held view is that they inhabited the Fylde, although there is no proof of this. The place-name *Portus Setantiorum* (the harbour of the Setantii) is known from Roman sources, but the location of the place itself is unknown. Several Roman coin hoards have been found in the past 150 years in the Fleetwood and Knott End areas. These four facts, each unconnected with the others, have led many people to suppose that a lost Roman site, Portus Setantiorum, existed at the mouth of the River Wyre, perhaps now washed away by coastal erosion. The answer may never be known.

pot and pan concerts beating of pan lids and metal pots by a group of women who disapproved of the actions of their neighbours. In Pendlebury in the late nineteenth century, for example, black-leg miners and their families were so treated.

A pot and pan concert.

potatoes Lancashire was the first county in England where **potatoes** were grown. They appear to have reached the county by the 1640s, about fifty years after they were introduced to Ireland, and several places in Furness and the Formby and North Meols area are claimed, without much authenticated evidence, to have been the location where they were first grown. One Marshside (Southport) tale says that an Irish ship carrying **potatoes** was wrecked there in 1565. What is certain is that by the 1670s they were a familiar crop in Lancashire, long before they became generally known in other parts of England, and that by the eighteenth century they had become a staple of the diet of the county's poor.

pother smoke and fumes, or an atmosphere thick with dust

potherbs chopped vegetables; typically, a mixture of all or most of cabbage, onion, leek, carrot and turnip sold, in places such as Preston, loose ready-mixed or in plastic bags for use in soup and stews. This is a fascinating instance of the survival of a very old word at the beginning of the twenty-first century, for 'herb' was the general medieval term for vegetables. Here it retains its ancient meaning, whereas in the most of England it has long since been restricted to the 'flavouring' herbs such as thyme and sage.

pouce naughty and badly behaved child

poverty knock euphemism, widespread in the 1830s and 1840s, for handloom weaving. That was the time when, as steam-powered weaving mills advanced, the old weavers were either forced out of work or compelled to change their jobs and lifestyles to conform with the new era of 'progress'. The term relates to the 'knocking' sound of the handloom (see *knickerty-knack*).

pow to cut hair (Lancashire pronunciation of the obsolete English word *poll*); an alternative meaning was the head itself

powfagged tired, exhausted; or puzzled, perplexed

powse rubbish, waste or worthless material. Taylor quotes the derogatory expression, current in the late nineteenth century, *'Theawr't a dirty powse'*.

Preston Guild England's greatest carnival (whatever Notting Hill might claim) has given a phrase to the language: 'Once every Preston Guild' describes something which is exceptionally rare or infrequent, because since 1562 the Guild has been celebrated only at twenty-year intervals (except in 1942, when the war intervened). The term was also used when promises of help or work were made, but not believed: *'Have you put that shelf up yet?'* 'No, but I'll do it', 'Aye, next Preston

Preston Guild: part of the weavers' procession in 1802.

Guild'. The earliest recorded **guild** was in the late 1320s, but the **guild merchant** — whose formal proceedings are the reason for, and the official focus of, the celebration — was established in 1179, and it is likely that there were **guilds** as early as the twelfth century. No other town in England has an event remotely comparable: over a million people attended each of the last two **guilds**, in 1972 and 1992, and planning for the **guild** now takes more than three years. The **guild** was originally the public demonstration of the commercial strength and political power of the town's merchants and craftsmen, and at the **guild court** the burgesses (who had the exclusive right to trade in the town) were enrolled as members.

priest holes There is hardly an old house in the county which is not claimed to have at least one **priest hole**. They are part of the popular mythology of history, but in many cases the 'holes' are likely to be simply the result of alterations and poor building design, where walls and joints did not meet quite as planned. On the other hand, Lancashire was by far the most Catholic county in England, and there were times when priests did need to hide. Some of the holes may therefore be authentic. The squire of Little Crosby, Nicholas Blundell, recorded in his diaries for 1715, during the first Jacobite rebellion, that he had had secret visitors (who were probably Catholics fleeing the government troops) and they certainly hid in a secret room in the house.

Proud Preston Preston has been proud to be known as **Proud Preston** for at least 300 years — Defoe notes the nickname at the beginning of the eighteenth century — and the title is probably much older than that. It may relate to the town's status, since the Middle Ages, as administrative centre for much of the county's business. This brought many lawyers and other professional men, and Preston was known to be a town of 'clerks and attorneys'. However, the town's badge is the Paschal Lamb which carries a flag on which the letters PP appear. One theory is that this stands for *Princeps Pacis* (Prince of Peace), and that after the Reformation this was reinvented as Proud Preston.

Pudding Feast (see **Aughton Pudding Feast**)

puddle to confuse or bewilder

punce to kick (cf *purr*)

punish to be needy, to want food

purr to kick (cf *punce*); but *purring* was a special form of kicking, curiously regarded as a sport, in which contestants used brass-tipped fighting clogs to try to strip the skin and flesh off each other's legs and shins. This entertainment continued in some areas, such as Clifton and Pendlebury, until the early twentieth century. (See also *up and down fighting*.)

puther (see *pother*)

putting (see **shrimping**)

putting-out For 300 years, *putting-out* in the textile trade was a mainstay of the domestic economy of hundreds of thousands of Lancashire families. The spun yarn was given out by middle-men (or, later, by the nascent textile firms) to cottagers and householders, who wove it into cloth on hand-looms in their own homes. The *putter-out* then came round collecting the finished cloth, and payment was given in return. An alternative was that the *putter-out* and the weavers might meet at a central collection point, where the cloth would be transferred and payment made. The system was also used for the spinning of yarn, though to a lesser extent. It disintegrated when the advent of the factory system not only put

The pynot, or magpie.

the handloom weavers out of their trade, but also concentrated production in new industrial premises rather than private houses.

put wood i' th' oil shut the door

pynot magpie

Q

Quakers The Society of Friends, better known as the Quakers, was founded in the late 1640s in Leicestershire by George Fox. In 1652 he travelled into Lancashire, and on the summit of **Pendle** (qv) had a mystical vision which led him to the house of Thomas and Margaret Fell at Swarthmoor near Ulverston. There the movement established its base and, from Swarthmoor, missionaries were sent out into other parts of the North. Some of the first Quaker meetings in the country were set up in Lancashire, and during the later seventeenth century and into the eighteenth this was the most fertile ground for the faith.

quoits Until the late nineteenth century, **quoiting** was a popular game in many rural areas of south Lancashire. It was often played in hollows in the fields, but, in some places, inns and alehouses had **quoit teams** just as many others had bowling teams.

R

rabbit-jumping This strange sport was apparently peculiar to the Clifton and Swinton area, where local contests were held in the nineteenth century. Participants, wearing *jumping clogs*, squatted on their heels and placed two fingers inside each clog with the thumbs outside, their arms passing between their knees. They then, in the words of Alfred Gaskell, 'swung their buttocks up and down to give them impetus for the first jump'. On the word 'go' they proceeded to a finishing line in rabbit-like jumps. Anyone losing his grip on the clogs was disqualified. Why didn't it catch on elsewhere?

Rachda' Rochdale. The name might be supposed to mean 'valley of the river Roch', but the older spelling of the name was Recedham (pronounced something like 'Rechdam'). The local dialect omitted the final 'm', making Rachda', and subsequently 'da' was assumed to be a short form of 'dale'. The 'ham' element in fact means 'a hall, homestead or settlement'.

rackancrook (numerous variants, such as *rackentithe, rackenhook, rack-and-hook*). Metal crane in the chimney on which pots could be hung over the fire. The word and the contraption were ubiquitous in Lancashire homes until the arrival of the primitive forms of kitchen ranges in the early nineteenth century.

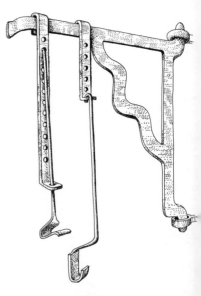

A rackancrook.

164

Radcliffe Shag fearsome bear-like dog (cf *barguist*) which once haunted the Radcliffe area. After the construction of the canal from Manchester to Bury, the beast roamed the banks of the canal and threw those walking along the towpath late at night into the water, though as one nineteenth-century historian noted, 'some were so sceptical as to assert that the ale barrel had much more potency in the matter'. (See also *Bezza Shriker*, *boggart*.)

rake to scratch

rake trackway or path up a hillside

ramble pub crawl

ran dan barley bread, the food of last resort for the poor at the end of the eighteenth and beginning of the nineteenth centuries, when Lancashire was in the depths of economic and social despair. Barley bread was tough, hard and heavy, and dark coloured, largely because barley has little gluten and so the bread did not rise, remaining a solid mass. Before baking, however, it formed a runny dough which, as several local writers recalled, had to be held into the oven until it had hardened sufficiently for the door to be shut, or else the mixture would flow out onto the hearth. An alternative name was *brown George*, perhaps called in ironic reference to George III.

rant frolic, a drinking bout, a wild time

rap This was another paupers' food in the years of hardship around 1800. **Treacle** (qv) and oatmeal were mixed together so that a solid sticky ball, almost dough-like, was formed. This was placed in the middle of a communal porridge bowl. Each person took a spoonful of porridge and then rubbed the spoon on the *rap* to transfer a little of the sweetness. *Rap* (the word means 'rub') comes from a time when the very poor desperately craved sweetness in their food but could only afford tiny quantities of sugar or treacle. Methods such as this meant that a very little went a very long way.

rappin' According to Peter Holland in his description of Swinton in the 1840s, it was customary among the poor for porridge (the only food which most could afford) to be served in a communal pot. When this was placed on the table the mother would rap her knuckles on the tabletop. The *rappin'* was a signal to the family to come and eat. Those who did not hear the *rappin'* lost their chance of food because all would have been devoured before they realised.

rearing putting the roof on a new building; an occasion for a small celebration, where by tradition the workmen would be given a meal and drink by the builder or owner, and in the case of public buildings there might be a commemoration with speeches and merriment. In cruck buildings, where the 'mirror image' halves of a great curved trunk were used as the supports for the ridge as well as the framework for the walls, the two limbs of the cruck would be raised, or *reared*, from the horizontal, having been laid out flat on the ground, and this may be origin of the term.

reasty (reesty, resty)   rancid, 'high' as in meat. The term was very often applied to bacon which had been kept too long and was going off. It meant 'rusty', and related particularly to the reddish discolouring of the fat which preceded rotting.

red-raw   self-explanatory term, used when, for example, something has been chafing and rubbing on the skin

red rose   The red rose of Lancaster is of course the county's symbol, contrasting with the white rose of York, and combined with it in the Tudor rose which commemorated the uniting of the two royal houses by the marriage of Henry VII and Elizabeth of York in 1485. According to Shakespeare, in the famous scene in *Henry VI Part 1*, the red rose, *rosa officinalis*, was adopted by the house of Lancaster when Warwick and Somerset, as representatives of the houses of York and Lancaster respectively, plucked roses during an argument in the Temple garden in London. This episode creates a powerful dramatic effect, since it foreshadows the Wars of the Roses:

'... this brawl today,
Grown to this faction in the
   Temple Garden,
Shall send between the Red
   Rose and the White,

A thousand souls to death and
   deadly night'

In reality, though, the white and red roses had been used as emblems by the two families long before the fifteenth century. The two roses were thus originally the badges not of counties but of royal houses. Their very close association with Lancashire and Yorkshire (rather than with the duchies of Lancaster and York, a quite different thing) is much more recent. We can view it as a response to the growing awareness of the county and the developing loyalties of its inhabitants during the nineteenth century, but its real blossoming has been during the twentieth century when, from being a relatively obscure symbol which appeared on a few coats of arms and badges, the Red Rose has come to stand for everything Lancastrian, in sport, tourist publicity, literature, local government and newspaper columns. Lancashire and Yorkshire are especially fortunate to have such badges, which now help to reinforce their very strong senses of identity.

red thread   In the eighteenth century in the Ribble Valley, it was customary to tie a piece of red woollen thread around the tails of cattle when they were turned out for the first time in the spring. This was held to secure the cattle from the evil eye.

reech   smoke (as in *reek* — the Scottish form is known today from the name Auld Reekie for Edinburgh, swathed as it used to be in dense clouds of smoke from coal fires). In parts of Lancashire including Wigan, chimneys were often cleaned not by sweeping but by stuffing lighted newspapers up the flue, which set the soot on fire and producing the typical thick clouds of sooty smoke, a practice known as *makin' a rooch.* The word also meant smoking tobacco: *'Neaw, win ye have a reech o' bacca?'.*

reed metal 'comb' on a loom which governs how fine the finished cloth will be. Its teeth keep the warp threads in place, and the number of teeth per inch determines the fineness of the cloth. The *reed* also formed a guide for the shuttle, keeping it in true horizontal alignment, and thereby helped to determine the tightness of the cloth. If the warp had not been properly threaded, so that two or more threads fell in the space between two teeth, the finished cloth would be badly marked along its long axis.

reel revolving frame on which the yarn was wound in hanks; a *reeler* would be in charge of the machine, which wound yarn from spools or bobbins into hanks, ready for further processing (such as dyeing) or for the market

religious rivalry The Catholic religion remained very strong in post-Reformation Lancashire, while Methodism was successful in attracting adherents in the later eighteenth century. There was considerable friction and rivalry between the three main denominations in the

Victorian period and well into the twentieth century. In towns such as Preston, there was unofficial job discrimination until the last twenty years, with some firms taking only Catholic workers. Children were brought up to be acutely conscious of the differences between the faiths. At rural Mawdesley in the 1920s, for example, the following abusive rhymes were called from child to child:

Catholic and Methodist to Church of England:
> *'Prodestant, prodestant, quack quack quack*
> *Go to the Devil and ne'er come back'*

Methodist and C of E to Catholic:
> *'Papish lout, pepper an' sawt,*
> *Can't afford a knife 'n fork'*

C of E and Catholic to Methodists:
> *'Methody bumps, kissed cay's* [cow's] *rumps*
> *Eitin' poddich aw' in lumps'*

rent dinner feast given by the landlord to the tenants on the day when the rent was paid

rhymes and verses Numerous Lancashire towns and villages were the subject of small verses, couplets and rhymes, used especially in children's games and songs. Here is an example from south-west Lancashire:

> *Prescot, Huyton and merry Childow* [Childwall]
> *Three parish churches all in a row*
> *Prescot for mugs; Huyton for ploydes* [ploughs?]
> *Childow for ringing and singing besides*

rid 'to dig virgin soil' in Taylor's 1901 definition. *Ridding* was the process of converting waste land to farmland, a medieval term which gave rise to place-names all over the Pennines of Lancashire and Yorkshire, for example, Ellenroad, Rhodes and Blackrod.

riddlins' loose dirt and other material which does not fall through a sieve or riddle; by association, therefore, rubbish, rough stuff, fragments, bits and pieces

riding the stang rough form of play or an impromptu mob punishment (the two are not too far apart in reality), whereby the victim was forced to sit astride a pole (the *stang*) and ridden round the streets, or carried to the *midden* (qv) and hurled into the muck.

An alternative was that two long poles were used, with a board across to serve as a seat. The victim was carried through the streets, fastened to the 'chair' with ropes, and the mob jostled alongside, banging pots and pans and making 'loud and discordant noises'. The final version, still current at the end of the nineteenth century in some parts of Lancashire, and with isolated instances as late as the Second World War, was that the victim was tied onto a handcart and pushed along the streets. This form of punishment was also common elsewhere in England and was often known as *rough music*.

riggin'-tree beam ('ridging tree') which supported the line of a roof in a timber-framed building

Riding the stang.

right in the same way as *like*, the word *right* is commonly used for what Nodal and Milner in the 1870s referred to as 'intensifying an expression', although they do not include *right* in their glossary, which might imply that its use is a more recent development. In some parts of Lancashire, such as Preston, *right* can be used, as a confirmation that the listener really understands, at the end of almost every sentence when telling a dramatic (or even not very dramatic) story: *'A' come through t' door, right, an' a' went in t' t' street, right'*.

right misery (see *'appy 'arry*)

ring games games played by children or young people, dancing in a circle and singing or chanting — usually about love, courtship and marriage; very widespread in the county until the early years of the twentieth century

ringing the pan John Harland says that he 'saw this ceremony performed in the neighbourhood of Burnley twice during the year 1868', and indicates that it was quite commonplace at the time. Couples who courted on a Friday night would find that the neighbours gathered outside the house, banging frying pans with shovels and pokers and chanting:

> *'Oh! dear a me!*
> *AB and CD* [naming the couple]
> *Court six neets eawt o' seven*
> *Un corn'd let Friday neet*
>   *olooan!'*

In the Ribchester area, the same custom was known as *jinglin'*

neet. Why courting on Friday was deemed to be inappropriate is not made clear by Harland, but the explanation is that this was *lads' neet out*, so staying in with your girlfriend was highly unsociable. Furthermore, courting *every* night (except presumably Sunday) obviously displayed an excessive and unnatural devotion.

rip rap firecracker, or a *jumping jack*; by association, a lively, excessively-spirited child (*come on, then, rip rap, settle down*)

ripstitch reckless person (one who tears his clothes), but often used for children who are high-spirited or over-exuberant

rive to tear (as in the almost obsolete standard English *riven*) *hoo rived 'er cloas*

roach coal pit

road way, as in the phrase *any road*, or *Ah've just come out o' t' road o' yon lot*

robber's knock rubbing your nose or a finger down a window pane (especially the windows of nervous elderly ladies) after you had breathed heavily on it, to produce a sudden shrill squeak; a game much favoured by small boys at night

Robbers' Walk The pathway between Horwich and Rivington was, according to one of those conveniently imprecise legends, once terrorised by a band of outlaws who preyed upon passing travellers, until one of their number was seized and hung from a tall tree on the orders of the lord of the manor. Subsequently, when the lord was away from home, and seeing 'upon the tall oak still ... the bleached bones of their companion', the five remaining outlaws slaughtered his lady and children. The five were swiftly brought to justice and executed, but their spirits haunted the mounds on the Rivington track where they had buried their hapless victims. Good stuff!

rody (roady)   streaked, especially as in old-fashioned bacon with its alternating stripes of fat (mainly) and lean (some)

Roberts, Robert   One of the greatest writers on working-class life in Lancashire, Robert Roberts was born in Waterloo Street, Salford, in 1905. He started his working life as an engineering apprentice at fourteen, but eventually studied languages, and became a teacher and lecturer. In the 1930s he began to write plays, short stories and radio scripts, and after World War II was closely involved in adult literacy work, teaching prisoners at Strangeways (amongst whom were companions from his childhood). He wrote two classic autobiographical books which, in vivid and moving fashion, recount his boyhood in the slums of Salford. *The Classic Slum* was published in 1971 and *A Ragged Schooling* posthumously in 1976. He died in 1974.

Robin Hood   As a result of Victorian sentimentality, Robin Hood is today associated solely with Sherwood Forest and the reign of 'bad' King John, but the legends associated with this largely mythical character were found throughout Northern England and were not connected with particular historical periods. He was a popular folk hero, often symbolised in May Day rituals, and local festivals in Lancashire often included Robin Hood in dances and pageants. For example, in the early sixteenth century, figures dressed as Robin Hood and Maid Marian were the lord and lady of the May in celebrations held in and around the collegiate church (now cathedral) in Manchester, while in the 1580s Puritans were actively trying to suppress the Robin Hood revels on May Day at Burnley. A local gentleman, Edward Assheton, complained of 'stirs at Brunley about Robin Hood and the May Games ... lewd sports tending to no other end but to stir up our frail natures to wantonness [with] embracings, kissings and unchaste beholding of each other [and] marching and walking together in the night time'.

Roby, John   A Rochdale man, John Roby published, between 1829 and 1831, two volumes entitled *The Traditions of Lancashire*, containing over forty stories associated with locations in the county. In reality, these 'traditions', which were very popular throughout the nineteenth century, are highly-romanticised fictional tales of Gothick character in the mode of Sir Walter Scott, woven around fragments of authentic tradition but of more interest,

The rock-cut graves at Heysham Head.

perhaps, as literary examples than as genuine history.

rock-cut graves Heysham Head is among the most important sites connected with the early Church in north-west England. The six coffin-shaped graves, cut deep into a single huge slab of sandstone just below the ruins of the eighth-century chapel of St Patrick, are perhaps the most puzzling or enigmatic feature of the area. Each grave has a socket at its head which would once have held a stone cross, and they are presumably of about the same date as the chapel itself, but nothing else is definitely known of their origin.

Roger-a-Moss (see **football**)

roke (see *rake*)

room space, allocation, as in *moss room* (qv) or *stoop and room* (qv)

roop hoarse or sore throat, when the voice becomes rough and rasping

Rose Queens Every summer, local newspapers in Lancashire are full of pictures of **Rose Queens** being crowned or officiating, with their attendants, at carnivals, school fetes, church garden parties and community processions. To be a **Rose Queen** is still regarded as a great honour, and those who make the choice have to decide with the greatest care, as fierce rivalries can be develop. The tradition in its modern form is well over a hundred years old, and is found all over the county — it is especially popular in towns. Its origins, though, are much older, since the choosing of a young girl to preside over festivals and wakes,

The rushcart, centrepiece of many rushbearing ceremonies.

suitably attired in flowers and finery, is recorded in seventeenth and eighteenth century sources.

rough music (see *riding the stang*)

roving frame In the spinning of cotton yarn the *slubbings* (qv), loosely-twisted strands of cotton fibre, are put through the *roving frame*, which gives them a stronger twist and makes them more regular and even. Thus the carded fibres are first given a slight twist to become *sliver* (qv), then combined and further twisted as *slubbings*, then twisted again into a stage part-way to yarn, as *rovings*, and then finally spun into the finished yarn.

ruckle, runckle to disturb, to push up untidily or in a heap (as in bedclothes)

rushbearing Strewing the floors of buildings with rushes, to give a softer and warmer and (initially at least) fragrant covering which could conceal dirt and filth, was an ancient custom. In late spring the old decaying material would be swept away, the floor was cleaned, and then fresh rushes would be cut and laid down. In many places in Lancashire, cleaning and re-rushing the church floor was an excuse for junketings of various sorts, and in some areas (especially in the south-east of the county) *rushbearing* became an important communal festival. At least some of these celebrations may have originated as pre-Christian fertility rituals, but by the later Middle Ages they were firmly attached to the Church. In the most elaborate instances, a *rushcart* (qv) was drawn around the village or town. *Rushbearings* were closely associated with *wakes* (qv) and generally died out in the early nineteenth century, although a few lingered on into the 1880s. In several places in south Lancashire, they have recently been revived after a break of well over a century.

rushcarts The centrepiece of the larger and grander rushbearings was the construction of a *rushcart*. A flat farm wagon would be used as the base, on which a towering structure made of bundles of rushes would be raised. The bundles would be carefully bound together with rope and twine, and then the 'architecture' was elaborately decorated with banners, flowers, ribbons and, latterly, with tableaux such as ornamental arrangements of agricultural implements and horse harness. Often accompanied by **morris dancers** (qv) or mummers, it would then be drawn around the streets and lanes, and bystanders would be pressed to give money, ostensibly to defray the cost of the *rushcart* but more probably to spend on drink. One nineteenth-century writer claimed that at *rushbearings* 'riot and drunkenness reigned supreme'.

S

sad heavy, solid, firm; used for cakes, bread and biscuits which have not risen successfully, and for heavy, soggy pastry, but also applied specifically to *sad cake*, a dense cake rich in fat with a very moist and sticky texture

Saddleworth The local historian, naturalist and novelist Ammon Wrigley, who was born at Delph in Saddleworth in 1862, described his home as 'a Yorkshire parish with a Lancashire population', and noted how its Yorkshire people spoke a Lancashire dialect. Cynically observing a characteristic popularly ascribed to Yorkshire folk, he also claimed that 'Yorkshire takes ... nearly every penny of its money [but] Lancashire takes its water, including that from the sewage works'. Saddleworth was in the West Riding, but on the wrong (or right, depending on one's perspective) side of the Pennines. For centuries it was a chapelry within the parish of Rochdale, and after 1834 was in the Oldham Poor Law Union. In 1974 it was transferred administratively to the Metropolitan Borough of Oldham.

St Cuthbert One of the most influential figures in the early English church, **St Cuthbert** (who died in AD 687) was ultimately bishop of Lindisfarne, but spent most of his adult life was as a monk, during which time he frequently travelled around the country as an evangelising missionary. Long after his death, his body was carried by the monks of Lindisfarne through Northern England to prevent it falling into the hands of the Viking raiders, and according to legend it rested for a time at Lytham. The truth or otherwise of this is impossible to ascertain, although Lytham Church has always been dedicated to the saint and there was certainly an ancient monastic site at **Kilgrimoles** (qv), the present St Annes.

St Patrick Although now inextricably associated with Ireland, little is known of **St Patrick** as an historical figure, but he was almost certainly born in Wales in the early fifth century. During his life he travelled widely, and persistent legends associate his name

St Patrick's Chapel, Heysham Head.

with Lancashire. The most notable story tells how he was shipwrecked in Morecambe Bay, just off Heysham Head. Though this story is unprovable, the ancient chapel on the headland has been known as **St Patrick's Chapel** for centuries. It was probably built in the eighth century, and so is two or three centuries later than the saint's own lifetime, but it is certainly Lancashire's oldest surviving church building. There is nothing inherently implausible in the notion that Patrick may at least have visited Lancashire, since the Irish Sea basin was his world.

St Paulinus According to the Venerable Bede, **Paulinus**, the missionary from Rome who converted the Northumbrians to Christianity in the 620s and who founded the

archbishopric of York, toured the North of England preaching and performing mass baptisms. Later legends claim that he visited a number of places in Lancashire, including Burnley, Whalley and Tockholes, and that the famous crosses in the churchyard at Whalley were erected to commemorate his visit. Unfortunately, and unromantically, historical evidence for such visits to the county is entirely lacking, and we now know that the crosses at Whalley were erected about 250 years later than Paulinus' time.

salt The Lancashire **salt industry**, much less well known than that of Cheshire, has had two main phases. In the twentieth century, brine and **rock-salt** have been produced at Stalmine and Preesall on the Wyre Estuary, where salt was discovered in the late nineteenth century during borings for coal. Until the eighteenth century, however, the county produced **sea-salt**, which was made by evaporating salt water in pans on or just behind the shore at, among other places, Warton (Carnforth) and Lytham, where the name **Salt-cotes** reminds us of this ancient trade.

salt cap oatcake soaked in water and sprinkled with a little salt; a main meal for the starving paupers of the early nineteenth century in areas such as Rossendale (cf *brewis*, *pigwhistle*)

Sambo's Grave Lancaster, like Liverpool, prospered in the Georgian period on the strength of the Atlantic trade, including the appalling human traffic in slaves from West Africa. In about 1736 **Sambo**, a Negro servant boy, was brought over to England with his master and died on arrival in the estuary of the Lune. He was buried on the shore just north of Sunderland Point, and there his grave can still be seen, with a brass plate (added in 1796) bearing a

---

Here lies
Poor SAMBOO
A faithfull NEGRO

Who (Attending his Master from the *West Indies*)
DIED on his Arrival at *SUNDERLAND*.

Full sixty Years the angry Winter's Wave
Has thundering dashd this bleak & barren Shore
Since SAMBO's Head laid in this lonely Grave
Lies still & ne'er will hear their turmoil more.

Full many a Sand bird chirps upon the Sod
And many a Summer's Sunbeam warms the Clod
And many a teeming Cloud upon him drips.

But still he sleeps - till the awakening Sounds
Of the Archangel's Trump new Life impart
Then the GREAT JUDGE his Approbation founds
Not on Man's COLOR but his - WORTH of HEART

The epitaph (1796) on Sambo's grave.

poignant and moving epitaph in verse. The grave always has fresh flowers and other small offerings left by visitors, for Sambo and the evil system of which he was a victim are not forgotten.

sand class In schools in poor areas before the advent of state education in the 1870s, a *sand class* might be held. A tray of damp sand was used, in which pupils drew their letters with a stick. The sand could then be smoothed over ready for the next child. It was a slow method of learning, for only one child at a time could be taught, but it was at least very economical.

san' forth (sanfer') the marsh samphire, which grows extensively along the muddy coasts of Morecambe Bay and the Wyre and Ribble estuaries. It is still picked and eaten, and in the past was a popular local delicacy, boiled and served with butter and a dash of vinegar, or else pickled.

sand grown native of Lytham St Annes or the Southport and Formby areas, where open sands and dunes were — and to some extent still are — the characteristic coastal landscape. *'I'm a sand grown 'un'* is a proud boast in both districts, where a very high proportion of the population has come from elsewhere, especially in retirement or to commute to a larger town or city.

sand knockers In parts of the Pennines, such as Smallbridge near Rochdale, *sand knocking* was a local trade until the early twentieth century. It involved crushing and grinding sandstones and gritstones into coarse powder, which was sprinkled on the floors of alehouses and butchers shops or, for domestic use, was scattered on a newly-washed floor as a scourer. The sand was ground over the flags with a block of stone or a wooden block so that the stones were smoothed and whitened. This method was the forerunner of the *donkey stone* (qv), which was later ubiquitous.

sands crossing Crossing Morecambe Bay on foot from Hest Bank or Arnside to Grange has become a popular attraction for Lancashire people, and in good weather it is a fascinating experience with very impressive views. In the past, though, crossing these sands (like the shorter sands crossings over the estuaries of the Cocker, Ribble and Mersey) was a dangerous necessity if travellers wanted to avoid the long detour by overland routes. An intimate knowledge of tides, quicksands and shifting channels was required, and over the centuries many hundreds of people were drowned. *Brobs* (qv) were used as markers, and guides were stationed at all the main crossing points; guide houses survive at, for example, Freckleton and Warton on the Ribble. Today Cedric Robinson, the Morecambe Bay guide, is still hard at work taking parties across the sands.

sauce pertness, impudence and, an associated earlier meaning, scolding or criticising shrewishly

The sands of Morecambe Bay, from Saxton's map of 1577.

scabby-headed baby *'I could eat a scabby-headed baby between two mattresses'*: peculiarly horrible phrase descriptive of extreme hunger, as used by the author's mother during her childhood in Openshaw in the 1930s

scar (see *skear*)

scorrock last bit or a little bit; Edmund Battersby, in his list of words used in Accrington, quotes *''E's etten every scorrock'*

Scotchmen originally, travelling pedlars (who often were Scottish or from the northern counties of England) but later, in the nineteenth century, the term and its variant *Scotch drapers* was used to describe credit traders of any sort

Scouse The distinctive modern dialect of Liverpool, with its remarkable vocal agilities, has become generally known as *scouse*. The origins of the dialect and the unmistakable accent are probably comparatively recent, and are held by many to result from the massive influx of Irish people to the area from the late eighteenth century onwards. Others identify a characteristically Welsh intonation or inflection, and it is certainly true that many immigrants came from the northern counties of Wales — and indeed from Scotland — in the same period. There is a reasonable amount of evidence that the earlier accent and dialect of Liverpool were more typically 'Lancashire', and *scouse* may therefore derive from the introduction of three Celtic accents and dialects 200-150 years ago, which merged with each other and with the existing local speech. *Scouse* is also, unusually, an accent which is actively extending its range. The decentralisation of population from Liverpool and Bootle in the twentieth century means that it is now found in places such as St Helens and (with markedly more refined overtones) Southport, where it has partially eliminated the older Lancashire dialects which were typical until the Second World War. It is important to note, however, that to many Liverpool people, the dialect and accent known as *scouse* is in fact considered to be specifically 'Liverpool Irish', and that within the city there are other local accents.

Scouser Derived from *lobscouse* (qv), a traditional dish of the poor, the term *scouser* to describe someone from Liverpool became more commonplace in the early years of the twentieth century, but has only become a standard national term since the advent of television. *Till Death us do Part*, with Alf Garnett raging at his son-in-law, the 'Scahse Git', has much to answer for.

-scough the ending of several Lancashire place-names (including Burscough, Tarlscough and Myerscough), from the ON *skogr*, a small wood

scrannel thin, lean, meagre, poor quality

scuffer in south-west Lancashire (especially Liverpool), a policeman

scutch to beat, to tear open. *Scutching* was a stage in the production of cotton and flax yarn. In the case of cotton, the bolls were beaten, and then the debris and fragments of stems removed; in the flax industry, the retted stems were cleaned and then *scutched* so that the long-stem fibres were separated and became a fine tangle of threads, which could then be combed ready for spinning. (See also *blowing room*)

seg callus, or small hard patch on the palm or heel caused by friction during work, but also used more generally for small growths and nodules anywhere on the

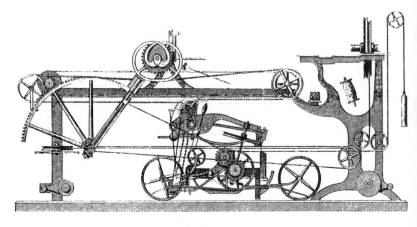

A self-actor.

body; a term of abuse for a stupid or slow person (in 1930s Manchester, *seg 'ed* [seghead])

self-actor In the late eighteenth century, when the principles of mechanically-powered spinning were perfected, the process involved several related stages which had to be done on separate machines: *carding, slivering, slubbing* and *roving* (qv). The latter three, by means of twisting and pulling movements, transformed the thick, loose strand of fibres into a tighter, longer and more even thread. The process was interrupted between each stage, and many workers were needed to perform the main tasks, together with such jobs as bobbin-shifting, which were necessary because the different machines were involved. The logical next stage was to try to combine as much of the process as possible in one machine, which would undertake a large part of the work automatically. The mid-nineteenth century invention of the *self-actor* was an important step in this direction, for it performed the *drawing*, twisting, winding-on and *copping* (qv) stages on one piece of equipment. *Self-actor minders* were skilled operatives, keeping an ever-watchful eye on all these processes more-or-less simultaneously.

sellin' calico man or boy with his shirt-tail hanging out of the back of his trousers, or (more poignantly) poking through the holes in his trouser seat

sen self; therefore, *mi-sen* (myself) and *tha-sen* (thyself, yourself)

sennit week; literally a 'seven-night', a term which has in the past fifty years become almost obsolete, unlike the equivalent word **fortnight** (fourteen-night). 'It was a week ago' would have been spoken as *'Twere a sennit-sin'*.

180

sett rectangular or square blocks of roadstone (usually granite) which were used for surfacing tens of thousands of miles of back streets in nineteenth and early twentieth century Lancashire. Such streets are usually referred to as *cobbled* (qv), which is technically incorrect, and many were tarmacked over in the 1950s and 1960s, though today, with pedestrianisation and traffic-calming much in vogue, *setted streets* are enjoying a renaissance.

Shakers The American religious sect known as the Shakers, perhaps best known for their beautiful hymn *Tis the gift to be simple*,

A boy sellin' calico.

developed from an obscure and secretive religious group which was established in Manchester in the early eighteenth century. In 1758 they were joined by Ann Lee, daughter of a local blacksmith. The group became convinced that the new Messiah would be a woman, and that Ann, who seems to have had a very dominating and persuasive personality, would be that person. In 1774, for reasons which are unclear (although very unreliable Shaker sources give official persecution as the explanation), most of the group emigrated to the United States. 'Mother Ann', as she had become known, died there in 1784.

Shakespeare, William The claim that William Shakespeare spent part of his early career in Lancashire has been raised for well over a century, and it has now been accepted by many people, even though historically-sound evidence is still lacking. It is true that there are circumstantial hints, of varying reliability and relevance, and it is also clear that the household of the earl of Derby did have close connections with Shakespeare (see **Malvolio**). Recent argument has centred on Shakespeare's supposed Jesuit links or crypto-Catholic faith, and the documented presence of one William Shakeshaft in the household of Sir Alexander Hoghton, is often taken as confirmation, it being assumed that the name is a version of the name Shakespeare. Those

Shawls.

unfamiliar with the county are apparently unaware that Shakeshaft is in fact a relatively common Lancashire surname. Argument will always rage, and even if it were proved that the great man did indeed spend time in Lancashire, it is not clear how this reflects upon the county or vice versa. As yet the verdict must surely be 'non proven', but I, as a historian, remain unconvinced.

shale to flake off, peel or become loose from the surface; brickwork, for example, is said to be *shalin'* when the surface flakes away

shanking (see **shrimping**)

shape, shaper to finish, complete, manage. In his book on the **Cotton Famine** (qv), Edwin Waugh records a conversation among men at a soup kitchen: *'Theer, thae's shap't that at last'*, said one of these to his friend, who had just finished his basin of soup.

shape to cooperate, do it properly, make a proper effort; for example, a child would be told to *shape* when not cooperating in pushing its arm into a coat sleeve

sharn clap (see *cow-slavver*)

shawls The classic **Lancashire** shawl was a warm, dark-coloured woollen cloth, large enough to cover the head (and so prevent draughts down the back of the neck), wrap around the shoulders and fall most of the way down the back. Most working women wore the shawl, and their 'uniform' was fairly standard — shiny black clogs, white *brat* (apron) and enveloping shawl. For domestic wear, and for special occasions, shawls of finer material, perhaps decorated with fringes, would be worn over the shoulders but not over the head. By the 1920s, shawls had tended to become smaller — covering the shoulders only — and were worn in conjunction with a hat or bonnet, while they were more likely than hitherto to be of a patterned material such as plaid or checked wool. They were thus becoming to some extent decorative rather than essential items of clothing. In areas such as Salford, it was virtually obligatory for a woman to wear a shawl when walking in public. One who did not do so might be damned as being *in her figure.*

shed space between warp threads on a loom (see also *picking*)

sheep, sheep, come over (see *blackthorn*)

sheppy, shepster, sheepster starling

shift to move, or remove house
Ah'm shiftin' ta Manchister

shilling to peel shrimps in areas such as Lytham and Morecambe is known as *shilling* (a dialect form of 'shelling')

shinparing fighting naked except for clogs shoed or tipped with brass or iron, the name graphically describing the purpose of the clogs; this 'sport' was once favoured by some sections of the Lancashire populace (see also *purring,* *up and down fighting*)

shippon cowshed

ship's timbers A favourite historical myth is that old buildings contain 're-used ship's timbers'. The Green Man public house at Inglewhite near Preston, for example, is said to have wood from Viking longships. Such claims are almost always unjustified, and archaeological and architectural evidence does not support the idea. If ship's timbers were recycled they would be used in other ships. Many properties do include re-used wooden beams, but these invariably come, logically enough, from demolished properties. People

*A sheppy, shepster, sheepster —
or starling.*

in the past were eminently practical and sensible, and the idea of hauling ship's timbers from the coast for building work miles inland would never have occurred to them.

shive slice, especially of bread *'Gie's a shive wi' butther, Ah'm clemmed'*

sholvers small freshwater fish of various sorts, such as minnows and stickleback

shop place *It were all over't shop; Aw'll gerreawt a' t' shop as soon as aw con*

shrimping The flat, sandy Lancashire coast is particularly suited to shrimps, and **shrimping** was a major trade in areas such as Southport, Lytham and Morecambe. The small, sweet shrimps from these areas remain a much-prized delicacy, and are one of

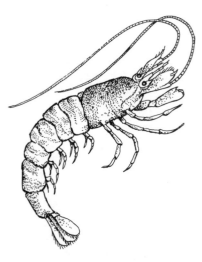

The common shrimp.

England's most notable regional foods. Shrimping (also known as *shanking*) was often done from carts or small boats using trawlnets, which were up to seven feet (2m) wide with a rigid beam, and were dragged along the bed of the sea. An alternative was *putting*, where a hand-held net was used in the shallows near the water's edge. The sand was washed off, and the shrimps and any other shellfish were then tipped into baskets known as *leaps* (qv) which were carried on the back. (See also **cockles**)

Shrove Tuesday While we still eat pancakes on **Shrove Tuesday** (also known as Pancake Day), the other elements of the festival have usually been lost. It was traditional in Lancashire for this to be an occasion for mischief. Children and young people would get up to tricks and a good deal of 'frolicsome merriment', as one Victorian writer put it, would take place. At Goosnargh, for example, the children went from door to door begging biscuits, apples, sweets and toffees — in 1888 the vicar recorded that 126 of them knocked on his door that day. At Poulton-le-Fylde, the apprentices had a half-day holiday, and they and other young people went from house to house begging for pancakes; if a housewife answered the door, custom dictated that she had to provide a pancake for the caller. **Samuel Bamford** (qv) records that, in Middleton in the 1790s, pancake-eating contests were held, and the losers were hurled by the friends onto the nearest midden.

shruff dust, parings, fine debris

shut to be rid off, to quit *'Howd te din, an' lie still a bit, till aw get shut on him'* (Edwin Waugh)

shutter to slide or roll down a slope: for example, snow might *shutter* off a roof; also used colloquially to refer to a stealthy or quiet departure *'Art shutterin' off?'*

shuttle-kissing (see *kissing the shuttle*)

side to clean or tidy, to put in order, put aside *Side the table, Side the cloas'*

side airs and graces, conceits, pretensions; often used in the favourable negative sense *She's got no side on her*

sike small stream or watercourse. The term is fast becoming obsolete, but survives in numerous minor place-names throughout the county, such as Syke Street in Preston and Haslingden.

sile to sieve or strain

Simblin' Sunday Mid-Lent Sunday (that is, Mothering Sunday), when in south Lancashire simnel cakes were eaten (see **Bury simnels**)

Simonswood An ancient legend tells how King John had 'a famous runner' down in London, who was eventually challenged to a foot-race by a man called Simon who came from Kirkby. Simon won, to the astonishment of those in the South who couldn't believe that a man from such a remote

place as Lancashire could possibly beat the national champion, and as a reward he was granted the position of 'keeper of the forest', which ever after was known as 'Simon's wood'. Unfortunately for romance, the place-name actually means 'Sigmund's wood', and is much older than the time of King John.

sink stone (see *slopstone*)

Sir Loin In August 1617, James I visited Lancashire during one of his progresses, and stayed at Hoghton Tower (I was once told, in all seriousness, that 'they rolled out a red carpet and it reached almost to the railway station'). During his stay, a loin of beef formed the centrepiece of one of

James I — the originator of the word sirloin?

185

the gargantuan feasts laid on for the king and his retinue, and the witty monarch is said to have taken out his sword and said to the beef 'I dub thee Sir Loin', thus giving the word sirloin to the language. He may well have made the jest (he is known to have had a somewhat ponderous and puerile sense of humour), but the word appears in medieval sources and so long predates the king's visit.

sithee historically, used in the sense of 'Look here' or 'Look you', but now generally employed (if at all) as a farewell: *'Right, sithee then'* — 'I'll be seeing you'

sithors scissors; the older pronunciation was very common until the 1920s, but has since largely died out

sitting up Before Victorian ideas of morality were imposed in the middle years of the nineteenth century, courtship was freer and easier for many Lancashire people. If a couple had been together for long enough and were regarded as *serious*, it was permissible for them to spend all or part of the night together, as a prelude to betrothal. The phrase widely used was *sitting up*. Hence, for example, in 1663 young Roger Lowe of Ashton-in-Makerfield wrote in his diary that he 'privately ingag'd to Mary to sit up awhile … the first night that ever I stay'd up a wooing ere in my life'.

skear in north Lancashire, a shoal or area of rocks below the high tide mark (alternatively spelled *scar*)

sken (with many variants, such as *sken ee'd, skennin', skenny*) cross-eyed or squinting, or with a crooked eye *'He skens ill enou' to crack a lookin' glass welly'*; but the word also, more generally, meant 'to look at' *''ave a sken at it'*

skew whiff (skew whift) awry, askew, on one side, off balance

skrike to shriek or cry out

skuse length of hollow plant-stem, used by small boys as a pea-shooter

slack shallow depression in between sand hills, usually boggy and sometimes filled with brackish water

slammock (slummock) to walk unsteadily or clumsy, to be ungainly

slance to steal small items and odds and ends; petty thieving; to pick up furtively; to pinch meat or other foods, or small items around the house (someone who took scraps of meat off somebody else's plate would be *slancin'*)

slancing taking another man's wife out for immoral purposes (*'No one misses a slice off a cut loaf'*); the word is clearly used, with considerably more dramatic intent, as an extension of the term for petty thieving

slated woman who was showing her underskirt, or more generally was bedraggled and untidily dressed

slatt'at drunk and quarrelsome

slatter to spill; hence, *slatterins'* for spillings, left-overs, dregs

sled 'a carriage without wheels', a sledge; such vehicles were used

A sled.

in parts of Lancashire until the late nineteenth century for transporting stone in quarries or down hillsides, peat from the moss, or similar heavy duties. In parts of Pennine Lancashire, the zig-zag tracks made for sleds can still be seen prominently on hillsides and valley slopes.

slink[1] A peculiarly unpleasant term for soft or diseased or rotting meat, or the meat of an animal which was stillborn or died prematurely soon after birth. The sale of *slink* was not approved by the authorities but, because it was cheap and the vendors wanted to dispose of it as soon as possible, it was often the only meat which the poor were able to buy.

slink[2] thin coat or mackintosh *Tekkin 'er slink wi' 'er*

sliver product of the carding machine; cotton fibre which has been combed and straightened, and emerges as a loose, soft and untwisted strand ready for the *slubbing* stage (qv)

slopstone washing place, also known as *sink stone*; a shallow sink carved from a single piece of stone and set on a stand or plinth. It would be fed by a single cold tap if piped water was available, or from a cistern or pail if not, and had a drain hole in the bottom

slow walking funeral procession

slubbing *Sliver*, the loose, soft strand of cotton fibre which results from **carding** (qv), is *slubbed* on a drawing-frame: several slivers are combined and twisted gently together, by which action a longer and more drawn-out strand is produced, suitable for winding onto **bobbins** (qv) and then sent on to the *roving frame* (qv).

sluft to hit or slap *Ah'll sluft thee*

slutch mud, filth, dirt

slurrin' to slide, as on snow or frozen ground

sneck catch or latch upon a door; a *sneck bant* was the string (*bant*) used to lift the *sneck*, but in the old

Lancashire style the door would be opened from outside by putting a finger through the 'finger hole' in the door and lifting the catch on the inside.

snig   common freshwater eel, which was extremely abundant in the slower rivers and lowland streams of the Lancashire plains. The eel formerly lived in the waterways and pools of the mosslands, and then, after these were reclaimed for agriculture, it adapted to the drainage channels and ditches of the same areas. The word *snig* is found quite frequently in minor place-names, farm names and field names in west and south Lancashire. The eels of the River Irwell were once particularly celebrated for their prodigious size — in the eighteenth century, it was said that grew especially fat by eating the grease which poured into the river from the woollen mills, but industrial pollution eventually led to their demise.

snig pie   Eel is a great delicacy, and was a popular feast-day food in eighteenth- and nineteenth-century Lancashire. At Widnes, which until the 1840s enjoyed a brief and in retrospect slightly unexpected career as a seaside resort and holiday town, there was an inn called **Snig Pie House**, where on Whit Monday the landlady was 'kept busily employed from morn till night' making and serving *snig pie*, the eels being caught on the spot from the Mersey. *Snig pie* was also eaten at local wakes — it was, for example,

a speciality at Flixton, higher up the Mersey, in the nineteenth century.

snirp   to overcook meat (a word noted in the Burnley area)

snod   smooth, as in *mi' clog 'ierons are snod*

snortch   to sneeze; an old farmer in the Fylde, explaining why he was ill, said *'I' coo snortched on mi'*

sny (snie)   numerous, swarming, very densely crowded (a crowded shopping street on a Saturday afternoon might be *snyin' wi' folk*); overrun (a house could be *fair snyin' wi' flecks* (qv))

sope   sup, a drop *A sope of ale*

soss   to throw down or lie down heavily; from this came the delightful although far from complimentary term *soss midden* (qv), which is known from eighteenth-century sources — a woman too lazy to move from her seat (a Georgian **couch potato**, therefore?)

sough   drain or sewer; a term especially found in a technical sense in mining, where a *sough* was a horizontal tunnel or adit used for drainage

soul cakes, soul caking   On the 1st November, All Saints Day, which was also All Souls Eve, children would go from house to house, chanting at each *'For God's sake, a so' loaf'*, upon which they would be given a *soul cake*, a small, round, flat biscuit (usually of oatmeal, resembling a Scottish oatcake) in which a few caraway or other seeds were pressed, or a butter print pressed on to make a decorative pattern.

sow, sowl   size used in the cotton trade; made of flour and water, and used by the handloom weaver for sizing the warp of the loom. After application, it was dried onto the warp with a *droighin' oiron*.

spanish   popular name for black liquorice; *spanish juice* was a drink made by children, who dissolved a stick of liquorice in water by shaking it up in a bottle

sparrow fart   What better term could there be to exemplify the no-nonsense Lancashire approach to life? As Taylor, writing in 1901, noted, it meant the very early hours of the morning, the popular phrase being *'Aw'st gerrup afore th' sparrow farts'*.

spaws   Although spa has a specific meaning as a spring whose water has medicinal or health-giving properties, and this meaning was recognised in Lancashire, the word *spaw* was also used more generally in the county to refer to many larger clear and bubbling springs, some of which were claimed locally to have special powers. Thus, near Bolton were (among others) **Turton Spa** — now a small spring which emerges from a footpath near the dam at Jumbles — and the *spaw* at Farnworth where, until the mid-nineteenth century, young people would congregate once a year for a *spaw fair*, and would drink a mixture of the spring water with sugar or liquorice, shaken up in bottles. In Rochdale and many other places, the first Sunday in May was known as *Spaw Sunday*, when people would go *a' spo'in*.

spear, speer   wooden partition beside the door of a cottage, opening directly into the front room. It provided a modicum of privacy for those inside the room, shielding it and them from the gaze of those standing at the door, but also (more importantly) acted as a screen to keep direct draughts out of the hearth area of the room.

spell   splinter of wood (the origin being the same as 'spill', a slip of wood)

spinning jenny   first commercially viable machine for spinning cotton, invented by James Hargreaves in about 1764. The name of this device, a major contributor to Lancashire's developing role as the world's first industrial society because it allowed multiple threads to be spun at the same time, derived from 'spinning engine', *ginny* being a common Lancashire abbreviation of 'engine' (which at that date simply meant any mechanical device).

spittle   baker's shovel or, in domestic use, a flat shovel for sliding bread or other foods in and out of the oven, or for baking on the embers of the fire

split-raisin   term used (with variants such as *split-fig* or *split-curran'*) to describe a particular type of parsimonious but meticulous grocer who was ever-anxious to avoid giving over-weight.

Split-raisin.

Proverbially, the dried fruit would be split with a thumbnail kept long for the purpose.

sprit sprout or shoot of a plant; *spritting-boxes* were the boxes in which potatoes were put to sprout before planting

squeezers mangle, an essential item for any Lancashire washday

stales pieces of stale cake, usually bought for a couple of pence from the baker, used for making *wet nelly* (qv)

stanging (see *riding the stang*)

stanner on the Fylde coast, a shingle ridge running roughly parallel with the shoreline. The lake at Fairhaven, between Lytham and St Annes, was created in 1893 by reinforcing the curving *stanner* which lay on what is now its seaward side

starr marram grass, the coarse, sharp-pointed and deep-rooted grass which was planted to stabilise the shifting sands of coastal dune belts, and prevent them encroaching inland and overwhelming farmland. *Starr* was also cropped in the eighteenth century because the leaves, tied in small bundles, made very useful kitchen brushes known as *starr besoms*.

starved frozen with cold

steaming The need for dampness in a weaving shed is well-known, and the Lancashire climate is traditionally held to have been especially suitable for the cotton industry for this reason. Methods of creating damp conditions in dry summers included: flooding the cellar of the mill to produce constant moisture in the building itself; using water to dampen the warp on the loom; and *steaming*, whereby steam from the engine was let out into the mill from overhead pipes using valves, and so maintained a constant high humidity. The advantage of this method was that if the atmosphere became too damp and the warp and weft sagged, the *steaming* could be turned off. For the workers, however, steaming was peculiarly unpleasant, creating a heavy, humid atmosphere which was very unhealthy for those (who were numerous) with respiratory problems and chest complaints, and meaning that their clothes were always damp and heavy.

Stiffkey, rector of Perhaps the most celebrated exhibit in pre-war Blackpool, Harold Davidson was the rector of Stiffkey in Norfolk, defrocked in 1932 for immorality (he had a penchant for fallen women). Because this scandal was a national sensation he was begged by **Luke Gannon** (qv), the Blackpool impresario, to go to the town as a tourist attraction. He did so, ostensibly at least to raise money for a legal appeal against the defrocking. Among other dramatic appearances, he lived for a time in a barrel and also fasted while lying in a glass case, and on another occasion was displayed 'amid the flames of an artificial hell', where he was prodded with forks by a mechanical demon. He later moved on to Skegness where, sensational to the last, he was mauled to death by a lion.

stoop   post, usually of wood as in **stoop-and-rail fencing**

stoop and room   method of mining coal whereby pillars of coal (*stoops*) were left to support the roof, while the coal was extracted from galleries or *rooms* in between. This contrasts with **longwall** working, where all the coal was removed along a long face, the roof being supported by pit-props while mining continued. In some parts of Lancashire, such as the Burnley coalfield, the alternative name was **pillar and stall**, using the equivalent dialect term **stall** for a space, a chamber.

strap   credit (buying **on the strap**)

Stretford goose   roast pork, with a savoury stuffing

stret man   miner whose job was to make the roadways through the new sections of the seam, so that the adjacent coal could be hauled out

stub   to dig up, uproot, grub out (as of tree stumps, for example)

Surey Imposter   In 1689 Richard Dugdale, a nineteen year old who lived at Surey near Whalley, was allegedly possessed by the Devil. He began to speak in strange tongues, to vomit stones, grew a lump in his leg the size of a fist which then worked its way up to his chest, and had extraordinary fits in which he leaped, danced and seemed to levitate. Large crowds flocked to watch the spectacle, and learned religious opinion was deeply divided as to whether or not he was (as in retrospect he clearly was) an imposter or fraud.

The Surey Demoniack:

OR AN

ACCOUNT

OF

SATANS

Strange and Dreadful Actings,

In and about the Body of

Richard Dugdale

Of *Surey*, near *Whalley* in *Lancashire*;

And how he was Dispoſſeſt by Gods Blessing on the Faſtings and Prayers of divers Miniſters and People.

The Matter of Fact atteſted by the Oaths of ſeveral Credible Perſons, before Some of HIS MAJESTIES Juſtices of the Peace in the ſaid County.

LONDON

Printed for *Jonathan Robinson*, at the *Golden Lyon* in St. *Paul's-Church-Yard*. 1697

A contemporary account of the Surey Imposter.

surnames Although surnames in the modern sense (that is, hereditary names which pass down unchanged in the male line from generation to generation) were becoming common in England by 1250, they were rather later to be adopted in Lancashire. Many seem to have arisen only in the late fourteenth century. However, in Pennine Lancashire 'official' surnames remained almost unknown among ordinary families until the nineteenth century, and most people were known instead by strings of first names which preserved oral genealogies: for example, *Ben o' Tom's o' Bet's o' Dick's*, in which Benjamin is the son of Thomas, grandson of Betty and great-grandson of Richard. Edwin Waugh quotes an extreme example, which he claimed was authentic and given to him in the 1850s: *Henry o' Ann's o' Harry's o' Milly's o' Ruchot's* [Richard's] *o' John's o' Dicks, through th' ginnel, an' up th' steps, an' o'er Joseph's o' John's o' Steens*.

swealing (swaling) the gamekeeper's practice of burning off the old heather from the moorland to encourage new growth of fresh heather shoots (the main food for grouse), and with luck to kill off any pests and parasites: *'We brun tops and t' flames creep along and destroy aw't muck. Pick reet day and then ... T' fire munnot git to t' roots, an it will if t' ground's too dree'*. The word derives from *sweel*, a great blaze, to burn, singe or destroy by fire, and other usages included *swaling t' chimbley*, that is, cleaning the chimney by setting the soot on fire rather than having it swept. A *swaling candle* was one that burned too high and too fast.

T

tackler[1] overlooker in a cotton mill. *Tacklers* were the men who repaired mechanical faults on the looms, 'overlooking' to ensure that all the machinery was running smoothly, and to check on the millworkers for lateness, idleness and other besetting sins. They were almost universally derided, and were legendary for their *gormlessness* (qv) — 'More brawn than brain' — and lack of humanity. Innumerable stories and jokes were told about tacklers, many of them collected in Geoffrey Mather's highly entertaining *Tacklers' Tales*.

tackler[2] humorous name for a sheep's head. Bill Mitchell in his book *Lancashire Mill Town Traditions* tells a story about a man who ordered a *tackler* from the butcher, but wasn't happy with its size: *'Tha doesn't mean to say as that's a tackler?'* The butcher replied, *'Neaw, but it will be when I've taken brains out'.*

talkin' bang speaking properly; standard English instead of dialect, which was *talkin' broad*

tally[1] living in sin (see *livin' up t' stick*)

tally[2] credit; *buying on tally* meant buying so that the sum owed was chalked on the *tally board*; the *tallyman* was a credit-trader

tansy The herb tansy (*chrysanthemum vulgare*) is a highly aromatic perennial with small, vivid yellow flowers, often used in the past as a flavouring (it has a bitter herbal taste) and because its juices gave a green tint to foods. At Radcliffe *tansy cakes* were eaten at Easter, and were used as prizes in local contests of *handball* (qv).

taste relish, a little bit of flavouring in a dull and monotonous diet:

> *'Will yo' land mi mother*
> *a saucepan*
> *Will yo' land mi mother*
> *a spoon*
> *Fer wer goon' t' 'ave a bit ov*
> *a taste*
> *To 'er tay this afthernoon'*

tater 'ash (see *'ash*)

Taylor, Francis Edward The extraordinarily long title of F E Taylor's 1901 book tells it all: *The Folk Speech of South Lancashire: a glossary of words which are, or have* been during the last hundred years, in common use in that portion of the County Palatine situate between Bolton and Manchester, including dialect words, children's words, local mispronunciations, colloquialisms and local slang, with an appendix of quaint sayings. The book is one of the most important attempts to record the vocabulary of the dialect, rather than just its pronunciation — as the author says, he includes 'every word that I remember using and hearing when a boy (fifty years ago)'.

teem, team   to put out, to pour

teanlaw, teanlagh   In parts of the Fylde, including Poulton and Kirkham, the festival of *teanlaw* (there are many variants on the spelling) was on All Souls' Eve. That evening, it was customary to light bonfires in prominent places 'to help deceased friends whose souls were in purgatory'. Detailed accounts survive of the festival at Poulton. Bonfires were lit at a cairn of white stones, in a field called Purgatory, and after the fires had died down, the stones were thrown into the ashes and left overnight. While this was happening, a group of men stood in a circle with pitchforks of burning straw raised aloft. At sunrise, any person who could not distinguish his or her stone would have bad luck for the ensuing year. *Teanlaw* died out in the mid-nineteenth century under the improving influence of the local clergy, but the farmer removed over twenty cartloads of refuse

from the field and it was noted that the soil was burned a deep reddish-black. The ceremony was evidently pre-Christian in origin — one Victorian writer notes that 'this farce was carried on in its pristine glory long after the Reformation, for rational Christianity, which had been almost lost previously [ie under Catholicism], progressed but slowly in the Fylde'. Today the shopping precinct in Poulton bears this ancient name.

teetotal   Richard ('Dickie') Turner was one of the six men who, with Joseph Livesey, signed the pledge in Preston on the 1st September 1832 (see **Temperance Movement**). He is alleged to have invented the word *teetotal* in September 1833 when, denouncing the idea that moderation rather than abstention was the best solution, he said with a stammer *'I'll be reet down and out tee-tee-total for ever and ever'*. While it is fairly certain that Dickie did say this, he was in fact using a colloquial phrase already well-known in Ireland and Northern England, including it in his speech because to local people it was already a familiar usage.

Temperance Movement   For centuries there had been groups and individuals who opposed the consumption of alcohol, primarily because of its damaging effects upon health and behaviour, but the modern Temperance Movement was founded by Joseph Livesey in Preston in the 1832, when he and six others signed a pledge to abstain from alcohol 'except as medicine' (from which derives the old phrase of the guilty drinker, that the beverage is 'purely medicinal'). The Preston movement was not original — other abstinence societies had been formed elsewhere, such as that rather optimistically founded at Skibbereen in County Cork in 1817 — but it was from Livesey's movement that the national crusade developed.

tenters, tenter frames wooden frames on which cloth was stretched to be dried in the open air, or was bleached in the sunlight. The cloth was fixed to the frame by large hooks and then stretched across, hence the phrase *to be on tenterhooks*. The *tenters* survived in many places until well into the nineteenth century, and names such as **Tenterfield** in many Lancashire towns and villages indicate their former location.

tenter minder, one who tends or looks after, such as the *engine tenter* in a steam-powered mill

tewit peewit or plover

tharcake Lancashire equivalent of the Yorkshire *parkin*, the latter being nowadays much better known. There are various explanations of the name, the romantic Victorian one being that the word was originally *thor-cake* and that it was eaten by the Norse inhabitants of the county before their conversion to Christianity, on feast days celebrating the god Thor. The much more prosaic reality is that it was almost certainly derived

from *th' hearth cake*, because it was baked in trays and dishes in the hot embers beside the hearth (rather than being oven-baked). It was made — as is usual with traditional dishes — in various ways according to the taste, pocket and inherited recipe of the individual family. The main ingredients were normally flour, honey, spices, and butter or lard.

Tharcake Monday first Monday after All Saints Day (1st November) and All Souls Day (2nd November). The association of *tharcake* (qv) or *parkin* with Bonfire Night is an ancient one. The 5th November was, by happy coincidence, the time of many pre-Christian festivals, and after 1605 these festivities were conveniently adaptable to the celebration of deliverance from Popery. Special spiced sweet cakes were already eaten at the beginning of November long before the seventeenth century, but from then on *tharcake*, toffee and, later, baked potatoes became a standard feature of Guy Fawkes' Night.

that used to mean 'so', and one of the commonest everyday forms in Lancashire speech *'It were that pricey Ah were flabbergasted', 'I'm that busy I don't know if I'm coming or going'*

thee The 'thee' and 'thou' form of address was universal in English until the seventeenth century. Its present-day suggestion of Biblical language results from its use in Thomas Cranmer's Anglican prayer book of the 1540s and the King

James' Bible, both of which were written when it was still standard speech. It survives in Lancashire and some other parts of Northern England as an integral part of dialect, although it is fast diminishing as Standard English takes over. That decline was set in train with the enforcement of 'proper' speech by the educational system after 1870, and has accelerated with mass circulation of the printed word, and with the ubiquity of radio and television. The form is seen in phrases such as *th' art* (you are), *th' all* (you will), *tha's* (thou hast or thou is — the latter a relatively modern hybrid), and *'ast tha* (have you).

thible   porridge stick or stirrer

A thible, used for stirring porridge.

thodden   vivid term for heavy, close-grained, excessively solid, as in bread or cake which has not risen properly; but used by analogy with people who feel stuffed up with a cold, or heavy and lethargic

Thornber, Rev William   one of Lancashire's first serious local historians. He was the incumbent of Blackpool St John and a native of Poulton-le-Fylde, and his *Historical and Descriptive Account of Blackpool and its Neighbourhood* was published in 1837. Thornber was particularly interested in old traditions and customs, which as an Anglican minister he usually regarded with disapproval, but which as a historian he found fascinating. His book records many Fylde customs which were already gone or dying out in the 1830s, and he includes a pioneering 'Glossary of old Words used in the Fylde, bordering on the Sea Coast'.

threap   to fight, quarrel, dispute. It appears in some place-names, meaning 'disputed land' (for example, Three Post Green, formerly **Threapers Green**, an area formerly disputed between the townships of Bispham, Mawdesley and Wrightington near Chorley), but it was also in widespread use well into the twentieth century throughout Lancashire to mean verbal argument between individuals. A particular implication was 'dogmatic and repeated assertion': *'He'd threap yo' eawt 'at black's white'.*

Three Dukes A-Riding   children's game, played until the late nineteenth century in south Lancashire, and also a country dance popular at **wakes** (qv) and fairs: lines of girls and boys advanced and retired, choosing partners from the opposite line

thrinter (see *trinter*)

throdkin solid cake made of oatmeal mixed with bacon fat and possibly a little chopped bacon. The dish was especially associated with the Fylde, and it is still eaten there by some older people — in the nineteenth century it was a staple dish. Meal, water and fat were kneaded well together, and afterwards placed upon a large, deep plate, often made of tin. The cake was about an inch and a half (4cm) thick, and was pressed down firmly before being covered with slices or scraps of fat bacon. When baked the *throdkin* was cut like a tart. It was extremely solid: one Victorian writer says that 'eaten fresh and warm it was not an unwelcome dish, and a little of it went a long way with the keenest appetite of a thresher'.

thronged, thrunged crowded, busy with people, a large quantity, plenty

throstle[1] song thrush

throstle[2] spinning machine for wool or cotton

thrums loose ends of a warp, in cotton weaving

thrutch[1] to shift or move about restlessly. Lying awake in the early hours of the morning, you might say to the person tossing and turning beside you in bed, *'Give over thrutchin', Ah caunt sleep fer it'. 'They olez say'n there's th' most thrutchin' wheer there's th' least reawm'* (Edwin Waugh).

thrutch[2] to push or force *'An' thrutch us like dogs agen the wo'* [wall]' (Ben Brierley)

Thrutch, the narrow gorge near Waterfoot in Rossendale through which the Irwell, the old road and the railway ran. A legend states that the Irwell Valley from here to the foot of Bacup was once a great lake. The Devil had his residence at Hell Clough, near Stacksteads, and used to bathe in the lake. One day the lake overflowed at the **Thrutch** and began carving a deep channel through the rock. Satan was bathing at the time, and as the water level fell he tried to carry an apronful of soil and stones to fill the breach.

A throstle, or song thrush.

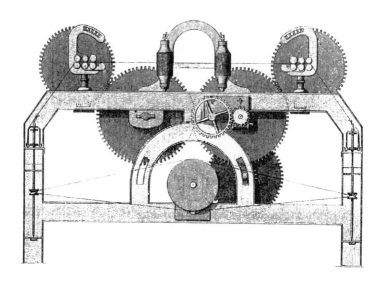

A throstle, or spinning machine.

Just as he reached the place, the apron strings broke and his load dropped above the river, where the tumbled heaps (actually the product of ancient landslipping) remain to the this day.

thrutcher child who, down a coalpit, helped to work the tub or bucket of coals from the pit bottom by pushing and shoving it from behind

thrutchings in cheese-making, the last-pressed whey

thwittle large butcher's knife

tig, tick well-known children's game, in which one person is *tick* or *tig* or *it* and has to chase after the others. When someone is caught, he or she becomes *it* in turn. There are numerous variations on this, such as complications

in which a specific place or object is 'home' and nobody could be caught at that place. The game is played all over the world.

Tim Bobbin literary pseudonym of **John Collier** (qv)

tip, tipcat variant on the game of *knur and spell* (qv), played in Burnley and surrounding districts until the early years of this century; the tip was a club with which a *bad*, or short thick piece of wood, was driven as far as possible

tipping up system of family financial management whereby all members of the household *tipped up* their cash wages to the mother, who bought everything out of the *kitty* and distributed pocket money to the earners; a Blackburn example from the early 1920s

Tipping up.

suggested a rate of 1d pocket money per shilling of wages

tit small horse or nag

titty-ups obsolete term for a 'forward or pert girl'; the derivation is obvious!

toe-rags Recently this term has been used all over England. It originally referred to rags which were stuffed in the toes of shoes too big for the wearer — a common problem when, for many of the poor, any shoes were better than no shoes, never mind if they fitted or not. *Toe-rags* were extremely insanitary, smelly and disagreeable, hence the use of the word as a form of abuse.

tollering boasting, showing off

tommy shops (see *truck*)

Tong Boggart particularly notorious ghost which lived (if that is the word) at Tong Fold in Bacup. In his pioneering history of Rossendale, Thomas Newbigging wrote that everyone in Bacup knew of the doings of the *boggart* (qv), and could tell the story of how 'his unearthly howlings and knockings ... kept the neighbourhood in a ferment of terror for weeks together'.

Tossets St Oswald's Day feast (the name is a corruption of the saint's name), which was celebrated near the beginning of August in and around Stalmine in Over Wyre, and was noted for its sports and games. It was traditional on that day to eat *tosset cakes*, thin, spicy biscuits thickly covered with fine sifted sugar.

tossing in the blanket In origin this was a form of 'folk punishment' or community retribution, but according to Harland, writing in the 1870s, the victim had by that time become the sufferer. When a woman jilted her sweetheart and married someone else, the deserted lover was placed on a blanket and tossed in the air by four people who held the corners. He was then 'fined' and the proceeds were consumed at the nearest public house. Harland claims that this procedure was still followed in the Burnley area. The custom was also associated, as a somewhat questionable form of entertainment, with events such as a twenty-first birthday or the end of an apprenticeship. (cf *buck thanging*)

tosspot drunk or rowdy; but in many Lancashire folk customs which involved plays, performances or acting by groups of characters dressed up, *Tosspot* was a 'comic part' — the dirty old man, the disreputable one who did suggestive things with the young man dressed up as a girl

Tower, the Lancashire's most famous landmark, symbolic of fresh air, fun and raucous entertainment for many millions of people since it opened in the summer of 1894, Blackpool Tower is now a Grade 1 listed building. It is visible for miles (*'Eh, Dad, Ah con see t' tower'*) and is an instantly recognisable symbol of the town, of seaside holidays, and of Lancashire culture in general.

tramps Apart from the common meaning of the word, this term also applied to casual workers who stood, ever hopeful and ever forlorn, at the gates of mills and other factories awaiting the possibility that a sudden vacancy might arise, a worker would not turn up, or a weaver would be late for work and sent home without pay.

treacle, trackle Until the import duty on sugar was lifted in the early 1880s, most poor families could not afford to use it to sweeten food or drinks. Honey was very expensive, and so the only source of sweetness for most people was treacle, the uncrystallised syrup left over from the sugar-refining process and therefore a comparatively cheap by-product. Many traditional Lancashire dishes of the urban poor included treacle, but in the hardest times even that had to be omitted as it was too expensive.

treacle-dipping very popular and thoroughly revolting entertainment at Lancashire *wakes* (qv) and other festivities. Several sources make specific reference to Southport, but others claim that the idea originated in Bolton.

(Neither place should be proud of the association.) Some silver coins were placed in the bottom of a large bowl, which was then filled with treacle. Then, as now, there were plenty of people who were happy to try to make money by undergoing public humiliation. These volunteers (often teenaged boys) had their hands tied behind their back, and then dipped their faces in the treacle and attempted to retrieve the coins with their tongues. After surfacing, choking and scarcely able to breath, their faces were coated with feathers and much amusement was had by all.

treacle mines The treacle mines of Sabden entered Lancashire folklore in the nineteenth century but their reputation was boosted in the 1930s when, according to Bill Mitchell, it was claimed that weavers were making parkin on their looms, using oatmeal for the warp and treacle strands for the weft. There have since been several somewhat embarrassing attempts to convert the joke into a tourist attraction, without conspicuous success.

Treacle Row As the use of treacle was widely regarded as a sign of poverty, cottages or terraces which were looked down on by the slightly better-off neighbours were often known colloquially as *Treacle Row*, a folk name which is found especially in the Pennine areas which were the stronghold of the porridge economy.

trial of strength The *Blackburn Mail* for the 5th May 1824 reported how Ralph Holden of Haslingden Grane had carried a stone weighing over 13 cwt (660kg) on his back for a distance of two yards (1.8m), in the presence of many witnesses. His reactions are not recorded, and neither is there any indication of why he chose to perform this prodigious feat of strength, but local reputation had it that Graners were more noted for physical strength than for brainpower.

trinter three year old animal, derived from 'three winter' (cf *twinter*)

tripe stomachs of the cow. This special delicacy of the county has today, with cowheel and **black pudding** (qv), become part of Lancashire's music hall joke image. It is not, of course, particular to Lancashire, since it was eaten, usually by the relatively poor sections of society, wherever cattle were kept. In the nineteenth century, the very poor could not afford even such cheap products as tripe, and had an almost entirely meatless diet, and its place in the folk memory of the county is comparatively recent phenomenon. Like many other sorts of offal, its consumption has since declined sharply, and it has an 'image problem', which is not helped by the apparent crudity of some of the best-known recipes: raw, sprinkled with salt and vinegar; or — particularly unpleasant to many — boiled with milk and onions to form a soft and slithery mass. It can be delicious, but

opinions have always been very mixed.

trippet game once played in east Lancashire. A *trippet* was a conical or tapered piece of wood about two inches (5cm) long and an inch (2.5cm) across in the middle, which was placed on a smooth stone. The player tapped it firmly on one end with a club or bat, throwing it into the air, and then hit it hard (as with rounders or baseball). The winner was the person who hit it the furthest distance. The game is closely related to *billet* (qv) and *knur and spell* (qv), and was also known as *peggy*. (See also *tipcat*.)

troughs In the hill areas of Lancashire, walkers may notice **stone troughs** being used for, among other purposes, flower tubs or cattle watering. Many of these originated in early industrial processes, such as *fulling* (qv) and dyeing, and have been moved to their present location subsequently. The dyeing trough pictured overleaf is probably 200 years or more old, and its curved undersides helped to carry the overspilling liquid away from the feet of the dyer. Today it is built into a field wall, but originally it would have been used in a shed or yard.

truck A hard fact of life for many Lancashire working people until the late nineteenth century, this was the system whereby there was a general shop in the vicinity of a coalpit or factory in which the owner or his manager had an interest. The workers were obliged

A dyer's trough, now used for watering cattle.

to spend the bulk of their wages there (or face dismissal), and they had to pay very high prices for the goods. Credit was also given, so that the men became doubly indebted to the owners. These places were known as *truck shops*, also colloquially referred to as *tommy shops* or *butty shops* (qv).

Tummus and Meary poem by Tim Bobbin (**John Collier**, qv), published in 1746 and the earliest significant example of the written literary use of the Lancashire dialect. There had been two or three earlier poems by John Byrom of Manchester, but those were little known and the dialect was not very authentic, whereas

Tummus and Meary (Thomas and Mary) was written in carefully-crafted dialect, and achieved great success and popularity. The poem is important not only for its use of dialect, but also because it had what a later reviewer called 'a certain coarseness' — that is, it dealt with everyday ordinary people and reflected their behaviour and attitudes, rather than high-flown classical or sentimental subject matter. Thus it set a pattern for almost all the better dialect poetry and prose later written in the county.

tundish funnel

turf Until the early nineteenth century, most poorer households on the Lancashire plain, especially around Bickerstaffe and Ormskirk, and northwards to Hoole and Longton, as well as many in the Fylde, the vicinity of Morecambe Bay and the north Lancashire fells, burned *turf* (peat) as their only fuel. With their single-storey thatched cottages built of mud and stone, their reliance on peat for cooking and heating, and their staple diet of oats and potatoes, the lifestyles and circumstances of these rural dwellers bore many similarities to those, now much better-known, of pre-Famine Ireland.

turnill, turnel large, shallow, oval tub which was used for, among other purposes, scalding the carcasses of pigs

twinter two year old animal, from 'two winters' (cf *trinter*)

twitchclock The black beetle was a familiar resident of almost all Lancashire homes until the mid-twentieth century, and so numerous in some that, according to Victorian writers, the walls seemed to move. In the lodgings in Wigan where George Orwell stayed in the early 1930s, the beetles swarmed all over the tripe stored in the basement of the shop, to his understandable horror and revulsion. (cf *blackclock*)

Two Lads The double cairn known as **Two Lads** on Wildersmoor above Horwich was the subject of several equally unlikely legends. One, current in the nineteenth century, held that it was the burial place of two sons of a Saxon king whose father had died locally in battle, while another claimed that they commemorated the two sons of Bishop Pilkington of Durham (who was born at Rivington), who had perished on the moor in the snow.

U

uncle pawnshop, pawnbroker *'Ah'll tek 'em clos' t' me uncle'*; also known by other similar names, such as *Uncle Joe*

Uncle Joe's Mint Balls This celebrated Lancashire confection is familiar to travellers on the main West Coast railway line because it is proudly and prominently advertised on a gable end just north of Wigan North Western station. The mint ball ('keeps you all aglow') was invented by Mrs William Santus in her kitchen in 1898, and has been produced according — naturally — to a secret and traditional recipe by the Santus family ever since.

up and down fighting A vicious and savage sport prevalent in south Lancashire until the 1840s, *up and down fighting* was viewed with the strongest disapproval by contemporary writers and local magistrates alike, but greatly enjoyed by some sections of the population. The two contestants in a fight could kick or punch anywhere on the body with whatever force, and could also attempt to strangle or break the limbs of their opponent. Contestants wore heavy iron-studded clogs, so that the injuries were often grotesque, and disfigurement or even death could result. Variants included *purring* and *shinparing* (qv).

V

Vimto The luridly purple herb- and fruit-flavoured beverage which would give 'vim' was invented by Noel Nicholas in Manchester in 1908, after years spent trying to perfect the recipe. It was originally marketed as a 'health tonic', although such claims were eventually forbidden on legal grounds, and became part of childhood for many people in the north of England (it was never as successful in the South). Advertising in the 1930s and 1940s promoted Vimto's image of health and vigour, suggesting that it was the ideal drink for hikers, cyclists, tennis players and 'outdoor types'.

virginity A traditional folk rhyme, recorded in the nineteenth century, casts considerable doubt upon the pre-marital behaviour of Lancashire girls (or at least those in the Warrington area) in the eighteenth century and earlier ('maid' means 'virgin'):

'The church at little Winwick
It stands upon a sod
And when a maid is married
*   there*
The steeple gives a nod
Alas! how many ages
Their rapid flight have flown
Since on that high and lofty
*   spire*
There's moved a single stone.'

W

waggin-fat   highly derogatory and entirely justified term for the early versions of margarine, the ingredients of which were extremely questionable; *waggin-fat* was used to grease the axles and hubs of carts

wakes¹   probably began as religious festivals in the medieval period, celebrating the patronal day of a local saint, and accompanied by feasting and entertainments. After the Reformation such events, which had often retained distinctly pagan elements, lost their religious content and became secular holidays. Most towns and villages of any significance had a *wakes day* and some of these, such as **Eccles Wakes**, were major popular attractions. The development of industry, growth of towns and the improvement of transport, as the railway network expanded, eventually changed the character of these holidays. By the 1880s the possibility of going away to the seaside was available for many, while the principle of longer holidays was also developing (by 1900 as much as a week was quite common). The traditional *wakes days* were therefore extended and transformed into *wakes weeks* and town holidays, whereby, in places such as Darwen or Nelson, most factories and mills would close for a specified week and the inhabitants would decamp *en masse*, usually to Blackpool. (See also *guisings*.)

wakes²   The alternative and equally familiar meaning of *wake* was a funeral feast. Here, too, there was the idea of a communal event or gathering, where special food was eaten and formal rituals observed. There is plenty of documentary evidence to show that *wakes* were held after burials by the early seventeenth century, and the custom is of course many hundreds of years older than that. *Wakers*, those present at the funeral, would be handsomely treated and given as lavish a spread as the family of the deceased could afford (see **ham**), while leading mourners would — finances permitting — be specially dressed for the occasion with new black gowns or coats, gloves and hats, and mourning rings (often thought to be a Victorian idea, but in fact traceable to at least the seventeenth century). (cf *arval*)

wakes entertainments *Wakes* were originally famed for the unruly and often ludicrous spectator sports which were an essential element in their enjoyment. Examples include *grinning matches* (qv), *treacle-dipping* (qv), eating a dishful of boiling porridge as fast as possible, and eating a pound (0.4kg) of tallow candles (with the wicks stripped between the front teeth). Some poor people would attempt anything for the possibility of winning money or a prize of food.

walking dialect term for *fulling* (qv), the cleaning of woollen cloth to get rid of its impurities, grease and dirt by washing with a cleaning agent such as *fuller's earth* or *lant* (qv). The surname **Walker** derives from this trade, while some place-names, such as **Walk Mill** in Cliviger, also recall its existence.

walking days (see *Whit walks*)

wamble to shake, stagger or tremble violently; to feel faint, sick or dizzy. A particular implication is the queasy and shaking feeling which results from acute hunger, a feeling which was all too familiar to many Lancashire people in the past.

warch (see *wark*)

Wardley Hall This sixteenth-century half-timbered manor house in Worsley, near Salford, has a human skull around which many stories and legends have accumulated. It was allegedly that of Roger Downes of Wardley, who was supposed to have been killed in a drunken affray at Epsom Spa in Surrey in 1676. The head was returned to Lancashire, and there began to haunt the house — stories of this sort are quite frequently recorded in older houses. However, John Harland, the local historian and folklorist, several times held the skull and noted, cynically, that it bore no appropriate marks of violence, although he acknowledged that Roger Downes not only lived but did lead a licentious time in London, dying aged twenty-eight in 1676. The story was effectively refuted by the fact that Downes was buried in Wigan Church with his head intact, as exhumation confirmed. A subsequent explanation for the skull was therefore that it belonged to a martyred Catholic priest, and more recently he has been identified with a good degree of confidence as Father Ambrose Barlow, who was hanged at Lancaster in 1641.

wark pain or ache, as in *bellywark*, *toothwarch;* in one of Samuel Laycock's poems, he says of his friend Isaac Bradshaw, a part-time quack doctor who sells remedies, *'He's yead-wartch pills, owd Isaac has'*

Warriken Fair anonymous sixteenth-century ballad ('Warriken' is Warrington) which is among the oldest surviving examples of Lancashire dialect. It is roughly datable because it refers to one Randle Shay, who lived in the reign of Edward VI (1547-1553). The story concerns the sale of a mare at the fair by the hero, Gilbert, who naively accepts a promise of future payment from the purchaser. His formidable wife Grace *swats him o'er th' face* and then goes after the money, which she keeps for herself. Perhaps Gilbert is the first Lancashire example of the little henpecked man married to a large and brawny woman, so beloved of the saucy postcard designers of the twentieth century?

wartch (see *wark*)

wash houses The public wash-house was a central feature of working-class life in the larger towns and cities until the 1960s, when the opening of the launderette and the increasing use of the domestic washing machine — as well as the wholesale redevelopment of the communities served by the wash houses — led to its rapid extinction. The first public wash-house was opened in Liverpool in 1842, at a time when the city was pioneering several important developments in sanitation and public health. The idea was originated by Kitty Wilkinson, the remarkable — and to many people, saintly — wife of an Irish labourer, who had encouraged her neighbours to use her house for washing during the 1832 cholera outbreak. Her pioneering efforts, undertaken purely on her own initiative, came to the notice of the city's medical authorities and were copied elsewhere in Liverpool and eventually in many other industrial towns. Wash-houses did not only have laundry facilities: most also included public baths, which gave the poor (and, indeed, the not-so-poor) the opportunity to wash themselves in comfort and with lots of really hot water, at a time when doing this at home was virtually impossible.

Waterloo porridge thin, watery porridge, without milk, sugar, treacle or bacon fat, which was the only means of subsistence for many thousands of the poorest people in Lancashire, including numerous out-of-work weavers, in the years around 1815 and the Battle of Waterloo. These were the darkest times in a long period of warfare, trade depression, and economic and social misery, and the name, given in irony, became a symbol in people's memories of those terrible days.

Waugh, Edwin Perhaps the greatest and most successful of the Lancashire dialect poets who flourished in Victorian period, Waugh was born at Rochdale in 1817, the son of a shoemaker. He had a childhood of desperate poverty, but from the age of twelve he worked for Thomas Holden, a Rochdale bookseller, and educated himself. In 1847 he became assistant secretary to the Lancashire Public Schools Association, and went to live in Manchester. He wrote poetry (often highly sentimental) in standard English in his spare time, and in 1855 he

Edwin Waugh.

published his first book, *Sketches of Lancashire Life and Localities*. In 1856 his first dialect poetry appeared, including the most famous of all his poems, *Come whoam to thi' childer an' me*. He became a full-time writer but, with his acute social conscience, he also made valuable notes and reports about social and economic issues affecting Lancashire's poor, especially during the **Cotton Famine** (qv) of 1861-65. He died at New Brighton in 1890 and is buried at Kersal.

Weavers Triangle area of Burnley along the Leeds-Liverpool Canal between Westgate and Trafalgar Street. Here the town's great cotton industry had its heart, with several large mills being built beside each other in the 1840s and 1850s, and taking their water supplies from the canal. In the years before the First World War, at least twenty tall chimneys marked this small area, but most have now gone, and the area and its surviving industrial buildings are now marketed as a 'heritage' site under the name the **Weavers Triangle**.

'weddin's nowt, 'ousekeepin's all' economy in managing the domestic budget was essential for all newly-married couples in the working-class areas of Lancashire, as this powerfully unsentimental phrase suggests

Weighvers' Seaport Hollingworth Lake, near Littleborough, was built in the 1790s to provide a water supply to the Rochdale Canal. Unlike many reservoirs it was easily accessible, close to increasingly populous industrial towns and had low-lying banks, so it quickly became a popular place for trippers, and Sunday and holiday outings. By the mid-nineteenth century there were funfairs, rowing boats, beerhouses and other entertainments on its north-western shore, and it had acquired the joking name of *th' Weighvers' Seaport*.

weighvers' talk (see lip-reading)

weind narrow lane or passage, usually in a town where it forms a side lane or street between buildings or separating back yards. The word is found especially in north and mid-Lancashire today (towns such as Preston and Garstang have many *weinds*, and their names often include the term, as in **Mainsprit Weind** in

Preston). However, the word is found in much of northern England and lowland Scotland, and was formerly used in other parts of Lancashire. (cf *back-cut*, *entry*, *ginnell*)

wells As in other parts of England where the Celtic influence was strong, Lancashire had many **wells** or springs which were claimed to have holy properties, including the ability of the waters to cure diseases, grant wishes and exercise similar miraculous powers. At Poulton-le-Fylde there was a well close to the site of the *Teanlaw festivals* (qv): if a sick person, escorted by friends, passed through the cairn of white stones which was the central feature of the *Teanlaw*, picked up three burnt white stones from the bonfire site, and then offered those stones to the well, a cure might be obtained. In traditional fashion, this well was also embellished with shells, pins, nails and rags of clothing, as votive offerings. At Sefton, the well of St Helen (a common dedication for holy springs) in the Thornton road cured rheumatism, bruises and other ailments, and until the mid-nineteenth century was thickly strewn with pins given as offerings to the waters. Sometimes wells and springs retain their special reputation. The well of Our Lady at the popular shrine of Fernyhalgh, just east of Preston, is perhaps Lancashire's best example.

welly almost, nearly (from 'well nigh')

we's in mid-Lancashire, used instead of standard English 'our' *'Comin' round we's 'ouse?'*

Westhoughton riot In 1812, Lancashire was in the depths of economic and social despair, with food shortages, civil unrest and mass unemployment. On the night of the 19th April, a group of rioters attacked the cotton factory at Westhoughton, and smashed and burned the building. Almost thirty were taken by the military and put on trial, four of them (including a boy variously described as sixteen or twelve years of age) being hanged at Lancaster. It was revealed at the trial that government undercover agents had incited the rioters, encouraging them to march on the factory, and had forewarned the authorities so that troops were in the area in large numbers. Events such as these exacerbated the sense of injustice, and fuelled the political agitation which led to the terrible events at **Peterloo** (qv) in 1819.

wet nelly Liverpool dish, almost universal among poorer families in the nineteenth century and for much of the twentieth, consisting of pieces of stale cake (usually bought for a couple of pence as *stales* from the baker) or pastry pieces soaked in sugar syrup, treacle or, more recently, golden syrup. People who lived in Liverpool in the 1920s and 1930s often recall that they were more or less brought up on *wet nelly*. The origins of the name are not certain, but it is assumed that Lord Nelson has something to do with it. Today, recipes are available which make a much more refined version, with the crumbs of cake mixed with dried fruit and baked in a pastry case, but this is a long way removed from the traditional form.

wh- The pronunciation of 'wh' varies widely across the county. In south-east Lancashire the sound was often added to words beginning with 'h', as in *whoam* , a standard way of saying 'home'. On the other hand, in the south of the county around St Helens and Warrington, 'h' was often not pronounced: in St Helens, 'whole one' might be said as *wole won* or *wole 'un*, while the phrase *e's a wom* meant 'he's at home'.

whack shortened form of *whacker*, friendly form of address from one man to another in Liverpool. The word probably derived from *pea whack*, a Liverpool version of thick pea soup which was one of the staple foods of the city's poor in the early twentieth century. (cf *lobscouse*)

wheel-gate (see *alley*)

whimberry, whinberry (see bilberry)

whisky distilling More usually associated with Scotland and Ireland, the illicit distilling of whisky (or other rough spirits) was by no means uncommon in parts of east Lancashire in the nineteenth century. The remote side-valleys of Rossendale, such as Haslingden Grane, had many isolated cottages and farmhouses which were ideal for concealing stills and the liquor itself, and were also conveniently near the packhorse tracks which crossed the high moors and were the regular routes for distributing the whisky. It was often carried in small bottles or cans wrapped up in bales of cloth. There were several prosecutions by HM Customs and Excise for illicit distilling in the area in the 1840s and 1850s, and examples of stills hidden behind chimneys, in cellars, or in one case in the engine-house of a small cotton mill, are also reliably attested. More tantalising, perhaps, are the suggestions that the distilling of illicit drink in parts of the area has not yet died out.

whisk-tail 'wanton female', a woman of ill-repute

Whit Walks For many decades, the great community event of the towns and cities of south and mid-Lancashire was the *Whit Walk*, also known as *walking days*. The Walks were organised by the different churches (strict segregation was the rule, and there was no ecumenicalism until very recent times). Bands of children and adults from each church would form separate processions, which converged on town centres or parks to hear addresses and sermons, enjoy entertainments, and partake of buns and cakes, and tea or soft drinks. The precise format of the *Whit Walks* varied from place to place, and also changed over time, but the basic

A packhorse route in Rossendale, used to distribute illicitly-distilled whisky in former times.

A traditional Whit Walk.

features remained largely un-changed into the mid-1960s when, in the face of declining religious attendance, the fast-altering culture in the age of mass media and entertainment, the introduction of bank holidays which do not coincide with the religious festival and, crucially, the disintegration of old-established communities as the planners and the bulldozers did their worst, they were abandoned. *Whit Walks* developed from much older Whitsuntide events (Robin Hood festivities were often held at that time of year), many of them deeply rooted in rural traditions, but they transferred very effectively to the new urban communities in the early nineteenth century. They were the highlight of the year — everybody dressed up, for Whitsun was when many people, adults as well as children, had new clothes and walked to show off their finery, and to those of us who had the privilege of participating in the Walks, they were an event never to be forgotten.

wick alive, lively, quick

wicks, wick 'uns creepy-crawlies; small living creatures such as insects, mites and lice

wicks couch grass

wicken mountain ash or rowan; the **Wiggin Tree** at the top of Parbold Hill takes its name from this, not from Wigan as is often thought

wide-mouthed spoon It was said in Rossendale in the early nineteenth century that a young woman who talked too much had *'eaten her porridge with a wide-mouthed spoon'*

wiend (see *weind*)

wife-selling Thomas Hardy's *The Mayor of Casterbridge* includes a famous episode of wife-selling at a country fair, a story based on an actual incident. There were a number of authenticated examples in Lancashire, and John Harland (qv), who was not only a careful and wise observer of folk customs and traditions, but also a senior reporter on the *Manchester Guardian*, noted in the 1870s that 'it is not uncommon for wives to be sold by their husbands'. Most such transactions were probably entirely private affairs between the three parties concerned, and such scanty evidence as is available suggests that 'token' sales of this sort were a makeshift form of divorce among ordinary and poor people. That the wife usually consented and went willingly seems likely.

Wigan Pier The debate as to the origin of the name continues. Perhaps the most plausible explanation is that it was applied as a joke to the chutes which projected into the Leeds and Liverpool Canal at Wigan, and were used for tipping coal into the barges waiting beneath. The name then stuck, was referred to in humorous postcards, and eventually was annexed by George Orwell, when he came to the town in the late 1930s and based his (to many

people) patronising and disagreeable book *The Road to Wigan Pier* on his observations. For so long a symbol of all that Lancashire was trying to forget — coal, grime, polluting industry, poverty and degradation — Wigan Pier has now become a symbol of the county's attempts to recall its harsher past, in the form of the heritage industry.

wiggin (see *wicken*)

will o' th' wisp In many parts of the county there were stories of the haunting *will o' th' wisp*. The rational explanation is that escaping methane and other gases from marshland and mosses or, commonly in Lancashire, from coal seams, spontaneously ignited and produced the characteristically ephemeral pale light which danced on the surface of ponds, wet ground or lanes. Such light was particularly visible in the days before street-lighting and the night-time glow of lights from built-up areas. Far more fanciful explanations naturally evolved, of *boggarts* (qv) or *feeorins* (qv) and all manner of supernatural beings. Barton, for example, records how, in the early nineteenth century, many local people refused to use the Long Causeway between Farnworth and Worsley at night, because of the ghostly fiery white rabbit which was held to haunt the dark lane across the moss.

Wilsons, the family of dialect writers from Manchester. Michael Wilson (1763-1840) is best-known for his lively verse-story, *Jone's Ramble fro' Owdam to Karsy-Moor Races*, which includes vivid descriptions of the 'fun of the fair' associated with the races on Kersal Moor outside Salford. His sons, Thomas (died 1852) and Alexander (died 1846), also wrote in dialect, and their collected works were published as *Songs of the Wilsons* in 1865, but it is known that much of their output was either unwritten or noted down on scraps of paper, and was therefore lost.

window-tackin' favourite pastime of small boys. A thread, with a button or washer on the end, is fixed above a window frame by looping round a pin stuck in the wood, while the other end of the thread is pulled by boys hiding round the corner. The button swings and then taps on the window. The householder comes out to see what is happening, sees nobody, goes back inside, and the noise is then repeated. It was great fun, as my grandfather, an acknowledged expert in the art in Manchester almost a century ago, would recount with great enjoyment when he was in his late eighties.

wint draughty passage between two buildings which caught the wind (Leigh area)

winter(h)edge in Rossendale dialect, a clothes horse or *maiden*

Winwick Church A very peculiar legend tells how Winwick was the place where St Oswald, king of Northumbria, was killed in battle. A church was to be erected nearby in a place which as yet had no name, but when the first foundation stones had been laid, a pig was seen running around the building site, screaming 'Weeick, Wee-ick'. It picked up a stone in its mouth and dropped it on the spot where the saintly Oswald had fallen. The founders, seeing in this extraordinary event a message, abandoned the earlier site and resumed building in the place the pig had shown them. Other almost identical stories of this sort, whereby the sites of churches were moved for some reason, are found in Lancashire and in other counties, but few have a pig as messenger from God. (See also **virginity**.)

wisket large shallow or flat wicker basket

witches The trial and execution of the **Pendle witches** in 1612 was the most famous of all the witch trials in seventeenth-century England. The story has been told many times, and embroidered, fictionalised or observed with cool objectivity depending on the perspective of the author. Ten people — two of them men — were publicly hanged at Lancaster on the 20th August 1612, the day after their two-day trial for witchcraft and other offences. We know now, of course, the truth of their tragedy, that they were the victims of the malicious and fabricated evidence of a teenage girl, Alison Device, who had implicated her own grandmother (who died in

Winwick Church, the subject of a curious legend.

prison) among the victims. In the hysterical contemporary climate of fear, matters were seen differently and these people stood little real chance of escaping death. Other alleged witches, from Samlesbury, were tried at the same time, while a fortnight earlier Jennet Preston from Pendle was executed at York for the same offence. The 1612 trials marked the high (or low) point of persecution in Lancashire, and thereafter juries were notably reluctant to convict. When, in 1633, nineteen people from the Colne area were sent for trial for witchcraft, again on the made-up evidence

of a child, they were acquitted. The reality, therefore, was that these were ordinary country people, falsely accused and wrongly executed. Theirs is a tragic and pathetic story, and the ludicrous images of pointed hats and broomsticks which now proliferate in and around Pendle do their memory no justice at all.

Wogdin pronunciation of Walkden, near Bolton. This version is usually considered 'common'. It is often instructive to listen to the announcements at Manchester Victoria, reciting the names of railway stations between Manchester and Wigan. The

THE

W O N D E R F V L L

D I S C O V E R I E   O F

WITCHES IN THE COVN-
TIE OF LAN-
CASTER.

With the Arraignment and Triall of

Nineteene notorious WITCHES, at the Affizes and

generall Gaole deliuerie, holden at the Caftle of
LANCASTER, *upon Monday, the fe-*
uenteenth of August laft,

1612.

Before Sir IAMES ALTHAM, and

Sir EDWARD BROMLEY, Knights; BARONS of his
Maiesties Court of EXCHEQVER: And Iustices
of Assize, Oyer *and* Terminor, *and generall*
Gaole deliuerie in the circuit of the

North Parts.

Together with the Arraignment and Triall of IENNET
PRESTON, *at the Assizes holden at the Caftle of Yorke,*
the feuen and twentieth day of Iulie laft paft,
with her Execution for the murther

of Mafter LISTER

by Witchcraft.

Published and fet forth by commandement of his Maiesties
Iuftices of Affize in the North Parts.

By THOMAS POTTS *Efquier*

LONDON,
Printed by *W. Stansby* for *John Barnes,* dwelling neare
Holborne Conduit. 1613

A contemporary account of the 1612 Lancashire witch trial.

'proper' ones say 'Walk-den', but others use the older, traditional form of *Wogdin*. (cf *ol it'thwood* or *hall-i-the-wood*)

Worktown In 1937 the national organisation known as Mass Observation was established, to record details of the everyday lives of ordinary people. During that year a team of observers researched and recorded Bolton (rechristened **Worktown**), and then subsequently observed **Worktowners** as they visited Blackpool for the annual holidays. The result, which was not published until 1990 when it was edited by Cross and Walton, is a fascinating insight into the lives and lifestyles of 'typical' Lancashire people in the years just before the Second World War.

woven mi piece reached the end, coming to the end of my life; a powerful metaphor from the handloom weaving era, used by the Rochdale dialect poet Richard Rome Bealey (1828-1887) in his popular and moving poem *My piece is o bu' woven eawt*, about approaching death:

> *'But now it's nee' to th' eend o' th' week*
> *An' close to th' reckonin' day*
> *Aw'll tak my "piece" upon my back*
> *An' yer what th' Mester'll say*
> *An' if aw nobbut yer His voice*
> *Pronounce my wark "weel done"*
> *Aw'll straight forget o' th' trouble past*
> *I' th' pleasure 'ut's begun'*

Written Stone The Written Stone near Knowle Green, on the south-ern slope of Longridge Fell, bears an inscription stating that it was placed there by Rafe Radcliffe in 1655. Predictably, a range of fanciful tales grew up around what was presumably a simple equivalent to the datestones so common on Lancashire houses built in the seventeenth century. Among these is the notion that the stone was the scene of a murder, and that it was haunted by a poltergeist which persecuted anybody interfering with the stone.

wuzzin' holes round deep holes in the stone walls of buildings, in east Lancashire; allegedly, bags or *hanks* of wet, just-dyed yarn were strung on sticks, which were then inserted into the hole and spun round (*wuzzed*) to dry the yarn

Wycoller The now-ruined hall at Wycoller provided the model for Ferndean Manor in Charlotte Brontë's *Jane Eyre*. Haworth is only six miles (9.5km) away (the two locations are now linked by the Brontë Way), and Charlotte knew and visited the romantic site. Slightly predictably, the ruins of Wycoller Hall were said to be haunted. A ghostly horseman would pay a visit on a wild and stormy night, the dreadful screams of a dying woman were heard, and the horseman and his fiery steed then rode off into the darkness. This was explained as being the ghost of a murderer, doomed forever to return to the place where, in the early seventeenth century, he had killed his wife.

Y

yammer to long for, yearn for; and, by extension, to cry, lament, whimper

yate gateway, such as an access point onto moorland or a gate across a road; **Yate** near Darwen takes its name from such a feature, and Tardy Gate, between Leyland and Penwortham, was formerly known as **Tardy's Yate** after a man called Tardy who constructed a private toll-gate there in the late sixteenth century

Yorkshire The old enemy? *'Be keaurfu' he'll put Yorksher on thi"*, meant that someone was trying to trick, cheat or deceive you, and to *come Yor'shur* meant that you were accusing someone of doing the same (*'doan come Yor'shur wi' me'*)

Yule loaf earlier version of the Christmas cake. In Lancashire a spicy fruit cake, not as rich and heavy as the modern variety, was baked or bought at a local market (there are records of this as early as the 1720s); they were often decorated with symbols, such as the head of a lamb — the use of this symbol arose from a confusion between 'yule' and 'ewe', Thornber recalling in the 1830s that in his childhood in Poulton-le-Fylde the name *ewe loaf* was used.

Bibliography

J Aikin, *A description of the country from thirty to forty miles around Manchester* (1795).

C Aspin, *Haslingden 1800-1900: a history* (Helmshore Local History Society, 1962).

W E A Axon, *A Lancashire Treasury* (nd, c1880).

J J Bagley, *The earls of Derby 1485-1985* (1985).

B T Barton, *History of the Borough of Bury and its Neighbourhood* (1874).

B T Barton, *A History of Farnworth and Kearsley* (1887).

E Battersby, 'Dead and dying words', in *An Accrington Miscellany*, edited by R Y Digby and A Miller (Accrington Library & Art Gallery Committee, 1970).

W Bennett, *The History of Burnley 1400-1650* (Burnley Corporation, 1947).

R K Bingham, *Lost Resort? The flow and ebb of Morecambe* (Cicerone, 1990).

E K Blackburn, *In and out the windows: a story of the changes in working class life 1902-1977 in a small East Lancashire community* (privately published, 1977).

J Blakey, *The Annals and Stories of Barrowford* (Blakeys of Nelson, 1929).

J E Bowman, *When every day was summer* (Owl Books, 1989).

Ben Brierley, *'Ab-o'th-Yate': sketches and short stories* (Clegg, 1896).

J B Brookes, *Lancashire bred: an autobiography* (privately published 1945).

E Cass, 'The Pace-Egg Play — A Traditional Drama in the Lancashire Cotton Towns', in *Transactions of the Lancashire & Cheshire Antiquarian Society* vol 94 (1998), pp 111-135.

H C Collins, *The Roof of Lancashire* (Dent, 1950).

H Craven and R Y Digby (eds), *A Bacup Miscellany* (2 vols , 1972 and 1975; Bacup Borough Council, Lancashire County Council).

A G Crosby, *A History of Lancashire* (Phillimore, 1998).

A G Crosby, 'The Bury Simnel: a traditional Lancashire food and its history', in *Transactions of the Lancashire & Cheshire Antiquarian Society* vol 94 (1998), pp 82-94.

G Cross and J K Walton, *Worktowners at Blackpool: mass observation and popular leisure in the 1930s* (Routledge, 1990).

R Eaton, *A History of Samlesbury in the Hundred of Blackburn* (1936).

K Entwistle, *From Bodeltone to Bolton-le-Sands: the story of a village* (Euromotor Publications, 1982).

J Fergusson, *She Knows You Know! The remarkable story of Hylda Baker* (Breedon, 1997)

H Fishwick, *History of the Parish of Rochdale* (1889).

A Foley, *A Bolton Childhood* (Manchester University Extra-Mural Department, 1973).

H Foster, *Don e want ony srimps? the story of the fishermen of Southport and North Meols* (Birkdale & Ainsdale Historical Research Society, 1998).

A Fowler and T Wyke, *Mirth in the Mill: the Gradely World of Sam Fitton* (Oldham Leisure Services Department, 1995).

R Frost, *A Lancashire township: the history of Briercliffe-with-Extwistle* (Rieve Edge Press, 1983).

A Gaskell, *The history and traditions of Clifton* (Swinton & Pendlebury Libraries, 1964).

A Griffiths, *Memories of an Atherton Pitman* (Leigh LHS, ed E Finch, 1990).

T Hampson, *Horwich; its history, legends and church* (1883).

J Harland and T T Wilkinson, *Lancashire Legends, Traditions, Pageants, Sports, &c* (Routledge, 1873).

F Hird, *Lancashire Stories* (1911).

B Hollingworth, *Songs of the people: Lancashire dialect poetry of the Industrial Revolution* (Manchester University Press, 1977).

G O Holt, *Regional history of the railways of Great Britain: the North West* (David & Charles, 1986).

E Horley, *Sefton: a descriptive and historical account* (1893).

How and Parsons, *An illustrated itinerary of the County of Lancashire* (1842).

J F Hughes, *Recollections of old Liverpool by a nonagerian* [sic] (1863).

A Kellett, *The Yorkshire Dictionary of Dialect, Tradition and Folklore* (Smith Settle, 1994).

D H Langton, *A history of the parish of Flixton, Urmston and Davyhulme* (1898).

E Z Lawson, 'Wheels within wheels: the Lancashire cycling clubs of the 1880s and '90s', in A G Crosby (ed), *Lancashire Local Studies* (Lancashire Local History Federation, 1993).

J Leyland, *Memorials of Hindley* (1873).

J Leyland, *Memorials of Abram* (privately published, 1882).

J Lumby, *The Lancashire Witch-Craze* (Carnegie Publishing, 1995).

R Mabey, *Flora Britannica* (1997).

G Mather, *Tacklers' Tales* (Palatine Publishing, 1993).

A Miller, *Upholland in old picture postcards 2* (1998).

W R Mitchell, *Lancashire Mill Town Traditions* (Dalesman, 1977).

T Newbigging, *A History of the Forest of Rossendale* (2nd ed, 1893).

G C Newstead, *Gleanings towards the annals of Aughton near Ormskirk* (privately published, 1893).

North West Sound Archive, *A textile dictionary of dialect and technical terms 1750-1960* (NWSA, Clitheroe, 1994).

S Nichols, *The Story of Vimto* (Carnegie Publishing, 1994).

W Nichols, *The history and traditions of Radcliffe* (c 1910).

L Pollard, *Great Harwood Gleanings* (Lancashire Libraries, 1978).

J Porter, *History of the Fylde of Lancashire* (1876).

M Presland, *St Helens: a pictorial history* (Phillimore, 1995).

W Rawlinson, *Memories of Burnley 70 years ago* [1820s] *told to 'Burnley Express'* (1892).

J Richards, *Stars in our eyes: Lancashire stars of stage, screen and radio* (Lancashire County Books, 1994).

R Roberts, *The Classic Slum: Salford life in the first quarter of the century* (Manchester University Press, 1971).

R Roberts, *A Ragged Schooling* (Manchester University Press, 1976).

W Robertson, *Old and new Rochdale and its people* (1881).

W Rollinson, *The Cumbrian Dictionary of Dialect, Tradition and Folklore* (Smith Settle, 1997).

S Schofield, *Short Stories about Failsworth Folk* (1905).

T C Smith, *The history of the parish of Ribchester in the County of Lancaster* (1890).

F E Taylor, *The Folk Speech of South Lancashire: a glossary of words which are, or have been during the last hundred years, in common use in that portion of the County Palatine situate between Bolton and Manchester, including dialect words, children's words, local mispronunciations, colloquialisms and local slang, with an appendix of quaint sayings* (John Heywood, 1901).

W Thornber, *A History and descriptive account of Blackpool and its neighbourhood* (1837).

J M Till, *A history of Longridge and its people* (Carnegie Publishing, 1993).

J G Timmins, *Handloom weavers cottages in central Lancashire* (Centre for North West Regional Studies, Lancaster University, 1977).

J K Walton, *The Blackpool Landlady* (Manchester University Press, 1978).

W Warburton, *Notes on Altcar Parish* (privately published, 1896).

E Waugh, *Lancashire Sketches* (1869).

E Waugh, *Factory Folk during the Cotton Famine* (Heywood, Manchester, 1881).

W Whittle, *Blackburn as it is* (Preston, 1852).

M J Winstanley (ed), *Working children in 19th century Lancashire* (Lancashire County Books, 1995).

P Wright, *Lancashire Dialect* (Dalesman, 1976).

H Worsley, *The dwindling furrows of Lowton* (Owl Books, Wigan, 1988).

M Yates (ed) and W Gibson (intro), *A Lancashire Anthology* (University of Liverpool Press, 1923).